FLIES IN THE
PUNCH BOWL

FLIES IN THE PUNCH BOWL

~

Art Theft, Cocktails, and High Society

Erika Simms

*Remember, Rome wasn't
built in a day!
Slackers.*

[signature]

·WP·

Wynkoop Press, Ltd.

All rights reserved.
Published in the United States by Wynkoop Press, Ltd.
www.WynkoopPress.com

Library of Congress PCN 2019900380
ISBN 978-1-7335295-0-1 (paperback)
ISBN 978-1-7335295-1-8 (ebook)

Cover design by Carlos Esparza

For Mark,
For Dad and Mom

FLIES IN THE
PUNCH BOWL

Chapter 1

On a drizzly evening in November, Seattle's finest—dazzling enough to be seen from space—were gathered for an elegant affair in the trendy arts district, where I lingered amongst them, shamelessly out of place.

Dressed to the nines in a flirty black dress and stilettos that cost more than platinum per ounce, I was flanked by my closest comrades, Lyla Finch and Evan Neruda. There aren't enough people in the world like these two, and when things go south, there's no one you'd rather have by your side. Hurled your car into a coin-op laundromat? Don't panic. Here's a shot of tequila. Go ahead, sink your teeth in.

Sworn members of the plebeian class, we never belonged in these affluent circles. If only we'd sought careers in technology and homesteaded the land of Silicon Valley, or discovered the cure for tomato blight. But that hardly stopped us from donning the masks when the call for a fresh thrill tugged at our sleeves.

"Should the gatekeepers of this glorious fete have doubted our overstated social status, I would have mesmerized them with an artful tale about my privileged life as the mild-mannered grandson of a reclusive adhesives baron," said Evan, the dimples in his Latin cheeks deepening as we entered the lively gallery.

Kaleidoscopic paintings hung from the satin-finished walls while sculptures forged from recycled materials left scuffs in the hardwood floors. Men with fat wallets and women with sparkling hunks of hardware filled in around us, the delicate aromas of antique roses and bergamot oil wafting from their skin. They chattered on like migrating geese in search of their next status symbol. Fancy waiters with dotted bow ties and silver platters swirled through the crowd, offering flutes of French champagne and hors d'oeuvres of chilled oysters and salmon mousse.

"The dump trucks must be queued up around the corner," said Lyla, her blue eyes sparkling as she appraised the price tag for a copper sculpture of a strangler fig suffocating a smokestack. "Open the gates, people. Here comes the cash." She adjusted the silk strap on her red cocktail dress, hemmed to a height that made her limbs look long. She turned to me. "The upper class must be minting Ben Franklins. Who's keeping an eye on those printing plates, Annabel?"

"A prehistoric government bureau with guards who speak in grunts," I said. "They're fiercely armed with Confederate muskets and dental cavities."

"You've been acquainted?" asked Evan. He combed his fingers through his dark hair, tucking the longer pieces behind his ears.

"Once or twice. The pleasure was all theirs." I motioned to the open bar across the gallery, where a green-eyed barkeep was twisting the cork from an earthy bottle of Pinot Noir. "Shall we see who's fastest off the line?"

A finicky lady with pineapple-blonde curls and cheeks rouged into the next century appeared from our periphery and outpaced us to the bar. Her pale legs were gangly, the result of subsistence on rice cakes and salad.

Evan leaned into my ear, his breath warm upon my cheek. "Sweep your fingers through your golden hair and bat your big brown eyes at the bartender so we can leap-frog this fussy dame."

"She spends her days sucking bonbons through her teeth," I said. "I can't compete with that."

"But you're a young little peach, all twenty-seven years of you." He pinched my cheek. "You even have the fuzz."

"Your five o'clock shadow is the only whisper of facial hair amongst us." I brushed his hand away and locked eyes with a server gliding toward us, a trio of crystal flutes perched upon his tray. "Forget the cocktails. This night calls for sparkling rosé."

We luxuriated in the fizzing sensation of brut bubbles dancing in our cheeks.

I raised my glass to toast the occasion, then abandoned the notion as a painting of a milk cow patterned in Ben-Day dots caught my eye. Memories of growing enamored with Pop Art while chipping away at an art history degree revisited me, and I couldn't help but chuckle at the satire. Certain destiny intended the painting to be mine, I glanced at the price tag and nearly swallowed my tongue. "How much can I get for my car?" I wheezed. "Do I really need two kidneys?"

Evan swatted my wrist as I reached for the canvas. "Annabel Riley, step away from the painting this instant. It is prohibited to touch the paint. The sign clearly says so."

"Breaking the rules without fear of consequence is my greatest talent in life," I said. "Besides, how severe could the penalty be—a night in the clink followed by an old-timey tarring and feathering?"

Lyla waved her finger in my face. "Unless you intend to walk away with that painting, don't draw attention to us."

Evan piled on. "What would your curator say if he could see this lapse in judgment?"

It was the curator of the modern art museum in downtown Seattle to whom he was referring, the affable man on the verge of petrification who had hired me into a position cataloging the museum's collections after my promising career in the field of art recovery and insurance investigations ended prematurely. Our shared love of Lichtenstein's comic strips and distant British descent had swayed him to disregard the blunder that led to my involuntary dismissal—paying out a giant settlement on a stolen Andy Warhol painting later deemed a forgery when the real one surfaced. By the time the fraud was discovered, the crook had disappeared into the wind. Few heads rolled with more finality than mine.

I shook off the memory two years expired and looked to Lyla to find a conspiratorial grin spreading across her face like unrefrigerated butter on a hot summer day. "If you want that painting, you must procure some bulky smocks to conceal it beneath as you slip through the exit a la Vincenzo Peruggia with the *Mona Lisa* at the Louvre a century earlier." She pointed to the back door leading to the cobblestone alley.

I choked on my rosé. "That scheme didn't work out so well for him. Two years later, police hauled him off in handcuffs."

"Then skip the smocks, rip the painting off the wall, and make a break for the door." She glanced to her right, then to her left, taking stock of the doughy bankers in our vicinity. "You could outrun every one of them. You'd be crossing the border by midnight."

"Have I the skills to execute such a primitive heist without capture? I wouldn't do well behind bars. I haven't the faintest idea how to whittle a bar of soap into anything other than a smaller, deformed bar of soap."

"They'll teach you," said Evan. "But watch your ribs. Prison kerfuffles are no picnic in the park and shivs made of chicken bones are surprisingly sharp."

I considered the implications of that bleak truth. "As I'm less than three percent confident I could hold my own in a clam-chowder-fueled prison brawl, I suggest Lyla lift the painting instead."

"The nonexistence of Chardonnay would make the slammer uninhabitable for me," she said, fluffing the thick fringe of black bangs feathered across her forehead. Her features were soft, her face precious enough to sell baby food when she was a newborn. It was her stint as a Gerber baby that had motivated her career in advertising, though the rungs of the corporate ladder at the creative agency Abbeson & Trott—or Absent Thought, she called it—were occupied by stiff suits who viewed her as too wet behind the ears to emboss her business cards with any title more honorable than *minion*.

"Last week you declared Chardonnay tastes like oily linguine," I said. "The absence of choice shouldn't concern you."

"Regardless of my flavor propensities, I prefer to be spoiled for choice, not restrained by it." Pink rosé sloshed over the rim of her glass as she planted her hands on her hips in a very Lyla-like fashion. "Everyone from the Bishop of Rome to the Incas with their llama hides would agree with me."

"The Incas were too busy throwing virgins into volcanoes to care about the plight of people facing lock-up with limited beverage options," said Evan, rolling his almond eyes. Restless in nature and of Argentine descent, he was rarely afraid to speak his mind, clamming up only when the subject of his vanished motorcycle, Macho, was raised. With fantasies of becoming the next Che Guevara, Evan had bought a rusty Norton 850 in Tijuana five years prior, saying to hell with his journalism degree and the dying news industry. When Macho disappeared from his hostel in Mexico City a few days later, the fuzzy glow of insurgency wore off, and he hopped the next chicken truck back to the States to beg the editor at the *Seattle Courier* to rehire him as a staff writer.

We polished off our rosé and helped ourselves to a glass of champagne. I said, "Let's see what other paintings are on our shopping list."

Effervescent conversations whirred in our ears as we slinked around the gallery like foxes on the prowl. Near the back, I spied a contemporary painting of an ombré fade of indigo watercolors with blocky white lettering that read: *Ooftah.* As I imagined the image with its kooky monosyllable hung above my dresser, the ear-splitting sound of a woman shrieking in disgust splintered the hum of voices. I spun on my heel to find a sour-faced mare, whose hair was crimped like an unsheared fiber goat, blubbering about a spill of champagne on her couture dress by a beastly patron with flippers for hands.

"Flies roam free in these parts," said Lyla. "Someone should tell her to zip it."

"You're volunteering yourself?" I asked.

"I'm not the one who can't mind my own business."

"I'll have you know I kept my New Year's resolution to mind my own business two weeks longer than you kept yours to cut back on carbs." I squeezed her lanky arm. "Not that you needed to. Your engine runs hot. The slab of cheesecake you gobbled at your company picnic last spring was incinerated before it left the folds of your intestinal tract."

As the customers of the gallery became engrossed in the spectacle, the back door flung open and banged against the wall. Paint chips sloughed off the indentation it left behind as a barrel-chested thug draped in black motorcycle leathers stitched with ornery motifs stormed in from the alley. His buckled boots pounded upon the floor. Stringy blond hair hung at his shoulders while coarse stubble blanketed his jaw. The cartilage in his nose was crooked, the crease between his eyebrows deep and mean. Acrid odors of cigarette smoke seeped from his skin as he stopped beside me and shouted from the fleshy depths of his diaphragm. "Where are the brothers who own this place?"

Silence devoured the room.

The man scanned it with cold eyes. "Come out, come out, wherever you are."

Dead air settled around us. In its undertow I trod as the man's agitation intensified. He cracked his neck, the octopus tentacles tattooed on his throat pulsating. "I will tear paintings off the walls if that's what it takes to get your attention."

Muffling a nervous squeak, a bright-eyed trust-funder with a ruby the size of New Hampshire nestled between her collarbones clutched Evan's arm and squeezed it like a ripe juice orange, sucking in wispy breaths.

Evan caressed her reassuringly. "Are you single?"

Dressed in a charcoal gray suit that fit as though he were born to wear it, a middle-aged gent with jet black hair and sapphire eyes shuffled hastily through the crowd. His skin was the color of a biscuit, his lips pursed in a way that made the apples of his cheeks seem artificially tight. A dirty martini with two green olives was gripped in his hand. "What seems to be the problem, sir?"

"Consider this your last warning, Domino," said the thug, drops of spittle expelled from his teeth. "Make things right or sink beneath the weight of cinder blocks to the bottom of Puget Sound."

Domino patted the air. "Please, calm down."

Choler filled the brutish man's eyes. "Don't tell me to calm down." He swiveled around and grabbed the crystal flute from my fingers, slamming it to the floor. Shards of glass sprayed around my feet as it shattered upon impact, the champagne forming a small puddle that would soon become sticky if not properly addressed.

"Hey, watch it," I said, riled by the hostile action as the stunned partygoers gasped around me.

The thug growled. "Shut your trap." He looked to Domino, his voice thinning to a hiss. "I would hate for you to wake up in the morning to find you've been relieved of your ears." He slid his fingers beneath his lobes in a slicing gesture that left little room for confusion.

"I prefer to keep my ears," said Domino. "Let's clear this up like gentlemen and you can be on your way." With an anxious tremor, he pulled a monogrammed wallet from his suit coat and extracted two crisp hundred-dollar bills.

"You can't buy me off with table scraps."

"Two hundred dollars is hardly table scraps," I said, finding the temptation to meddle irresistible—a fact I weakly blamed on the alcohol making my brain cells soggy. "That's like seventy pounds of apples or half a bottle of that premium champagne you wasted." I pointed my toe to the mess on the floor.

Lyla clapped her hand over my mouth. "Now would be a good time to stop talking."

"You think you're Domino's protector?" said the thug. "I could snap your neck with a squeeze of my thumbs."

I shuddered. "That sounds effective but violent. Allow me to clarify, I've never met Domino before tonight. My allegiance to him is nonexistent." I gulped and offered the proof. "If ever he and I found ourselves wandering the shores of that bear-infested archipelago up near Alaska—what's it called, Kodiak Island?— and a half-ton grizzly with a war hammer for a snout deemed us a threat, I'd kick Domino in the shins and run off without remorse. I may even toss some berries and salmon fillets to the bear for good measure."

The thug's nostrils flared. "You sure do talk a lot. You think I couldn't make you disappear?"

I processed the sum of his threats. "You've made some excellent points. I'm going to mind my own business now."

"Too late." The man lurched forward and captured me by my wrists. He tightened his grip, his calloused fingers pressing divots in my skin as he dragged me into his burly arms and spun me around to face the gallery owner. "No more second chances, Domino. Give me what I'm due or she'll be next."

Chapter 2

"Enough!" said Domino with sudden authority. "Let go of her. We'll speak outside." He motioned to the exit leading to the dark cobblestone alley, then spoke to his bewildered guests with forced composure. "There's nothing to be concerned about, ladies and gentlemen. Merely a case of mistaken identity. More champagne, more salmon mousse!"

With an indelicate touch, the motorcycle thug pushed me away, then followed behind Domino, leaving the mess of broken glass and spilled champagne for someone else to clean up.

As the back door rattled on its hinges, the room began to thaw. A big-boned dame with a miniature poodle curled up inside her lizard skin handbag ordered everyone to lock the doors before the hoodlum returned to murder us all. Beside her, a refined gent whose sideburns were peppered retrieved his cell phone to summon law enforcement with their clubs and guns and walkie-talkies.

Evan and Lyla rushed to my side, champagne splashing from their glasses like seismic waves in a swimming pool.

"Are you all right?" asked Lyla, combing her fingers through my hair. "Your golden tresses look like a crow's nest."

"I'm fine." I released a deep breath. "I just need to shake this off. Let's take the floor and show these thoroughbreds what a proper foxtrot looks like."

"In no galaxy is that a good idea," said Evan. He threw his arm around my shoulder in an exaggerated gesture that tested the seams on his guanaco suit. A generous gift from his older brother of less athletic build who had done well flipping houses, the garment fit Evan snug, but gave him a more distinguished appearance than his twenty-nine years of age would suggest. "Don't think we've forgotten how you stunk it up on the dance floor at your younger sister's wedding last summer, jerking your arms and shaking your hips like a malfunctioned sprinkler."

"That's because I was doing the sprinkler. You don't know good rhythm when you see it."

"What the patient needs is a fresh glass of champagne," said Lyla. She hurried off to procure the loot and returned minutes later with a clean glass and full bottle in hand. "The bartender was too preoccupied with an internet tycoon to notice my skillful sleight of hand."

My pulse regulated as I sipped from the champagne.

"Your valor in addressing that bruiser was impressive," said Evan. "I almost thought you were flirting with him."

Lyla smacked his arm. "Not funny. Annabel could've been hurt. That tattooed ape towered over her."

"Men who behave with the rough social skills of an early hominid are hardly my type," I said. "Besides, Lyla would throw fists before she'd let me walk off with the lone bad boy in the room."

She gave me a playful shove. "Only in certain circumstances."

"What did he mean when he said *you'd be next?*" asked Evan.

"I'm not sure, though I'm certain he didn't mean next in line at a lemonade stand replete with Dixie cups and a banner printed in comic sans font," I said. "Domino may have brushed off that confrontation as a case of mistaken identity, but he knew what it was about. The thug addressed him by name." I took a long drink from my glass and gazed out across the gallery, where the glitzy patrons were dropping the notion of contacting the police in favor of debating topics more pressing: the stock market, the futures exchange, the fashion faux pas of the royal couple. Soon the room would be buzzing like a hornet's nest, the unexplained intrusion all but forgotten.

"Let's take a final lap of the gallery to polish off our champagne before Domino returns," said Lyla. "By now he's realized we're imposters." She shivered as the air-conditioning tickled her bare shoulders and paused to slip on a black cashmere sweater.

While I waited for her to fiddle with the buttons, my eyes wandered to an abstract art installation, where giant facial features were hung from the ceiling by thin wires: a bloodshot rubber eyeball, an eyebrow formed from broom bristles, a wax nose the size of a Jurassic mushroom. Titled *Deconstructed Capitalist*, the piece was a confusing take on a subject so overplayed, it ought to be a curiosity shop, where propaganda buttons and the shrunken heads of CEOs would sell like hot cakes.

Evan frowned at the work of art. "I pray our city council doesn't blow our tax dollars on something so hideous for the sake of public enrichment. I'm not afraid to threaten to move to Canada."

As Lyla gave up on her buttons to pile on with a quip about the sleep disturbances in which the piece would result for the poor sap duped into buying it, the enticing hum of a rumor mill churning nearby caused my ears to perk up. I followed the sound to find an expensive couple of mismatched ages sliding epicurean cocktails down their gullets while discussing a topic for which I felt compelled to eavesdrop. I inched toward them, nudging Evan and Lyla to inch with me.

"Rumor has it, Byron is sweetening the reward for the return of his stolen surrealist paintings with a sizeable sum of cash and a scarce magnum of Walla Walla Syrah," said the wrinkled man, adjusting the felt beret perched upon his gray head of hair. "As if the initial reward weren't sweet enough. It practically exceeded the value of the paintings themselves."

The smooth-skinned girl furrowed her tweezed eyebrows. "I fear Byron's efforts are in vain. Three months have passed and still police have no leads." She sighed. "Such a horror for Byron—his magnificent vacation in the Périgord soured by the discovery of the theft upon his return."

The aging man nodded. "I heard he was inconsolable in the weeks following the crime. His wife was dosing him with a tablespoon of calf suet every night before bed. It's a wonder he stayed so trim."

"Is calf suet fattening?"

"No one knows."

The girl picked at her manicured fingernails and flicked a sliver of cuticle to the floor. "Byron said the paintings were the prize of his collection. Pity he failed to put protective measures in place." She suspired with judgment. "He fancies himself a cunning entrepreneur, yet he hadn't the ability to lock his doors? Maybe the papers were right to label him a brainless inventor with more money than sense."

"Don't believe everything you read in the papers. Byron swears up and down he locked his doors and armed his alarm, and his wife swears up and down she checked twice."

"If that's true, how did the thief waltz into Byron's mansion and lift the paintings from the walls of his foyer as if he were invited in?"

As the couple pondered the question, I crept several inches closer, a clandestine move proven poorly executed as my bare shins collided with a steel banana stalk jutting out from the sculpture of a dead banana tree. Knocked off-balance, I twisted like a circus contortionist and fluttered my hands, groping the hindquarters of a suited man nibbling on a crab cake. He spun around with raised eyebrows, leaving me to utter a clunky apology as Evan and Lyla dissolved into laughter.

I dragged them away by their sleeves. "Are you done splitting your sides?" We repositioned ourselves near the bar, and I dabbed up the champagne sloshed onto my satin dress with a cocktail napkin. Then I crumpled it into a ball and tossed it at Evan.

He released an evacuative sigh as it bounced off his lapel and landed at his feet. "Fortunately your legs bore the brunt of the impact with that steel banana stalk." He motioned to my shins, where the first purpling of a bruise was peeking out. Soon it would have a pulse of its own. "Had you damaged that sculpture, you'd be hocking your soul to pay for it."

"Three hundred grand," said Lyla, regaining her composure. "Why would anyone spend that much on the sculpture of a dead banana tree when they could purchase the entire plantation in the jungles of Laos and still have change left over for the harvesting equipment?"

"Heavy wallets make the hips look wide."

"Even so, what motivates one to sculpt something so uninspired?"

"According to the artist's bio in the brochure, while studying at a distinguished institution in Manhattan, he roomed with a surly photography major of Irish descent who kept a coffee-stained copy of *The Dharma Bums* on his dorm room bookcase—"

Lyla reached across me to zip his lips. "It was a rhetorical question."

Evan unzipped them and chucked the imaginary key that hadn't been in play. He turned to me. "Why were you intrigued by that couple's conversation? I thought that theft happened three months ago. It was all over the papers at the time."

"The crime may be old news, but if the victim ups the reward, that'll be hot off the presses," I said.

"And?" asked Lyla. She sipped the last drops of her champagne and deposited her empty glass on the bar.

"It means the crime was never solved. The victim is desperate for the return of his paintings."

"*And?*" She really managed to drag out that single syllable.

I deflated.

Evan finished his champagne in a triumphant swig. "Listen to me, Annabel. It's time to silence the inner voice urging you to seek vindication for the Warhol blunder, and ignore whatever whispers of unfinished business you say linger." He wiped his palm across his mouth. "Lesser people have forgiven themselves for far worse."

"What you need is a hobby," Lyla said to me.

"I have plenty of hobbies."

"Finding new uses for avocado shells doesn't count."

"What do you call this?" I swept my hand through the air to emphasize the ritzy gallery swinging and swelling around us.

"I call it drooling over ridiculous art you can't afford in a lifetime."

"That's where you're wrong. Once Evan writes his best-seller, I'll waltz into a gallery like this and open a suitcase stuffed with cash to purchase whatever painting my heart desires." I looked to Evan and snapped my fingers before his face. "Hurry up, will you? I'm relying on you to bankroll my hunger for contemporary art."

Loosely titled *A Sophoclean Tragedy for the Urban Man*, Evan's elusive manuscript had been in the works since the dawn of man, but had yet to present itself as little more than a chicken-scratch outline on the back of a cable bill. But what he lacked in progress he made up for with passion, a fact confirmed by the impromptu poetry recitals he would deliver, out of the blue, when his kettle of creativity took on a rapid boil.

"Before we depart this glamorous affair, I must bump into the young maiden who earlier latched onto my arm," he said, changing the subject. "With that buttercup by my side, I could quit my job and sail the seven seas with nothing but the constellations to guide me."

"It'll never work," I said. "She spreads caviar on her peanut butter sandwiches. We both know how queasy you get around fish eggs." I puffed out my cheeks. "Besides, once Domino realizes we crashed his event—"

Heavy palms thumped down upon my shoulders from behind. Startled, I swiveled around to find staring back at me with jet black hair and sapphire eyes, the man whose name had just rolled from my lips.

Chapter 3

Few things are as spellbinding as a trio of vivid martinis in chilled coupe glasses, whispering two simple words: *drink me*. Or perhaps three simple words: *drink me, please*, because there's something to be said for manners. Lyla's Bijou with its herbaceous Chartreuse, Evan's Hanky Panky with its bitter Fernet Branca, my sweet Mary Pickford with its maraschino liqueur—standard libations from the era of debauchery that would surely address us with the sandpaper brogue of a hardened rum runner if only they could speak.

Located three doors down from the Titan Gallery in a historic brick storefront that once housed the city's first printing press, the Empire Martini Bar proved to be the pot of gold at the end of the rainbow we sought after Domino kicked us to the curb. In a manner devoid of compassion, the man had demanded we leave, pointing his finger in our faces in a gesture even children arguing over the last bites of chocolate bar on the playground would find rude. After threats to call the police were then lobbed, we agreed to remove ourselves from his gallery without protest, save an irreverent peace sign flipped over Lyla's shoulder on the way out.

Warm lighting from ensconced sixty-watt bulbs cast a glow across the intimate martini lounge, where the faint smells of dusty books lingered in the air, like the forgotten library of a horse-and-buggy antiquarian. Soft strumming from an acoustic guitar filled in the background as animated banter amongst thirsty customers added a spirited purr. Clever twenty-somethings with horn-rimmed glasses and scarves bunched around their necks settled into stools at the bar. Bantering thirty-somethings with fitted flannel shirts and Converse sneakers gathered around the tall tables sprinkled throughout.

Handsome with surfer-blond hair, chiseled features, and slate-gray eyes, the bartender who served our martinis returned to check on us. He was Lyla's type, of that I was certain, and the fact wasn't lost on her, either.

With cheeks glowing like a neon vacancy sign on a cold, cold night, she lavished him with praise—her martini with its flavors of the forest floor every bit as heavenly as she had hoped. A dribble ran down her chin as she took a sip to demonstrate.

With a flattered grin, the bartender offered her a napkin and excused himself to produce the tab for a pair of preppies dressed in chambray shirts and khakis hemmed to their ankle bones.

I leaned into Lyla's ear. "Your heavy-handed approach to issuing praise is entertaining."

"It's impossible to be excessive in the flattery of one's bartender," she said, fishing the cherry from her glass. "It's like knowing the friend of a cousin of a senator. There isn't any downside." She looked to the bartender as he cleared the preppies' empty glasses and ran a rag across the bar. "What gives this martini its bombastic flavor?"

"Green Chartreuse," he said. "Some say it's an acquired taste."

She rolled the liquid across her tongue. "I'm familiar with this taste. I acquired it last year when Annabel and I lost ourselves in Boston's confusing solar plexus and stumbled into a speakeasy in search of directions and something stiff." She cupped my knee. "As Annabel can attest, the cocktails were smooth but the clientele was iffy. A bed of clams could have done a better job filtering out the riffraff." She scrunched her nose. "Half the guys there were tanning parlor regulars with skin shinier than a body builder's biceps on competition day."

The journey Lyla described in curious detail was one upon which she and I had embarked to visit a mutual friend from undergrad working for a craft brewery in Davis Square. We had flown the red-eye to get the cheapest price on airline tickets, rented an economy car the size of a jelly bean, and spent the evening of our arrival puttering around town while waiting for our host to extract herself from the copper kettles.

"I could never live in Boston," said the bartender. "Between the rain that falls in inches and the hot-headed cab drivers, it's too much for this California transplant to endure."

"You're allergic to the rain, yet you live in the Pacific Northwest?" said Evan, sipping from his martini. The aromatic flavors of saffron, rhubarb, and cardamom nipped at his tongue.

"The dark days of winter haven't arrived, and I can already feel the cones in my eyes atrophying from lack of sunlight. How do you locals do it?"

"We've learned to worship the incinerating qualities of the sun for the few months it shines, then spend the rest of the year healing our sunburns and drowning our sorrows in unhealthy doses of vitamin D," I said. "What brought you to Washington State?"

"A cliché romance that fell apart within the first three months, after which time I spent the next five months weeping into my bran flakes."

"You don't strike me as the blubbering type."

"I'll take that as a compliment, though I've decided to return to my hometown of San Diego. In two weeks, I'll stuff all my earthly possessions into my Mini Cooper for the drive south."

Disappointed to hear of his impending departure, Lyla frowned. "Seattle will miss you. Bigger and better things await?"

"Opportunities to put my political science degree to use with any luck." He crossed his fingers. "Maybe I'll lobby the Olympic Committee to add surfing to the summer games."

"I'm sure you'll be persuasive." She offered a partial smile. "Say, as the bartender in a classy place like this, ever ask your customers, *Penny for your thoughts?*"

"The monetary nature of that proposition seems imbalanced. And it's a terribly moth-eaten thing to say."

Lyla's cheeks tinted pink. It was a question she couldn't have cared less to have answered, but rather than change gears and ask the bartender his name already, she opted to describe the respectable death that old phrase died when the last real outlaw shot the sheriff at a saloon with swinging doors in the ghost town of Tin Cup, Colorado.

The bartender looked confused.

Lyla corrected course. "What's your name?"

"Dane," he said.

Her eyes lit up. "Dane is a name of great refinement. It makes me think of those thickly-pelted rescue dogs from the Alps."

"I believe you're thinking of the St. Bernards, a species known less for refinement and more for heavy drooling."

"Regardless of their drool, I hear those hounds save many lives every year. What do they carry in those tiny barrels collared around their throats?"

"Folklore says it's brandy."

"Pity. I hoped for Armagnac liqueur."

There it was, the Armagnac liqueur—one of a handful of French things Lyla loved to reference when it fit neatly into conversation. She had never actually been to France, though the coastal region of Provence topped the list of destinations she most wanted to see once she procured herself a proper love interest. Anyone could go to Paris, she would say. But Provence? That was the place for lovers. That was the home of perfumed herbs and soft-curd cheeses.

A quartet of middle-aged women with the rosy glow of celebration cast across their cheeks shuffled into the martini bar, hooting and hollering and waking the dead. With ribboned gift bags in hand, they beckoned Dane for a predictable round of cosmopolitans. As he stepped away to serve them, I felt certain that if anyone came to the bar with bells on that night, it was very likely them.

Lyla's eyes flickered as she watched him walk away. "A charmer like Dane would be the cure to all that ails me. I bet he's a tender-hearted gentleman and a virtuoso with an espresso machine." She swirled the liquid in her glass. "How are your shins, Annabel?"

I lied. "Never better."

"Have you learned your lesson to mind your own business?"

"Not a chance."

She tapped her heel on the rung of her stool. "Be honest. Were the paintings stolen from that entrepreneur even any good?"

"Depends on your taste for surrealism. A similar piece by the artist is in our collection at the modern art museum. An outspoken docent once likened it to the illegitimate offspring of an Antikamnia skeleton calendar and a Grateful Dead concert poster."

Lyla cringed. I mean she really cringed. A Parisian waiter

offended by an Alabaman's pronunciation of the word *croissant* would take pause.

"Independent of how you feel about melting, morphing objects, the paintings were worth big bucks. Our curator valued the museum's piece at a quarter-million dollars."

She whistled. "That's a lot of chili peppers. Why is the culprit still at large? Surely the entrepreneur had security cameras that recorded the crime."

"No cameras for the paintings, windows, or doors." I resettled in my stool. "No way to verify how the thief pulled off the crime without smashing his way in or triggering the alarm."

She startled at the details. "Why didn't the guy have cameras?"

"That's the million-dollar question." I took a drink from my martini and set the glass on the bar. "The entrepreneur wasn't the only instance of such an oversight. A wealthy socialite who was robbed while hosting a private party at her estate last month—an *expo peinture*, she called it—didn't have security cameras, either. Police suspect the thief blended in with her party guests, snuck into her conservatory, lifted a rare abstract landscape off the wall, and snuck out undetected." I clicked my tongue. "Totally brazen."

"I've never heard of an expo peinture. Is that a mustard-based dipping sauce?"

"Technically it translates to painting expo. The socialite's application of the phrase is imperfect, but she felt it fit her glamorous soiree centered around showing off her expensive art collection while slurping raw oysters flown in from the coast."

Evan gulped the contents of his glass. "I remember when news of the theft from the socialite hit the papers. Our social columnist from the *Seattle Courier* had been at her party the night of the crime. He said the socialite commented to her guests that only their conscience and the big guy upstairs would be watching should their fingers become sticky."

"Did the news say why she didn't have cameras?" asked Lyla.

"In an interview with the press, the socialite claimed the electromagnetic buzz emitted by the devices disturbed her yoga practice," I said. "Particularly her plow pose."

"Seems like an unsatisfying explanation."

"Not everyone is meant to be inverted."

Dane returned and leaned his elbows on the bar. "So, what's the big occasion? You three are dressed like your next stop is a box seat at the opera."

"Exclusive gala at the Titan Gallery three doors down," said Lyla. She stretched her hand out like a red carpet rolling across the Hollywood stars.

Dane was impressed. "Rarefied air you must breathe. Other than the free brochures, I can't afford anything in that gallery."

Evan squeezed Lyla's thigh. "Lady Finch was two breaths away from buying an eighty-thousand-dollar painting of a Spanish toreador drawing a velvety cape across his shoulders." He could never resist a good put-on.

Dane straightened his posture. "I didn't realize we had a *lady* in our presence."

"Neither did I," I said, chuckling beneath my breath. Dane seemed to be buying it, a fact that amused me given the non-royal picture of herself Lyla had painted moments ago. I wanted to ask him, do you really think a lady of nobility would know the first thing about men who frequent tanning parlors?

"The owners of the gallery must have been honored to have a lady on their guest list," said Dane. "Why didn't you buy the painting?"

"Sir Neruda is to blame," said Lyla. She clapped Evan's shoulder. "The toreador's cape triggered a random musing from him about one compulsively peeling the layers of an onion back, only to discover nothing in their hands but a pile of peeled onion layers." She rolled her eyes. "Such musings run rampant in the Neruda bloodline, and my chateau in Chamonix is hardly the place for endless jabber about allium vegetables."

Dane looked to Evan. "You're a descendent of the poet Pablo Neruda?"

Evan shook his head. "No relation to the poet, though I am a man of great complexity myself. Often I've been told my genteel disposition comes second to only that of the Earl of Nottingham." He placed his hand on his chest, coughing back laughter. "Guilty as charged."

I smirked. "Your imagination is a thing to behold."

He turned to me. "My most charming quality, wouldn't you say?"

"No shortage of confidence, either."

"Are you flirting with me?"

"Don't flatter yourself."

He straightened his collar. "Just because you hope our history will one day repeat itself doesn't mean you must flirt with me every time you get a bit of champagne in your system."

Whenever the mood was right, Evan loved to bring up our air-quotes history, which had been as lacking in depth as an inflatable kiddie pool. In the wake of the Warhol debacle, Lyla and I were blowing my last paycheck on expensive cocktails with ingredients we couldn't pronounce at a bar in Belltown when Evan spotted us from across the bar. He was funny, handsome, and Latin. He couldn't decide which of us he liked better, so he offered to buy both of us breakfast in the morning.

Evan went home empty-handed that night, though months later, we came to appreciate his brand of humor. He was dating a brunette with an attitude the size of Cleveland, who while helping him move into an apartment in Ballard, had unearthed a photograph of Evan posed with his motorcycle, Macho. Raised under a rock, the girl had referred to the vintage Norton 850 as a scooter, and likened it to a Vespa she saw dilly-dallying through a yellow light at milkman-delivery speeds. Affronted, Evan had assured her Macho could chase banditos across the border if he were so inclined, and when this clash spilled onto the sidewalk near a breakfast joint with the best waffles in town, Lyla and I stumbled into it. Unwilling to tolerate the girl's insults, Evan had begged us for earmuffs. When recognition of our faces then set in, he suggested we revisit his breakfast offer once he was back on the market.

As to any other history between Evan and me, I can neither confirm nor deny such allegations.

Dane studied Lyla with his head tilted like a fuzzy puppy begging for a biscuit. "I've never met a noble lady before. Should I ask for your autograph or a lock of your hair?"

"A lock of hair would be creepy," she said. "But if you asked for my number, I'm sure we could find some trouble to get into."

"I can do better than that." He reached for his wallet.

"Slow down, King Charles. I'm not that kind of girl."

"You haven't seen what I have to offer." From within the folds of his leather wallet, he removed a simple white business card and held it like the queen of spades between his thumb and forefinger. "Do the words *18 Laws* mean anything to you?"

"I might have seen an oppressive sign at the royal swimming pool with such a title," she said. "Thou shalt not enter the water with a peeling sunburn, lest the shed skin cells clog the pool filters—"

"She means the words 18 Laws don't ring a bell," I said, cutting her off. "What's on the card?"

Dane offered a sly smile. "The directions."

Chapter 4

Printed on the white business card in the uncluttered font of an antique typewriter were the cryptic directions to 18 Laws. My eyes widened like pupils under the influence as I ran my fingertips across the grained papyrus. Redwood tree pulp and octopus ink were used in the production of that card, I just knew it.

Dane leaned in close and lowered his voice. "Hidden beneath the frail bones of an abandoned building in the old industrial district, a resurrected prohibition speakeasy known as 18 Laws roars to life every Saturday night with unrestrained revelry and unbridled decadence." He paused for effect.

Our interest was piqued. "Go on."

"Between the walls of 18 Laws, luxurious cocktails flow like a river charging its banks while every shade of intrigue drips from the rafters. Nothing worth having comes easy, though. You must unravel the clues to find it—down a darkened stairwell, where the masonry walls crumble like a forgotten headstone, and behind the rusted hinges on the boarded-up doors that invite no one but the eternally lost to enter."

"Well…" I said, looking to Evan and Lyla as Dane's words hung in the air. "This could provide for some fresh entertainment."

"Or a trip down the rabbit hole," said Lyla, studying the card. She squinted her eyes, furrowed her brow, and sucked her cheeks in tightly—an odd expression of the face if ever I've seen one. "These directions are as clear as a glass of buttermilk."

"Bleh, buttermilk," said Evan. He plucked the card from her fingers.

"You have until midnight tomorrow night to find 18 Laws," Dane continued. "After that, this opportunity expires." He uncapped a pen and wrote his number on the card. His penmanship was neat, his sevens hashed with a cross through the spine. "When you arrive at the speakeasy, you must charm your way past the doormen by whispering into their ears. Call me at eight tomorrow evening for the magic words."

Lyla recoiled. "The last time I whispered into a strange man's ears, I wound up with two burly arms wrapped around my torso like a constrictor snake sucking the last breath of life from its prey."

I swiveled to face her. "What?"

"I thought I saw Evan standing in line ahead of me at the dry cleaners and snuck up behind him to whisper something gooey in his ear. The guy mistook it for a pickup line and latched his arms around me like it was love at first sight."

Evan rolled his eyes. "I fail to comprehend how you confused me for that sasquatch."

"It was a moonless night. Anyone could have made the same mistake."

"But you were standing inside the dry cleaners beneath two-thousand lumens of fluorescent lighting."

"Splitting hairs."

"I'm confused. Are you two together?" asked Dane, glancing back and forth between the pair. "And what's a lady doing picking up her own dry cleaning?"

"I'm not hairy enough for the lady," said Evan. "She prefers her men like Afghan hounds."

"Don't blame your romantic failures on body hair," I said to him, retrieving the card for safe-keeping.

Dane scratched his head and pressed forward. "The directions to 18 Laws may not be shared with anyone. If a bottom-feeder with a tribal tattoo slimes up to the door, the proprietors will have my head." He paused and looked to Lyla. "Not that a lady would keep such company."

"No bottom feeders," I said. "Got it. What happens if we get stuck working through the directions?"

"Call the number printed on the back of the card for a hint."

"The number you wrote down?"

"No, there's another number on the other side." Dane motioned for me to flip the card over.

"Two numbers? Seems cumbersome." I glanced at the back of the card before tucking it inside my handbag. "If you're the keeper of the password, why aren't you the keeper of the hints?"

"The decision wasn't mine."

I finished my cocktail and ate the red cherry, tossing the stem into my glass. "Can we skip this dance and get the address? Even with a hint, it could take us all night to make sense of this gibberish."

"Spoil the experience?"

"You'd be doing us a favor. Wrangling Lady Finch's impatient demeanor is a challenge even greater than navigating other peoples' nut allergies."

"I can't give you the address. But look on the bright side. It's not like you have to sacrifice a goat."

Lyla bit her lip. "I'm not sure how I feel about this."

"You would prefer to sacrifice the goat?"

"No, I'm not sure how I feel about this escapade. How do we know you aren't sending us blind into the underground lair of some ruthless Ukrainian loan shark to whom you owe an astronomical debt? They break kneecaps as payback."

Dane brushed off her concerns. "Ukrainian loan sharks are the cuddliest teddy bears in the toy store."

Carried on the wings of a gust of wind, a forty-something gent with a slick suit and gelled sideburns entered the bar. He had *smooth operator* written all over him, an observation confirmed by the tan line on his finger where his wedding band ought to be. He settled into a stool and issued Dane a familiar nod.

"One of my regulars," said Dane, returning the gesture. "He's a generous tipper."

"What happened to his wedding ring?" I asked.

"He lost it swimming with the dolphins in Tahiti. A dolphin from the pod sucked the ring into its blowhole."

"Seriously?"

"How the hell should I know?" Dane clucked over his shoulder and walked off to greet the man.

~

A cloud of exhaust puffing from the tailpipe of a rusty Pontiac blasted us in the face as we left the martini bar and emerged onto the sidewalk. Evan signaled for a taxi, and a yellow cruiser with rattling engine and doors spackled in grime pulled to the curb. The cheap vinyl in the backseat, which smelled of drugstore cologne, bulged beneath our tailbones.

As the taxi cut through the bustling streets of Seattle, we discussed 18 Laws and the opportunity with short expiration to pickle ourselves in a beautiful aquarium of top shelf martinis from the storied caverns of a prohibition speakeasy. The proposition felt irresistible.

We arrived at our apartment building in lower Queen Anne—a three-story brick structure boasting the elegant flourishes of prewar construction—and stumbled out onto the sidewalk in a disorderly fashion.

Mature maple trees stretched their aging branches in a tired canopy overhead, depositing beneath them an autumnal gift of fallen leaves the size of baseball mitts. We rubbed our shoes on the door mat to avoid grinding the foliage into the carpet inside.

Taped to the interior bank of mailboxes, a handwritten note fluttered at its edges as the door swung shut and locked behind us. Lyla paused to read its contents, flicking her finger against the page. "According to section D of our rental agreements, it is illegal for tenants to prop open the doors to this building. Violators will be... *persecuted?*"

"In other words," I said, "go ahead and shove a phone book in that door. Just don't be surprised at the hell that rains down when a solicitor lets himself in."

Lyla ripped the note from the mailboxes and wadded it into a paper ball. "This poorly penned reminder deserves the same fate as the authoritarian note from last week reminding tenants about the prehistoric plumbing." She tossed it into the recycling bin. "I'll damn well flush whatever I please."

From my handbag, I pulled the keys to my apartment and peered up the staircase to the second floor, where my charming abode of linoleum countertops, turquoise bathroom fixtures, and pine floors was situated. The kitchen barely fit a loaf of bread, the toilet ran until the handle was jiggled, and the dual-spigot water faucet spit out a blend of lava and glacier melt. But such matters were of little concern to me. "Shall we reconvene at my place tomorrow night—dressed to kill—and see if we can crack the directions to 18 Laws?"

"How do you define dressed to kill?" asked Lyla, kicking her toe at a nickel resting on the carpet. "Pelt of a mountain lion tossed over the shoulders—paws attached, head attached, rodent in its teeth?"

"You could never pull off that look."

Evan gestured down the tastelessly papered hallway to his door. "Let's meet at my place instead. There's an unopened bottle of Stoli in my cupboard that isn't going to drink itself."

Lyla picked up the nickel and placed it in her pocket. "I could be persuaded by such a bribe. If the hunt for 18 Laws proves to be a wild goose chase, what shall we do instead—fan each other with lotus leaves while eating peeled grapes?"

Evan shook his head. "We'd have to swing by the market for grapes. That's inconvenient."

"If we're met with defeat, we'll retire to our favorite taproom near the arts district for a round of consolation pints," I said. "They have a Belgian pilsner on tap so magnificent, the critics are calling it the lone Stradivarius in a symphony of spoons."

Evan and Lyla nodded in unison. "We agree to those terms."

"A final point of clarification," said Lyla. "Dane said 18 Laws is located in an abandoned building. What happens if we bumble into the wrong one and find ourselves in the clutches of a salivating Count Orlok sizing us up as his next meal of peasant and claret?"

I gave her a cockeyed look.

"He hasn't brushed his teeth in a hundred years."

"We'll offer him a breath mint."

Chapter 5

The following evening, we reassembled in Evan's apartment of Art Deco furnishings with a bottle of Stoli, two limes, and a liter of soda water. Handsomely attired in our Saturday night best—Evan in his tailored shirt with trousers and vest, Lyla and I in our little black dresses—we looked like the first stars to roll off the assembly line from the golden age of Hollywood.

With cocktail in hand and lips pressed to the rim, I produced the directions for 18 Laws and studied the cryptic contents:

1. Start where once the Byzantine Empire held its rule
2. Find your way to the opposite of a gyrocompass find
3. Right at pennies in a dollar less the quintessential prime
4. Left where pedagogy was first at three but lost at twenty-nine
5. Left at once M90
6. Follow the forgotten trail until the mean of ten and two
7. Abandoned you will find her

As the words swirled through my mind, I took a seat on the 1940s Le Corbusier sofa with stiff leather cushions and steel frame Evan bought off Craigslist at a screaming deal. *Streamlined* was the word he used to describe it, which I'm certain meant it was stuffed with shoebox inserts.

"Thoughts?" asked Lyla, settling in beside me.

"Clear as dishwater," I said, my optimism fading like newsprint in the sun. My eyes wandered to a prismatic wall poster depicting a symmetrical alignment of vertical color bars from Ellsworth Kelly's *Spectrum IV* series. Reminiscent of a television test pattern, the image triggered a high-pitched sine wave oscillating in my ears, a voice announcing: *This is a test. This is only a test.*

I glanced at Evan sitting on the retro swivel chair at his desk. "Does the well-connected social columnist at the *Seattle Courier* who owes you a favor for getting the duck sauce out of his tie at last year's holiday party have access to the address?"

"I don't know how to reach him," said Evan. "For the past two weeks, he's been recharging his batteries on a remote atoll off the tip of the Seychelles—a nature reserve known more for giant tortoises than cell reception."

"Then we'll search for the speakeasy online," said Lyla.

"Already did so while on hold with the cyborgs from the credit card company earlier today. A whole lot of nothing is all I came up with." He sipped from his glass. "It may be time to bribe the gnomes in your brain to start turning the cogs."

"The gnomes have been mighty greedy these days." She looked to me. "Can you get your hands on some bronze coins?"

"For what reason?" I asked.

"We need to speak with some Byzantines."

"I doubt we're meant to hop a 747 to ancient Istanbul, the flight a long one with food service that leaves much to be desired."

"I'm not opposed to packing a lunch."

I took another glance at the card and flipped it around in my fingers. "What if the answer lies not in the meaning of the words, but in the words themselves? If you subtract the word *Byzantine* from the riddle—"

"Scratch it out from the directions? I need a pen."

"This is a mental exercise, Lyla. Now, add the words *martini* and *bar* after the word *Empire*."

She processed the instructions. "The Empire Martini Bar?"

I nodded. "I believe that is where our hunt for 18 Laws will commence."

"You're sure of this?" asked Evan.

"I wouldn't bet the farm on it, but it's a reasonable guess."

"Good enough for me." He tossed me a pen.

I made the notation on the card. "The next step references a gyrocompass."

"Is that the self-balancing scooter mall cops ride around on?" asked Lyla.

"A gyrocompass is a navigational gadget prized by seafarers throughout history. If you'd stayed awake during the shipwreck documentary I twisted your arm into watching with me last week, you'd know the gyrocompass was cherished for its ability to locate true north."

"Which means we need to head south down the street that runs north-to-south in front of the Empire," said Evan, finishing my thought. He tossed me a paper map for the Seattle metro area. It crinkled my dress as it landed in my lap.

"Paper map, seriously?" I said. "Aren't there more mapping sites online than sandcastles in Death Valley?"

"I'm occasionally old-fashioned."

As I unfolded the map, Lyla leaned over to examine it with a craning of her neck that resembled a prairie dog peeking out from its earthen burrow. I told her this much, but she failed to see the humor. She did, however, find the street in question. "Bromwell Street," she said, pointing to the map.

I set the map on the floor and noted the answer, then proceeded to the third step. As a left-brained person who could barely calculate a fifteen percent tip without counting on my fingers, I knew we'd need Evan to produce the quintessential prime.

While he searched for the answer online, Lyla and I conferred on the number of pennies in a dollar. We arrived at quick consensus on one hundred. It was also the number of reasons Evan was ill-prepared to cultivate houseplants, as evidenced by the ficus wilting into extinction on his desk.

"You wouldn't believe the passion the adorable math brains in Vermont hold for the quintessential prime," he said after several mouse clicks. "The number is forty-seven. Since one hundred less forty-seven is fifty-three, we'll turn right at Fifty-third Street." He polished off his cocktail, collected our glasses, and disappeared into the kitchen. Moments later, the ice-clanking, lime-cutting, water-fizzing, spoon-stirring sounds of three vodka sodas being mixed echoed out. When he reappeared, three highballs were balanced in his hands.

"What did I do to deserve the first class treatment?" I asked, eyeing the generous pile of lime wedges floating in my glass.

"Your darling Lyla sliced up extra limes for you before you arrived."

I turned to Lyla and squeezed her cheek. "You're a doll."

"Let's move on to the forth step," said Evan. He headed for his desk, pausing before the multi-paned encasement windows to gaze into the darkness outside. Perfectly timed with a cold draft of air leaking in through the frame was the hissing and clattering of the cast-iron radiators coming to life. It was a quirk of prewar apartments that seemed charming at first, but proved to be annoying as hell with the passage of time.

"The next step references the word *pedagogy*, along with the numbers three and twenty-nine," I said, reading from the card. "We could be looking for an educational landmark."

"What do the numbers mean?" asked Lyla.

"Could be a reference to the address." I stood from the couch to stretch, rotating in a circle with my arms pressed out over my head. Above Evan's couch I spied an antique poster of a 1930s Duesenberg convertible zipping along an oceanfront roadway dotted with feathery palm trees, striped beach umbrellas, and slender seagulls aloft. Suspended in the distance, a highway marker signed *Florida US 94* identified the road while a banner floating across the top labeled *Naples to Florida* indicated the direction. At the bottom of the image, a blue pennant with the words *Go by road!* encouraged vintage travelers to skip the train and explore by highway instead.

"New poster, Evan?" I asked.

"I bought it from a used bookstore in Wallingford last week." He straightened the frame. "Highway 94 went the way of the rotary dial phone back in the forties when the American transportation giants got a bee in their bonnets over short intrastate highway segments. Once a lengthier stretch of road connecting Miami to Michigan was laid, the old signage was sent to some junkyard to rust into oblivion. Funny thing is, that junkyard was demolished thirty years later to make room for a theme park."

Lyla's eyes lit up. "That's the answer to the clue."

"A theme park?"

"No, a different kind of park." She retrieved the map from the floor and studied it. "Last month, a partner at Absent Thought dragged me to a client presentation in this part of town. Upon our arrival, she was horrified to discover her assistant had arranged for a budget coffee service, and sent me on the hunt for something gourmet. It was a miserable endeavor that involved hoofing it ten blocks in the pouring rain while the pain from my tarsus-twisting heels radiated up my spine." She huffed. "When I returned with the goods in hand, I learned everyone had grown impatient, stuffing their bellies and filling their bladders with the coffee service better saved for the peasants."

"Hold on, Lyla," I said. "How lengthy is this tale?"

"Patience, Annabel." She shook her finger. "Infuriated, I stormed out and whiled away the next forty minutes inhaling vehicle fumes. When my phone began ringing off the hook—the fussy partner demanding my return—I stopped by a post-age-stamp park to ignore her incoming calls. I then noticed a placard affixed to a crumbling pillar of bricks that identified the park as the site of the first schoolhouse in Seattle's third school district. Tragically it burned to the ground in the winter of 1929. Needless to say, the chalkboards and pencil erasers never stood a chance." She pointed to the map. "The school is located at the intersection of Fifty-third and Logan Street."

Evan jumped from his chair and sucked in an eager breath. "Tonight we celebrate triumph!" It was a presumptuous response akin to a politician inflating the celebratory balloons before the results of the campaign have been announced; the red, white, and blue bunting advising against it.

I was that red, white, and blue bunting. "Don't pull out the streamers just yet. We still have three more steps to work through, starting with *Left at once M90.*"

Evan cued up an internet search while Lyla and I gathered over his shoulder.

After sifting through the results, we arranged our findings into three categories: automotive, military, and miscellaneous. The automotive bucket included a motorway in Scotland, a highway in Michigan, and a Japanese motorbike. Comprising the military results were the sniper rifle of the Irish Republic Army, the assault rifle of the Yugoslav army, and the camouflage pattern of the Swedish army. Lastly, the miscellaneous category provided for a high-tech light bulb, a galaxy in the Vertigo constellation, and the FAA code for the Mendota airport. But the answer remained a mystery; the old-fashioned pointing finger extending from a black cuff with the caption *This way, folks!* failed to reveal itself.

Evan swept his fingers across his unshaven chin. "We could follow the trail to the burned-down school and see if we can find the meaning of M90."

"Tread through an urban park after dark?" asked Lyla.

"It's either that or we dust off the stack of weird tarot cards you bought in the French Quarter three years ago and see what gems of wisdom they yield."

"The last thing I need is a two-headed horseman judging my personal hygiene habits."

"Then what do you suggest?"

"I say we drop this fool's errand in favor of finding another private party to crash."

"We saw how well that turned out last night," I said. "I still have imprints in my skin from that motorcycle thug's ragged fingernails." I motioned to the Swiss railway clock mounted above Evan's desk, the red second hand shaped like a signaling paddle marching along the arc of black tick marks. "It's past eight. Let's call Dane for the magic words and see if he'll tell us the meaning of M90." I punched in his number and set the phone to speaker.

"Be sure to speak in a soft, feminine voice," said Evan.

"As opposed to the gruff, masculine voice I would otherwise use?"

Dane answered on the third ring. His voice was rushed. A jazz band from Portland was setting up to play, and the needy musicians had him standing on his head.

"These guys are a pain in the ass," he moaned as we exchanged greetings. "They think a martini bar gig is beneath them, but as far as I can tell, money is money, and Gibson guitars don't grow on trees."

"Here, here," I said. "What should we tell the doormen at 18 Laws?"

"The magic words are *deuce five*."

"Got it. How about a hint on the meaning of M90? That fifth clue refuses to don its clogs and dance an Appalachian jig."

"Like I said last night, call the number on the back of the directions for a hint."

"That feels an awful lot like giving up." I looked off into the distance, an idea taking shape. "You're moving back to San Diego, right?"

"That's right."

"Remember Sir Neruda from last night?"

"The Latin guy with the genteel disposition?"

"That's him. As luck would have it, he knows the food writer at the *San Diego Beacon*. If you'll tell us the meaning of M90, Sir Neruda will convince the guy to write a glowing article about your stupendous bartending skills. Every martini bar in the city will want to hire you. Politicians will, also." I glanced at Evan to find him slicing his finger beneath his chin in a *cut! cut!* gesture.

"I'm a sucker for free advertising," said Dane after an extended pause. "Here's what I'll tell you. To solve the fifth riddle, you must step back in time."

"What does that mean?"

"That's all I've got." His voice muffled. "The talent needs something stiff to prime their pumps. Gotta go."

As the call disconnected, Evan looked at me with reproach. "I don't know the food writer at the *San Diego Beacon*. That isn't even a real paper." He walked to his bookcase, selected a worn copy of Voltaire's *Candide*, and flipped through the pages without reading the words.

"What are you doing?" Lyla asked him.

"I'm thinking."

"Seems like an unnatural way to think."

"As unnatural as the artificial maple syrup in which you drown your pancakes?"

She ignored the question. "That book is falling apart. You should support the spine."

"This book is bomb proof. It's been to the moon and back."

"Was that a humble brag?"

"No, the shopkeeper at the used bookstore told me so."

Accustomed to the pair's occasional squabbles, which I generally credited to Lyla being an only child and Evan being the younger of two, I tuned them out and allowed Dane's hint to spin clumsy pirouettes in my mind. A news story I'd once read about scientists from the land of the rising sun cracking the Gordian knot of superconductors while unwinding over a round of happy-hour specials came to mind. I thought, if those lab coats could accomplish such a feat while navigating the path to three sheets, we could identify the meaning of M90 over a round of vodka sodas.

I shared this opinion with Evan and Lyla, who were less convinced.

"You're being stubborn," said Evan. "Let's call the number for a hint. I'll dial the phone."

"Not just yet," I said, glancing around his apartment, deep in thought. My eyes landed on the wall above his desk, where an unidentified green splatter once lived. "Did you repaint your walls?"

"Last week," he said. "I could no longer tolerate staring at that waxy green patch every time I kicked back in my chair to contemplate the meaning of life. Now I can spin around and lose myself in the vintage Florida coastline." He gestured to the poster of the Duesenberg convertible.

I lingered on his words. "You mean you take a step back in time?"

"Something like that."

I grinned, the answer flashing before my eyes like a ribbon of magnesium in an antique camera. "I know how to find the meaning of M90, but we need to leave right away." I checked the clock to find the hour hand prancing toward nine. "The history museum closes in fifteen minutes." I pounded my cocktail and slipped into my woolen peacoat. "I'll explain everything on the way over."

Chapter 6

Like a speedy roadrunner escaping the absurd machinations of its clumsy pursuer, we pulled ourselves together and raced for the door at a dizzying pace. We climbed into a taxi idling at the curb and bribed the haggard driver to go heavy on the gas pedal for an extra five bucks.

On the heart-stopping drive over, I explained my hunch to Evan and Lyla that Dane's vague hint was pointing to a street once called M90. Since our destination was a historic speakeasy, I guessed the road would have been in use during the 1930s. It was a map from that era we would need to procure.

I laid my hand on Evan's knee as I described the role his vintage poster played in drawing that conclusion, then lurched into his lap as the taxi took a corner at fifteen over. The driver glanced in his rearview mirror and snickered, the sagging skin on his cheeks bunching at the folds.

Lyla bonked her head against the window and forced her way to the middle of the backseat. "Move over, will you? I'm sustaining head injuries over here."

I granted her a millimeter of space. "That better?"

"Much." She smoothed her black bangs. "Aside from some rusty canteens, what do we hope to find at the history museum?"

"The reason for this escapade is to consult with the expert in the history of our city." I pulled the seat belt across my lap. "His name is Claus Vandenberg. He spends his evenings tucked away in the archives room."

"How do you know this Claus Vandenberg?" asked Evan, jamming his knees into the center console as the cab driver slammed on the brakes to avoid collision with a panel van coated in political stickers. Angry honks and lowbrow hand gestures were exchanged.

"I cut my teeth working for Claus during an internship at the history museum my senior year of undergrad. As you'll see, he's a quirky, hermit-like individual who prefers the company of the characters prancing around in history books to those with reliable pulses."

"The term *hermit-like* warrants definition," said Lyla. "It makes me think of a fossilized eccentric who gets himself in a tizzy over speakers blasting rock and roll." She glanced out the window. "And webbed feet."

"You have an active imagination," I said, feeling nostalgia wash over me as I recalled the side of Claus that was contrary to what his museum persona would suggest: the side that reminisced fondly of Woodstock, drove a '67 VW Beetle colorful enough to put a school of mandarinfish to shame, and wore his gray hair too shaggy for his age. He had taught me the virtues of meticulous record keeping and a few tricks for firing up the carburetor on a vintage Bug when the mercury dipped below forty.

"I've heard getting those quirky types to warm up is like cracking the shell of a macadamia nut," said Lyla. "We should arm ourselves with an irresistible cocktail of flattery and appeal to butter the man up." She looked to me. "Are you familiar with the Renaissance?"

I rolled my eyes. "The Renaissance, seriously?"

"You'll be the poet Edmund Spenser, Claus will be Queen Elizabeth the first, and with a few words of flattery—"

"No one is Edmund Spenser. We don't have time for that."

Ten exhilarating minutes later, we arrived at the museum and sprinted to the entrance. Warm air brushed past our cheeks as we gripped the handles to the heavy doors and pulled hard. Inside, an atrium arched across the expansive foyer while educational exhibits were staged around us and suspended overhead.

A high-school volunteer with Sun-In-streaked hair and metal braces manned the information desk, an escritoire of veneer so white, every celebrity in Hollywood would hear their teeth holler in envy. Busy organizing a stack of brochures, the girl jumped to her feet to find us rushing toward her like a band of crazed gypsies riding a chariot pulled by insane, charging horses.

I cleared my throat and spoke with authority as we stopped inches from her face. "We need to speak with Claus Vandenberg. Please notify him Annabel Riley is here."

The girl adjusted the nameplate pinned upon her blouse. "The closure announcement sounded over the intercom ten minutes ago. Come back tomorrow during business hours." She handed me a glossy brochure.

I denied the brochure and clicked my heels on the polished stone floor, imagining how slippery it likely became when tourists spilled beverages from their clumsy hands. "We must speak with Mr. Vandenberg at once regarding a preservation emergency."

"On a Saturday night? I don't think so. Please leave."

Make me is what I wanted to say, though I drew Evan and Lyla into a huddle instead. "This girl is incorrigible. Since when were teenagers such sticklers for the rules?"

"Give me a minute alone with her," said Evan. "I'll introduce myself as an exiled prince from Denmark whose bank account is bursting at the seams. She'll be putty in my hands."

"What is it with you and these boastful theatrics?" asked Lyla. "You're starting to sound like an arrogant windbag."

"This coming from the girl who introduced herself as a renowned apiculturist to the beekeeper at the farmers' market in order to get a free jar of honey?"

"Why do you find that ruse questionable? The beekeeper's honey was more nectarous than most, and I was two dollars short of buying the jar. The bundle of radishes cost more than I thought."

"When the beekeeper asked for your thoughts on colony collapse, you rattled off some nonsense about the deadliness of malaria amongst the first Anglicans in the Carolinas. Wrong colonies, Lyla."

"How was I to know the beekeeper was referring to honeybee colonies? At least I wasn't using my cover story to get a date."

Evan smacked his forehead. "In what version of reality would I look to score a date with a petulant youth barely old enough to tie her shoelaces?"

I raised my hand to silence him. "We can all agree you both have some notable achievements notched into your belts, but now is not the time to relive them. Our young volunteer is dialing security." I smacked Evan's shoulder. "Batter up."

With a flirtatious wink, he stepped into the girl's personal space and spoke to her with romance in his voice. "You must be Spanish. I can see it in your eyes."

The girl lit up like a Christmas tree, a reaction that was so wonderfully, eye-rollingly predictable.

"It appears we've found the right man for the job," I whispered to Lyla. "Did you hear that bit about her Spanish eyes?"

Lyla sneezed and dug around in her handbag for a tissue. "Every nauseating word."

"Nauseating or not, the girl is doing swan dives into Evan's eyes."

Lyla blew her nose and shoved the crumpled tissue into her coat.

"Remind me not to go digging through your pockets later."

Her face was somber. "It's a minefield in there."

Charmed and disarmed, the young volunteer succumbed to Evan's persuasions and placed a call to the archives room. "Claus will be out momentarily," she said to us. "Wait for him by the door signed *Museum Personnel*." She pointed the way and batted her eyelashes, hopeful her coaxed amenability had earned her Evan's seven digits.

Evan thanked her with the aw-shucks charm of a rodeo cowboy, then yanked me and Lyla away by our sleeves. "We need to get out of here before any more of this gets caught on camera. I may run for political office someday."

Sepia photographs of Makah and Nootka whaling parties dressed in animal hides and onion-domed hats flanked the nondescript door for museum staff. The restrooms nearby displayed signage with humanoid figures shaped like popsicle sticks. En route to the lavatories, a janitor pushed a wheeled bucket and mop across our path, soapy water dripping down the sides.

Evan ducked into the restroom while Lyla turned her attention to an exhibit of logging tools from the early deforestation of Aberdeen: drag saws, felling axes, sledgehammers, marlin spikes.

"Shopping for protection in case the Ukrainian loan sharks come out to play?" I asked, joining her before the display.

"While the crude axes wielded by the libertines of the timber industry would make for solid defense, it would be impossible to loot this weaponry buffet without getting caught. Everyone knows museums are bursting with rabid guard dogs and security cameras."

"Not necessarily. The history books overflow with successful museum heists made possible by inadequate security measures."

"You're suggesting I test their safeguards?"

"For some rusty saws? Hell no. The risk of tetanus is too high."

Evan rejoined us and said to me, "Do you recall from your days working at this museum if their security measures are up to snuff?"

"You want to lift a taxidermy chipmunk from the wildlife diorama?"

"No, I want to know if the little monster who left a chewed wad of spearmint gum in the water fountain will get caught."

"You'll have to leave a complaint in the comment box," said Lyla. "There aren't any security guards to notify." She paused. "Which means if ever we wish to quit our day jobs, we can knock off this museum and be set for life."

"Not exactly what I meant," I said. "But go ahead and give it a try. See what happens."

"The challenge would be knowing what to steal," said Evan. "Remnants of nets from the sponge fishing display wouldn't be worth much on the secondary market, but nuggets of gold from the mining exhibit would."

"Sponge fishermen made it this far west?" asked Lyla.

Evan gave her a funny look.

"There's clearly too much uncertainty in establishing value," she said. "Let's focus on private collectors instead."

"Private collectors can be a crap shoot," I said. "Take the wealthy socialite whose abstract landscape was stolen from her conservatory last month. Despite its rarity, it was the least valuable painting in her collection by many magnitudes."

"How do you know that?" asked Evan.

"After the theft occurred, the socialite's insurers contacted our curator at the modern art museum to weigh in on the value of the painting. He appraised it at four thousand dollars, small potatoes compared to every other painting the woman owned."

"Why was your curator involved in establishing value? I thought that's what gallery appraisals were for."

"The artist fell into obscurity decades ago, so there were insufficient auction records to support the gallery's appraisal. The socialite's insurers wanted the opinion of an expert."

"Who was the artist?"

"His name escapes me, but I recall he hailed from some mossy firth in Scotland and fell into obscurity once tastes for abstract landscapes moved on. According to our curator, the socialite considered the painting the prize of her collection only because it had been passed down to her by a distant aunt who engaged in a romantic tryst with the artist while traveling to Scotland to escape the cultural wilderness of her hometown. How the thief managed to bumble the crime by stealing the only painting in the socialite's conservatory that wasn't worth huge dollars is a head scratcher."

The door signed *Museum Personnel* drew open, and the sound of cork-soled Birkenstocks shuffling across the threshold served as prelude to the man of the hour: Claus Vandenberg. His aging face was creased like the folds of a linen napkin forgotten in the cupboard, his hair white and unkempt. He greeted us with a wrinkled hand extended from the frayed cuff of his sweater. "Annabel Riley, how many years has it been?"

"Too many," I said, introducing Evan and Lyla with formality that subsided as we recounted the details of our search for 18 Laws.

Claus removed the wire spectacles hooked over his collar and set them on his nose. He reviewed the directions and our notes. "Let's speak in my office."

We followed the man through a bright hallway with ecru walls to the archives room, where the familiar smells of musty attic and tanned leather, and the familiar sights of mahogany bookcases spilling over with hardbound tomes, rekindled memories of my days spent working alongside Claus in the warm, windowless room.

From an archives drawer, he selected an antique map and directed us to gather around a cartography table. He laid the delicate papyrus—faded and brittle like an aged bale of hay— flat upon it.

"Have many streets changed names since the 1930s?" asked Lyla, overlaying her modern bearings atop the antique depiction.

"Some," said Claus. He drew our attention to our last known turn from the directions, then traced his finger southward forty blocks until arriving at an unfamiliar intersection in the pulseless heart of the old industrial district. "During the roaring twenties, a prominent businessman named Alfonso Barretto operated many businesses in this area and solicited the city council to name the main artery in his honor. But due to a clerical error, the letter *o* was dropped from Barretto's name, and signage for Barrett Street was hung instead. When the mistake was discovered, the city scrambled to stamp out new signage, though in a gesture that ingratiated Barretto with everyone from the mayor to the woodworkers milling chair legs for his furniture shop, he forgave the mistake and urged the city to accept his donation to build a playground for the children."

"This Barretto fellow sounds like a stand-up gent," I said.

"So he led everyone to believe. When prohibition was repealed, the man's corruption was revealed. With roots deep in organized crime, Barretto had been operating his businesses as fronts for illegal operations. After a jury found him guilty of extortion and racketeering, he was shipped off to some penitentiary to fade into obscurity. Some, however, theorized Barretto continued to run his operations from behind bars." Claus raised his white eyebrows. "Anxious to distance themselves from the scandal, the city changed the name of Barrett Street to Commerce Street. It was the least controversial thing they could think of."

"What is the connection between Barrett Street and M90?" asked Lyla.

"In your notes, you've indicated the Irish Republic Army kept in its arsenal a sniper rifle called M90, manufactured by the Barrett Firearms Company."

Her jaw dropped. "Alfonso Barretto was supplying weapons to the IRA?"

"No, I believe the author of the directions was simply being clever." Claus rerolled the map. "Turn left when you arrive at Commerce Street, then continue six blocks—the mean of ten and two. There you should find the abandoned building in which the speakeasy is located."

"Incredible," said Evan, a magnificent smile spreading across his cheeks like that of a deep-sea diver uncovering the sunken cache of gold doubloons stashed away by a peg-legged pirate once rumored to have sent half his shipmates marching down the plank, trust issues an obvious ulcer amongst his crew.

"Abandoned buildings litter the old industrial district," I said with a more neutral expression. "How will we know which one we're looking for?"

"Barretto owned a boutique hotel rumored to have housed a speakeasy in its basement during prohibition," said Claus. He accessed a file cabinet and sifted through a collection of historic photographs, then returned with a black-and-white picture of a three-story brick building boasting a grand entryway with round pillars. The sign affixed to the front of the building read: Meland Hotel, Sleeping Rooms 50¢ Nite & Up. "This photograph was taken during its heyday."

"The Meland Hotel," I said, studying the building and the black roadster parked at the curb with curved body panels, round headlights, chrome bumpers, and squatty windshield. It seemed to be waiting for nefarious mobsters running from the Feds while bootlegged bottles of rum banged around in the trunk.

Evan sucked in an excited breath. "That roadster rolled straight off the set for *American Graffiti*. Paint it yellow, pop the hood, add a set of racing tires…" He cooed with delight. "If only I could afford a Ford deuce five-window coupe that isn't infested with mice."

"Next to his mistress, Barretto's deuce five was likely his most prized possession," said Claus.

"Did you say *deuce* five?" I asked.

Claus nodded.

"Dane instructed us to say those words to the doormen at 18 Laws. Curious the modern-day owners of the building are familiar with Barretto's vehicle."

"Perhaps they have a copy of this photograph, as well." Claus motioned to the image. "As you can see from the address, the Meland Hotel was located on the sixth block of Barrett Street. I suspect you will find the speakeasy in its basement."

"How will we identify the hotel? Looters would have stripped the signage away decades ago."

"The cornerstone should still be located between the lowest layer of bricks on the front of the building." Claus placed the photograph in the archives drawer and ushered us out. "If you don't mind a short walk, the D-line from the train station two blocks away will drop you off near the intersection of Logan and Commerce Street. It's the last stop on the line." He glanced at his watch. "You must hurry, though. The trains are running on the weekend schedule. If you miss this train, the next won't arrive for another hour."

We bid Claus farewell and exited onto the sidewalk.

"Should we skip the train and order a ride?" asked Lyla.

Evan scrolled through the ride app on his phone. "Not for forty bucks. Surge pricing is a bitch." He pointed down the puddled sidewalk toward the train station. "Ladies first."

Chapter 7

We arrived at the train station to find a motley collection of strangers standing upon the covered platform, shivering in the damp cold. Compelled to observe the first-come-first-serve nature of mass transportation, we took our place near the back of the line and waited for the train, where a thirty-minute ride with a cross-section of the city's urban inhabitants would deliver us to the decaying industrial district. From there, we'd imagine ourselves stepping like forest pixies through the garden of earthly delights as we continued our hunt for 18 Laws.

"Why are there so many people riding the commuter train on a Saturday night?" asked Lyla, appraising the crowd. "Surely they aren't taking hot laps around the city for the hell of it."

"This is the main line between the city and the outskirts," I said. "It's the only mode of transportation that's practically free."

The train tracks quaked as the bell announcing the arrival of the D-line sounded across the platform. In a sloppy shuffle, the waiting passengers assembled themselves for entry, avoiding eye contact and the touching of shared surfaces.

Ravenous for an unlikely Conradian adventure within the radius of our city, I imagined myself tiptoeing through the jungles of Borneo as I stepped aboard the train and slid into an open seat beside a middle-aged woman cradling a carton of eggs. Her fingers gripped the cardboard cups as the eggs nestled inside awaited their destiny in a mixing bowl of cookie batter.

Three rows back, Lyla settled into an empty seat beside a heavily pierced teen with an impressive assortment of studs and spikes pinned through his ears and nose. Throw him to a herd of Styracosaurus seventy-five million years into the past, and the horned beasts would recognize him as their own. They may even brunch together on Sundays. From the edges of her corneas, Lyla caught the teen ogling her, and the eye roll she flashed him could flip a tanker on its side.

Two rows forward, Evan sat beside an ivory-haired lady with a schoolgirl grin. She gazed at him, thinking, *Oh, my, imagine the possibilities!* Indeed, the afternoon she was cooking up for them was a nice one: bridge with the blue-hairs at noon, bread crumbs to the geese at three, a dinner of Salisbury steak by five.

As the chime announcing the next stop sounded through the train, the keeper of the eggs stood for the door. A zombie of a woman hovering in the aisle banged into my knees and collapsed into the cushion. Deprived of sleep like one kept up through the night by feral dogs barking for pork chops, she rubbed her fists across her droopy eyes. Her muscles went limp and her head slid toward my shoulder, the greasy matting of hair draped over her forehead like jellyfish tendrils brushing across my cheek.

I gagged and jumped into the aisle.

Evan appeared at my side, chuckling. "Nice maneuver."

"Tips are encouraged." I wiped my face with my sleeve. "I see you've made a new friend in the geriatric community."

"How could you tell?"

"Your cheeks are red."

"Myrtle wouldn't stop pinching me."

"Did you make bingo plans for Wednesday?"

"Bingo is so passé." He motioned to Lyla clamoring up behind us. "Have you and the lost band member from the Anti-Nowhere League forged an unlikely romance?"

She crinkled her nose. "Not in this lifetime. He smelled like Pop-Tarts and microwaved fish heads. I thought for sure he was going to launch into a stick-it-to-the-man rant and look for me to join in."

"Were you prepared to do so?" I asked.

"No, but I was prepared to be Dutch."

"Which would accomplish what, exactly?"

"People who speak Dutch don't understand English."

"Except for those who do."

"Regardless, the suggestion of windmills and pickled herring is enough to convince any weirdo to leave me alone." She glanced down at the zombie slumped over in the seat. "What's her deal?"

"Feral dogs and midnight deliveries of leaf blowers," I said.

"Does she have a pulse?"

"I'm not sure."

"She probably missed her stop and is destined for a frigid night at the train depot. She'll need a warm bottle of milk and a bassinet if she hopes to make it through the night."

As the train continued winding along its tracks, the passengers dwindled with the passage of each stop. Before long, it rolled through the outskirts of town and stopped at a dingy platform in the rundown curtain district, where developers had converted grungy commercial buildings into tiny apartments during the eighties. Offering the cheapest rents around, the district served as home to many urban dwellers who relied on the commuter train for transportation into the city.

Seats opened up in a wide swath as the bulk of the passengers disembarked, leaving only us three and the zombie sawing logs.

"Where is this train taking us, the bowels of the city?" asked Lyla, wringing her hands as the doors slid shut and the train pressed forward, the bright lights of the city fading into a distant blur. "I hope Dane isn't sending us into some lawless dystopia, where luck is the only rabbit's foot we'll have on our side."

Evan patted her shoulder. "I think you misunderstand how the rabbit's foot works."

Minutes later, the train slowed to a stop at a poorly lit platform dumped in the forgotten industrial district. We stepped off and shivered as the doors slid shut behind us.

Odors of cigarette smoke, diesel fuel, and destitution hung in the air as a deserted webbing of crisscrossed train tracks expanded into the distance. Mangled sections of chain-link fence and broken chunks of concrete littered the ground, along with shards of broken glass, splintered scraps of wood, and a clapped-out El Camino with bullet holes in the hood. A dilapidated warehouse with crumbling smokestack stood hauntingly alone, save a row of decrepit bungalows withering beside it, which only the Grimm Reaper called home. Even the stars in the sky seem dimmed.

I looked to Evan and Lyla and said, "Welcome to Eden."

Chapter 8

Spits of drizzle fell upon us from the grumpy clouds looming overhead as we left the seedy train station. Lyla and I huddled beneath her umbrella while Evan allowed the pellets of moisture to dampen his dark hair.

We arrived at Logan Street to find a tired two-lane roadway dotted with rundown storefronts, dilapidated row-houses, and rusty stop signs at every intersection. The road was absent cars and the sidewalk absent people, a lost cat lapping water from a neglected fire hydrant the only sign of life.

"Our sanity is officially up for debate," said Lyla, wrestling with the umbrella as the wind pulled at its spines. "Look at us, strolling like gawking tourists through the roughest part of town, where even the children's tricycles are weaponized."

"What happened to your adventurous spirit?" I asked.

"Rolling into the Thunderdome with nothing but a water gun mounted to the grill of a Fisher Price buggy is hardly my definition of adventure."

Greasy puddles and potholes the size of Bolivia greeted us as we arrived at Commerce Street, the forgotten road once named for the mobster Alfonso Barretto. Six blocks farther, a deserted neighborhood unspooled before us with the dark silhouettes of abandoned buildings moaning beneath their collapsing roofs. Mangy bushes flanked the forgotten structures, their cornerstones buried beneath a bulkhead of shrubbery.

Lyla sneezed and passed me the umbrella while she retrieved a tissue from her handbag. "We must be turned around. Soft tissues such as the brain require warmth and oxygen to function."

"Based on the directions, we're on the right track," I said. "We need to find the cornerstone for the Meland Hotel."

"By digging around in the shrubbery? No, thanks. A colony of black widow spiders has almost certainly taken up residence in these old structures, and I'm telling you those little bastards can be cantankerous. I say we retreat to our favorite taproom for a round of pints."

"We're not throwing this urban safari a retirement party until I'm three sips shy of a monumental hangover."

We strained our eyes to see the fuzzy details of each building as we pressed forward: the slumping entryways, the crumbling walls, the unruly juniper branches scratching at our skin like the hideous fingernails of the Wicked Witch of the West as a ghostly voice hissed, *Ready or not, here I come!*

I stopped in my tracks to shake off the thought. Lyla paused beside me to adjust the zipper on her boots, the joints in her bony knees cracking as she bent down. "Wait—" She stood up. "There's a vehicle creeping along at a snail's pace two blocks down." She motioned toward a set of headlights illuminating the empty road.

"It could be someone else looking for 18 Laws," I said.

"Or a madman trolling for used gallbladders."

"Why would anyone be in the market for used gallbladders?"

"How should I know?" Her pupils shrank as the headlights neared. "My mother will never forgive me if my face ends up on a milk carton. We must hide." She pointed to the hollow carcass of the nearest building.

"Specters, spiders, and grave robbers be damned?" I asked with exaggerated horror as Evan and I followed on her heels.

We ascended the rickety stairs to the drooping entrance, where sticky cobwebs brushed past our faces and clung to our clothes. Images of the hallowed country estate from *The Turn of the Screw* swirled in my mind, though in a lucky twist of fate, the Victorian apparitions chose to leave us alone, and I shook off the goose bumps like a pro.

Evan and Lyla flattened themselves like pancakes against the boarded-up doors while I took post behind the pillars. A heavy silence settled over us, until Lyla broke it in an elevated whisper. "Hiding in the shadows of this creepy front porch makes me feel like the fleeing lovers from *Guillaume de Palerme* taking cover in the forest from the Emperor of Rome."

"You're referencing thirteenth-century French poetry at a time like this?" I whispered, recalling the poem from level-one French class in undergrad where Lyla and I first met. She had declared the poem her go-to citation in the unlikely event we ever found ourselves in a situation like this. Indeed, her brain had sopped up all sorts of useless nuggets from that class, though little stuck with me other than a few useful sayings for getting myself out of trouble when presented with a plate of dissected frog parts for dinner at a Michelin-starred restaurant.

"I've been waiting a long time to use the reference," she said.

"So I'm the princess and you're the benevolent wolf?"

"Why would I be the benevolent wolf?"

"Because you're the one who spotted the headlights."

Evan shushed us as a modern Town Car with shiny rims pulled

to the curb. Dressed in a patent cap and navy suit, the driver emerged, hustled to the rear doors, and opened a large umbrella.

A dazzling woman attired in a splashy cocktail dress and red-soled stilettos stepped from the vehicle and cocooned herself in a cashmere shawl. Her male companion appeared behind her in a tailored chesterfield coat. He took the umbrella by the handle, the woman by the arm, and guided them down the walkway. "Watch your heels, darling."

"Thank you, love," the woman replied. She tiptoed around a crevasse lurking in the pavement. "These shoes cost more than my last chemical peel." Her voice was proper yet pained as the arches of her designer heels forced the stretched tendons in her feet to suffer in silence.

"Your radiance is astonishing, darling. Need I keep an eye on you tonight?"

"Don't be silly, love. I haven't eyes for anyone but you. Though, I do intend to leave a sparkling imprint of my freshly plumped lips on Julian's cheek. I simply cannot get enough of his delicious compliments. Last weekend he likened us to the *Incroyables* and *Merveilleuses*—the eighteenth-century aristocrats of French fashion." Enraptured by the horn-blowing memory, she beamed.

"A fitting comparison." The man motioned to a trail of brick pavers wrapped around the building. "Shall I walk in front?"

"Yes, love, but step carefully. Rat-bite fever sounds dreadful. Let's save that for someone else, shall we?" The woman smacked her lips together and allowed the man to take the lead as they ambled down the path.

As the pair disappeared around the corner, we emerged from the decrepit entryway and dusted ourselves off. I peeled away a string of spider web clinging to a button on my peacoat as Lyla smoothed her black satin dress.

"Should I ever find myself marooned upon a remote tropical island, I hope to be wearing that woman's blinding dress," she said. "Natives diving for conch shells two hundred miles offshore will come to my rescue before I've contemplated my stomach's ability to digest the fibers from the palm fronds."

"Why would anyone eat the fronds when the dates are so plentiful?" I asked as we headed down the path.

Spongy patches of moss and a tangled matting of ivy lined the pavers. An overgrown evergreen tree stood sentinel halfway down, detritus from decades' worth of storms settled at its base. In search of solitude, a grouchy raccoon had made its den in the branches and would soon hammer a sign into the crinkled bark inviting visitors to bugger off.

At the rear of the building, a crippled wrought-iron fence tipped with spears like those from a medieval battle weapon surrounded the perimeter. Crabgrass carpeted the ground while maple trees sagged from age, their branches twisted and gnarled.

Paces farther, we arrived at a darkened stairwell descending into the frail bones of the old hotel. I stared into the pitch-black nothingness. "Let's see if this stairway leads to 18 Laws."

Musty odors and a suffocating darkness devoured my senses as I inched down the steep risers, the gradation in light degrading from dark to darker. The air was frigid, biting in a way that made the hair on my forearms stand at attention. And while I wasn't descending into the catacombs of a fourteenth-century monastery, I knew I'd prefer not to find myself there alone should the ground start shaking or the ghouls start howling.

A dim light sparked to life at the base of the stairs, casting a murky glow across a heavy door. I gestured for Evan and Lyla to follow me and rapped hard to signal our presence. As the door drew open the width of a sliver, a goony-looking man with cleft chin and squinty eyes peered out.

"You gawt the words fah me?" he asked in a scrappy Boston brogue, an accent out of place in the Pacific Northwest.

"Deuce five," I said with great anticipation.

The man chewed on the words and pulled the door open.

Inside, we lingered in a tiny foyer no larger than the narrow space between two loafers tucked in a shoebox. The temperature was warm, the walls the color of artichokes.

With bulky arms protruding from a tight white shirt, an ogre of a man guarded a second door. As I waited for one of the men to speak, I absorbed the details of their stereotypical appearance. When an organized crime boss in the movies said, *I've got some guys*, these were the sort of guys to whom he was referring.

Squinty Eyes motioned to the door guarded by the ogre. "If you want in, you gawta tell me what deuce five means."

The question caught me off guard. "I'm sorry?"

"I said, what does deuce five mean?"

"Dane from the Empire Martini Bar sent us with instructions to say deuce five, nothing more."

"I don't care if Pope John Paul the Second sent you. Unless you tell me what deuce five means, you nawt gettin' in."

"Uh, boss…" the ogre said in a dopey voice. "Pope John Paul hasn't been the Pope in a long time."

"I don't care who the freakin' Pope is."

"That's rather dismissive of the Pope," said Lyla.

Evan leaned into my ear. "These low-IQ goons have *grease the bouncers* written all over them." He extracted a twenty from his wallet. "Gentlemen, meet my friend Alexander Hamilton."

"We don't accept bribes," said Squinty Eyes.

"Might a basket of steemahs sway you?" asked Lyla.

"Forget the clams," I whispered. "Claus told us the meaning of deuce five at the museum." I looked to Squinty Eyes and addressed him with confidence. "Deuce five is a reference to the Ford deuce five-window coupe owned by Alfonso Barretto."

Squinty Eyes shook his head. "You gawt it wrong."

"How can that be wrong? We saw the picture of Barretto's roadster parked in front of the Meland Hotel."

Evan pressed his lips to my ear. "The expensive couple out front mentioned a man named Julian. He sounded important. Follow my lead?"

"What do you have in mind?"

"My name is Worthington and I'm a rich businessman who built my fortune shorting the housing market. You're my wife, Phoebe, and you have a spoiled Maltese terrier." He leaned into Lyla's ear. "You're my mistress, Henrietta."

She balked. "I refuse to go along with Henrietta."

"Suck it up and follow my lead." Evan turned back to the men and pressed forward with the freshly minted cover story—thin, as those concocted in moments of desperation often were. "Did Julian put you up to this? That sneaky devil. He owes me advice on rebalancing my investment portfolio since the Venezuelan government bonds he suggested blew up my second-quarter returns."

"Huh?" said Squinty Eyes.

"I'm facing double-digit losses and it's cramping my five-star lifestyle." Evan wrapped his arm around my waist. "I promised my darling Phoebe a romantic getaway on a private island near Bora Bora, where scientists have discovered the fountain of youth. If you believe the local aborigines, two sips of that nutrient-rich batter will knock a decade off your age." He pinched my cheek. "Darling Phoebe will never forgive me if I deny her the chance to slather herself in that youth-restoring nourishment."

I elbowed him in the gut. "Not that darling Phoebe needs it."

Squinty Eyes summoned the bedeviling sort of laugh one might hear from a wily auto mechanic who's just found a leak in the radiator pump, and hold on to your hats, ladies and gentle-men, this replacement is going to cost you dearly. "Cute story," he said. "Get lawst." He pushed past us to open the door, and booted us into the cold.

"Time to call for a hint," said Evan. He punched the number from the back of the directions into his phone. It rang until an automated voice instructing us to leave a message picked up.

"Brute force it is," said Lyla. She took Evan's phone, launched the internet, and typed *deuce five* into the tiny search box. Several results filled the screen. The first directed us to an angry website geared toward gun-nut enthusiasts, where a collection of black pistols were displayed upon a charming series of backgrounds: an office desk, a bed sheet, an evidence table in the police impound. "The speakeasy could be the front for a weapons-smuggling ring," she said.

I shook my head. "Only in Hollywood."

She continued sifting through the results. "This looks prom-ising." She tapped the screen as a busy website dedicated to gambling loaded. An icon of a domino caught my eye and I urged her to click it. On the next page, variations of domino games were explained: Matador, the game for businessmen guzzling Manhattans; Chicken Foot, the variation for the milk-and-cookies children gathered around a breakfast nook. Individual dominoes were also displayed, including a tile with two black dots arranged atop five, labeled *deuce five*.

"Prohibition speakeasies were a hotbed of vice," I said. "The password must be a nod to elicit gambling activities." I turned to the door and delivered a forceful knock.

Squinty Eyes opened the door and scowled. "I thawt I told you three to get lawst."

"We have the answer to your question," I said. "Deuce five is a gambling reference."

Squinty Eyes' lips flattened as he gnawed at the information.

From behind him, the ogre spoke up. "Uh, boss… I think they got the answer right."

"Shut up, you big loaf, I'm thinkin'."

Loaf? Lyla mouthed to me. I shrugged.

He chewed on the answer a moment longer, then drew the door open, his façade cracking like a chocolate-shelled, creme-filled, foil-wrapped egg on Easter Sunday. His cheeks puffed out and his belly filled with laughter. "I see what's goin' awn here. Julian put you up to pullin' a wicked prank awn me."

"Should we let them in, boss?" the ogre asked.

"Yeah, yeah, deeze guys are awright."

Chapter 9

Carbon filament Edison bulbs glowed from industrial fixtures while ornate tin ceiling tiles and a massive steel clock added a whisper of Steampunk charm. Sultry music spilled from the brass instruments of the jazz ensemble and enlivened the ritzy crowd—the movers and shakers, the *in the know*—who had united as one at 18 Laws to sip prohibition cocktails while prancing their way from one titillating conversation to the next.

We dropped our belongings at the coat check and headed for the bar. Carved with elegant flourishes, the mahogany relic from the 1920s was situated against a flecked brick wall and bore the abrasions of its age. Simple stools followed its contours while a scaffolding of shelves boasted top shelf offerings. Propped against the bar with irony, a timeworn sign read: In compliance with the 18th Amendment, no intoxicating liquor allowed on the premises.

Baby-faced with green eyes, button nose, and cinnamon hair, the young bartender presented us with a martini list attached to a tiny clipboard. Then he left us to consider our choices.

Evan flopped his menu on the bar seconds later and spoke in a voice that was smooth like the sands of Guardalavaca. "Lost in Havana."

"Your quick decision-making is impressive," I said, eyeing on the menu his martini of choice.

"Decisive action is the credo by which I live my life. What strikes your fancy?"

"The Sapindaceae sounds bewitching: vodka, lychee liqueur, vermouth, and a plump lychee fruit soaking up the glory."

"I'm intrigued by the Gaelic Mythologist," said Lyla. "Though, I must verify the quality of the garnishes." She gestured for the bartender's attention. "The maraschino cherries you serve aren't the waxy, freakishly red cherries one often encounters in a drinking establishment, are they? I'm not sure how I feel about corn syrup and red food coloring these days."

"We import our cherries from Dalmatia," said the bartender. He extracted a cherry the color of burgundy wine from a lidded container and passed it to Lyla on a fancy toothpick. "The mountainous regions of Croatia are rugged, but the liqueurs preserving these cherries are pure silk."

She swallowed the cherry in two bites. A satisfied smile unfurled across her face. "Based on this cherry, I am certain the Gaelic Mythologist descended from the heavens." She read the ingredients aloud. "Scotch, sweet vermouth, orange bitters, lemon, maraschino… Yes, please."

With the dexterous sort of handiwork that made me question the laws of physics, the bartender mixed the ingredients of varying hues like a Brasileiro dancing the samba. Paper-thin slivers of ice slipped through the strainer and floated on the surface as he filled each glass. He selected a twist of lemon for Evan's cocktail—an enticing combination of spiced rum and orange curaçao—then slid two cherries into Lyla's martini and a lychee into mine. "We import our lychees from Guangdong," he said. "The fruits from China have the softest flesh."

Two suited men of dissimilar heights arrived at the bar and ordered the finest bottle of champagne.

"Celebrating something, gentlemen?" asked the bartender. He selected a chilled bottle of Dom Perignon. The liquid sparkled as it poured into their crystal flutes.

The taller of the men sipped from his champagne with his pinky extended. "I've just spent a hundred thousand dollars on a contemporary painting—a spectacular rendition of Georges Seurat's *A Sunday Afternoon on the Island of La Grand Jatte*. It's the masterpiece of an artist from Manhattan in which the faces of Seurat's Victorian folk have been overlaid with those of over-cooked rock and rollers." He peered down the extended bridge of his nose to the bald man standing beside him. "My attorney advised me on the purchase."

The attorney caressed the thin sprouts of hair speckling his forehead. "It's a sound investment."

"Congratulations on your acquisition," said the bartender. He topped off their glasses. "The brothers will insist on joining you in a toast."

"And we'll insist on a glass for you, as well." The attorney handed him a credit card. "Keep the champagne chilled while we mingle."

As the men disappeared into the crowd, a stiff-postured gent wearing a black fedora arrived at the bar. Anguish was evident on his face. "I need a strong drink to soothe the sting of treachery."

The bartender weighed the severity of his claim. "What sort of treachery, sir—Brutus versus Caesar?"

"Worse." He pinched his fingers together like crab claws. "Last night, I was *this close* to getting my hands on a life-sized installation of a Swingline stapler with metal staples the size of croquet wickets. Inscribed with various numbers—long numbers, in the thousands—each staple represented the patents taken out by the inventors who contributed to the progression of the stapler from the iteration used by Louis XV to the Swingline we know today." He moaned. "Some hedge fund twit with Chiclets for teeth and eighty grand in his wallet beat me to it."

From the shelf, the bartender selected a bottle of Pernod absinthe and mixed the emerald antidote. "This should soften the blow."

The pained man sipped from the martini. His posture relaxed. "Ordinarily I'd have my attorney sue the other buyer, but he's currently hiding out on a nude beach in Aruba bronzing his nether regions."

"Your attorney or the other buyer?"

"My attorney. He recently weathered a nightmare of a divorce. The local naturists and hurricane-strength daiquiris are helping him erase the ordeal from his memory."

"An effective strategy?"

"We'll know in two weeks. Problem is, he looks like a newt with a comb-over and has as much personality as a celery stalk." He sighed and took another sip. "What's this drink? I feel mended already."

"Death in the Afternoon, sir. Historians say it was a favorite of Ernest Hemingway."

"Bravo, bartender. I must lobby the fine brothers who own this place to give you a raise." He handed the bartender a credit card the color of a slinky. "Keep my tab open."

As he adjusted his collar and sauntered off, it struck me that high-end art was the topic du jour at 18 Laws. I wondered, would we experience a dramatic intrusion from a brute with bruised knuckles as we had when lingering amongst a similar vein of affluence at the Titan Gallery the previous night?

I turned to Lyla. "If a motorcycle thug with octopus tentacles tattooed on his throat storms in, it's your turn to play hostage."

"Hardly a risk with the muscle guarding the doors out front." She sipped from her glass. "As long as a band of raving mad stilt walkers smoking cloves cigarettes don't stomp in and sneak up from behind me, all is copacetic."

"Don't tell me you're still carrying around baggage from that night on Bourbon Street three years ago when you tripped over a crack in the sidewalk and knocked a stilt walker off his poles."

"His beaked mask gave him the grotesque appearance of a medieval plague doctor." She trembled. "I can still smell the odor of cloves wafting from his cigarette as he lay flopped upon his tailbone, cursing me out in a strange tongue of gypsy and bayou."

I chomped the vodka-soaked lychee from my glass. "You need to seek help."

"A partner at Absent Thought feels the same way. Last month, he hired some street performers from Union Station to work a private party—some jugglers and a ventriloquist that creeped the shit out of everybody. Next morning, he discovered the performers had taken his Bentley for a spin, leaving behind smudges of face paint and smoldering cigarette butts. Apparently the smell of burnt tobacco sticks to leather the way mildew sticks to a kitchen sponge."

"That isn't remotely the same thing."

"Enough with the street performers," said Evan. "Let's explore this place."

Frothy conversations echoed in our ears as we made our way around the speakeasy. Near the back, we spied a small room with an oversized chesterfield couch and a trio of hefty club chairs arranged atop a knotted rug the color of an oyster shell. Metal bookcases displayed a collection of antique cigar boxes and chemistry supplies.

Masterful reproductions from legendary expressionists hung from the masonry walls: Paul Klee's *Senecio* with its geometric face; Wassily Kandinsky's *Improvisation 35* with its mosaic of symphonic imagery; Ernst Ludwig Kirchner's *Street, Berlin* with its chic dames ambling down a red carpet.

Posed for a picture before the madams, a silver-haired woman wearing maroon lipstick that made her lips look thin smiled for the camera. She saw her reflection in the painting of the fashionable dames, a fact that amused me. I hate to break it to you, darling. It's just a pair of prostitutes.

Platinum-haired and painfully underfed, a twittering lady dressed like a 1920s flapper took notice of Evan and hurried her twiggy legs over to his side. Twice his age and half his size, she smiled flirtatiously, hooking her bony elbow through his, a giant rock sparkling on her finger.

Disinterested in breaking up her holy matrimony, Evan extracted himself from her clutches. "I've promised the refined gents who own this place I'd join them in a debate of practical strategies for rowing tin baths around the Isle of Man."

"I'll go with you," she squeaked.

"No, that's all right." He motioned to Lyla and me. "My darling wife, Phoebe, and my mistress, Henrietta, will ship me off to Timbuktu if I introduce another ingredient into the mix." He bid the woman adieu and pulled us back into the main room, where the saxophonist was dancing his fingers along the brass keys of his instrument.

"For the record," said Lyla, "I officially renounce the name Henrietta. It makes me sound like an old maid from Holland who dines on figs and quail." She polished off her cocktail and guided us to the dance floor, where a comely lady plucked from the pages of *Town & Country* magazine exchanged airy kisses with a flamboyant man whose chestnut bouffant formed a gentle wave across his forehead. The man laid his smooth hands upon his chest and thumped them twice to mimic the beating of his heart.

"Schmooze city," I said, watching him dance in a circle to show off his slick mulberry suit, shiny cufflinks, and shimmery tie. His face was structured, his eyes amber, his lips parted into the saccharine grin of a smarmy Don Juan.

Evan gestured to a big-boned dame with diamonds the size of chestnuts dangling from her ears, blazing a path through the dance floor to capture the man with the glossy bouffant. "She looks hungry for some *amore*."

"Think her diamonds are real?" asked Lyla, snickering.

"Of course they're real. She dined on endangered rabbit kidney and a glass of Chateau Lafite Rothschild Bordeaux for dinner."

"Then she'll be gnawing her way through those diamonds halfway through the night. Have you seen French portions?"

The well-upholstered woman squeezed the man in a tight embrace, then shoved her hands into his coiffed hair to ruffle it like a pilgrim rubbing soiled trousers across a washboard.

On the verge of suffocation, the man wriggled free and dashed away, leaving the woman to lick her wounds and declare her intention to find someone strong enough to hold her.

I wrapped my fingers around Evan's bicep. "You've been looking ripped these days. Think you're up to the task?"

He pretended to flex. "No one says *looking ripped* anymore."

"How about pumping iron, is that on the table?"

"*Pumping iron* fell from the vernacular when we were still in diapers."

Lyla gestured to the young bartender, who was cracking an egg for a pink Clover Club martini. "Speaking of diapers, how old do you think our bartender is—eighteen, nineteen, tops?"

"He's twenty-three," a firm voice answered from behind us.

We turned to find staring back at us with jet black hair and sapphire eyes, the owner of the Titan Gallery—the man named Domino. We felt ourselves shrink as his intruding corneas seared our skin. "What the hell are you doing in my speakeasy?"

Chapter 10

Paisley wallpaper and a crystal chandelier ornamented the small room inside which Squinty Eyes locked us without explanation. Two white Verner Panton ribbon chairs were arranged beside a hopsack Florence Knoll couch and steel coffee table that gave the space a modernist feel. In the corner, a well-stocked bar boasted an enviable variety of top shelf spirits, two medallioned bottles of AsomBroso Reserva Del Porto tequila anchoring the shelves.

"Are you sure the door is locked?" asked Evan, gesturing toward it.

"I tested it twice," I said, recalling the handle's unwillingness to budge after the bouncer shut the door with us deposited inside.

Lyla was slow to catch on. "If you wish to get cast for a role on the big screen, you must practice your delivery—enunciate your words, animate your gestures, faint to the floor if it feels right…"

I faced her square on and gave the handle a hard shake.

She gasped. "This isn't good. I've watched this scene play out in the movies. In five minutes, Domino will send in his thugs to take us out back and feed us to the fish." She seized a sculpture of parrot wings from the coffee table and wielded it like a butcher knife. "We must arm ourselves."

"He's not going to feed us to the fish," I said. "Domino isn't moonlighting in organized crime."

"If that's true, why did he have his bouncer lock us in here?"

Evan walked to the bar. "Until Domino arrives to explain himself, I'm going to see what we have to work with." He selected a bottle of Hangar 1 vodka from the shelf and lined up three shot glasses.

Lyla replaced the parrot wings with an indelicate thud. "Ever hear the saying *curiosity killed the cat*?"

"Curiosity killed the cat, but satisfaction brought it back." He lifted the first shot and knocked it back clean. "What else is there to do? Our phones don't have reception; I already checked."

The lock on the door disengaged and the man with the silky bouffant let himself in, grinning in the disingenuous way that made me wonder if I was about to be talked into buying a high-mileage convertible. I stepped back to allow him passage as Evan hid the evidence of his curiosity.

From the shelf, the man selected the bottle of AsomBroso and prepared himself a generous pour. When he spoke, his voice was creamy. "During the reign of King Louis XV, custom dictated the highest-ranking member of the court unfold his napkin before his dinner guests."

Lyla and I exchanged confused glances. *What?*

"For eons, customs have governed our society, yet here we are, a herd of mannerless morosophs who believe the bleached bones of those customs should be tossed to the sharks." He set down his glass and wiped his hands together, sloughing off the remnants of those bleached bones. "With that in mind, tell me who you are."

It was an odd request for our names, and I found myself answering in an unintended question. "My name is Annabel?"

"Annabel who needs neither surname nor introduction?"

I hesitated. "My last name is Gurglebloom and I work in a pea factory splitting peas for split-pea soup."

As the man suspired with impatience, the door drew open and Domino entered. He conferred in whispers with the man whose glossy bouffant was glimmering beneath the light of the crystal chandelier before addressing us as one. "My brother, Julian, and I are quite startled you've found our establishment. Our speakeasy is a secret to which few are privy."

I straightened my posture. "You two are brothers? You own this speakeasy, as well as the Titan Gallery?"

Domino nodded. "Tell me, who leaked the address?"

"No one leaked the address. We solved the riddles ourselves."

"Impossible."

"We're clever folk." I motioned to Evan. "He can count to eleven on one hand."

Domino grit his teeth.

"Why have you corralled us like livestock in this glorified animal pen?"

"Don't be dramatic. Livestock aren't as cunning as you three."

"You didn't answer my question."

"Nor do I intend to. Instead, Julian and I have an irresistible proposition to share."

"First class airline tickets to Tahiti?"

"Not quite. For the remainder of the night, you may enjoy our luxurious VIP room with drinks that never run dry. In return, you will forget 18 Laws exists. You'll never come here again, and you'll never speak of it to anyone."

"What's with all the secrecy?" I asked.

"That's none of your business."

"I was taken hostage by a tattooed ape at your gallery last night. The least you could do is show us some respect."

"Why do you think we're allowing you to stay?"

I paused. "What was that confrontation about, anyway? You brushed it off as a case of mistaken identity, but that thug asked for you by name."

"You're making a mountain out of a mole hill. Let the moles rest." He lifted the cuff of his suit and glanced at his watch, its intricate movements typical of a premium brand. "Julian and I must return to our guests. Our bartender will be in shortly to tend to your drinks. When you're ready to leave, press the button by the bar to notify him." He straightened his suit coat, opened the door, and crossed the threshold with Julian on his heels.

Lyla stood from the couch to inspect the button as the door locked behind them. "This is too weird for my taste. Let's summon the bartender and tell him we want to leave."

"What's the hurry?" asked Evan. "Rather than rushing out of here, we could live it up like people with money to burn would do."

"You're suggesting we shrug off our captivity in favor of doing shots?"

"As far as false imprisonment goes, this place isn't terrible." He lifted the two remaining vodka shots in search of takers.

"Have you lost your mind?"

"This speakeasy may be a mystery, but so is Stonehenge. It's not like people go around questioning Stonehenge."

"Questioning Stonehenge is exactly what people do," I said. "I agree with you, though. We're here with the kings and queens of society and we have this swanky VIP room all to ourselves. Let's run up a monster tab on Domino's dime." I joined Evan at the bar, accepted a shot glass, and shuddered as the burning liquid drained down my throat.

"You've both lost your minds," said Lyla.

I wiped my hand across my mouth and pointed to the remaining vodka shot. "Are you going to take that?"

"And risk arsenic poisoning? No, thank you."

"Suit yourself."

"Wait—" Lyla swatted my hand as I swallowed the contents of the glass and poured myself another. "I think that vodka is laced. Look at Evan. He's catatonic."

I glanced over to find him gazing off into space, grinning a mischievous smile. "The vodka is fine, Lyla. He's picturing life in a distant galaxy, where a group of eight-armed cephalopods have gathered around a supper table to share in their last meal before riding off into the sunset, planet Earth locked in their sights." I whispered into his ear. "They'll need at least two sedans for all those tentacles."

He jolted back to reality. "What?"

"Lyla thought you were tripping on arsenic. She was seconds away from administering mouth-to-mouth."

"Why did you stop her?"

"It all happened so fast. Where'd you go?"

"I was imagining the expression on my editor's face if a giant buttercream-frosted birthday cake were to roll into his office Monday morning with me popping out of the confectionary monolith."

"Buttercream requires refrigeration."

"I'm aware of that."

"Is it his birthday?"

"Who knows. Point is, I'd be holding in my crafty hands a story about 18 Laws."

"What will you say, Domino and Julian are pretentious snobs?"

"I'll publish the directions to 18 Laws and urge every booze-hound in the city to crack the code. My editor has had a Kalahari thirst for scarce content like this ever since our social columnist retreated to the Seychelles."

"That's the worst plan you've ever concocted," said Lyla. She latched onto his shoulders. "Domino did not mince words when instructing us to forget about this place. Do you want to know what happens when he discovers the details of his private speakeasy splashed across the newspaper?"

"My pursuits to become an investigative journalist have been slow to launch, but I can remedy the situation by cracking open an electrifying story that leaves my editor grinning like a possum eating sweet potato pie."

Lyla released his shoulders. "Or you could stop accepting the crappy assignments better saved for the junior interns who haven't grown their permanent teeth."

Evan brushed off her retort and pulled his phone from his pocket. "My editor will want pictures." He swept the room with the lens. As I offered the camera a flirty grin, Lyla pushed her lips out in a pout. Evan gave her a funny look. "Stop making duck lips."

She huffed and stepped from the frame. "Clearly you have never seen the cover of an *Elle* magazine." She lifted a bottle of Sipsmith gin from the shelf and coughed as she swallowed a shot, her senses overpowered by the Christmas tree flavors.

"Stick to wine coolers," said Evan.

"Hummingbird syrup? I never touch the stuff."

"Don't act like you didn't polish off an entire bottle of Boone's Strawberry Daiquiri at my tiki party two weeks ago. I smelled your hiccups." He appraised the shelves. "We just need to find…" His voice trailed off as he locked eyes with the distinct red label of a rare bottle of Pappy Van Winkle bourbon. For a brief moment, he contemplated cartwheeling across all seven continents, then lifted the bottle from the shelf, pulled the cork, and drank from it freely. "My God, this liquor is smooth." He handed me the bottle. "Try it."

I luxuriated in the seductive aromas of caramel and spice before taking a long swig. But as the high-end bourbon offered my taste buds a warm kiss, it took a wrong turn and got sucked into my lungs. I jerked my neck forward and expelled a rattling string of noises that masked the sound of the door unlocking.

The baby-faced bartender entered and sucked in a sharp breath as he spied the evidence of our indulgence—the open bottles of liquor, the empty shot glasses, the devil-may-care expressions on our faces. His cheeks reddened and his button nose twitched as he rushed over and yanked the bourbon from my hands. "Did you stick your tongue in our bottle of Pappy's?"

"I didn't stick my tongue in the bottle," I said. "I'm not seven."

"Domino will be furious." He stormed off to rat us out.

I bit the inside of my cheek. "I think we're about to discover the size of Domino's leather-soled oxfords when he kicks us to the curb."

"We don't know if they'll be oxfords," said Lyla. "I didn't see his feet, did you?"

I looked to Evan. "How expensive was the Pappy's?"

He grimaced. "The promise of your first born should cover it."

With our coats draped over his forearm, the defiled bottle of Pappy's in one hand and Lyla's umbrella in the other, the bartender returned with stern instructions to leave. He flopped our belongings into Lyla's arms and swiftly lost patience as she passed them around with unnecessary commentary: "A velvet cape for the lady, a feathered fan for the queen, leg o'mutton sleeves for the lord…"

"What are you doing?" he snapped.

"If the brothers of the royal court insist on sending their squire to do their dirty work, I must engage in this theatrical bit."

"Hurry up. The car Domino called for you will be here soon." He handed me the bottle of bourbon. "We can't serve it to our customers now. It's yours."

Amazed, I slid the bottle into my handbag. "Tell us one thing before we leave—why is the speakeasy called 18 Laws?"

The bartender released an aggravated sigh. "Did you take American history in high school?"

"Who didn't?"

"Study the Constitution?"

"Of course."

"And the Eighteenth Amendment?"

"Yes."

"Then you can figure it out yourself."

As the door to the deceptive world of 18 Laws slammed shut, I shoved my hands in my pockets and felt my throat chill. In silence, we ascended the dim stairwell into the blackened night, the sky charred the color of coals.

"Dethroned," I said. "Now what?"

Evan rubbed his hands together. "Now we high-tail it back to our apartment building so I can write my article."

"Why must you poke the bear?" asked Lyla. "Nothing good can come of writing the story. Drop it."

"Spoons get dropped, as do plates of roast beef, if one isn't careful. Stories that are guaranteed crowd pleasers? Never."

Our unadjusted eyes struggled to see the placement of our feet as we made our way to the front of the Meland Hotel to catch our ride. Near the lone evergreen tree with the grouchy raccoon, Lyla tripped over a raised brick and fell on all fours. The contents of her unzipped handbag spilled across the unlit path.

"No!" she yelped, pawing at her scattered belongings like a backyard canine pawing for grub worms.

Evan pulled out his phone and shined a light on the path, where Lyla's wallet, lipstick, and sunglasses were strewn about.

I nudged Evan. "While you help the duchess regain control of her monarchy, I'll go hold the driver." I hurried to the front of the building and rounded the corner to find a silky black limousine idling at the curb. From within the shadows of a gnarled tree, I paused to practice the aloof nod-shrug combination that said, *I'm part of the club; I've been here before.* I'd wield it with confidence as the driver opened the door to the backseat, where a bottle of champagne would be lounging on ice. Like affluent prairie dogs, we'd stick our heads out the sunroof and let the fire hose of bubbles spray into the night.

As I grew quite certain our evening would unfold in that precise manner, a corpulent man in a fine suit emerged from the darkness near the hood of the limousine. With limbs trembling and backbone sagged, he stepped into the stationary beam of the headlights and threw his arms into the air.

Perplexed, I maintained my place in the shadows and watched with sudden alarm as a second man wearing motorcycle leathers materialized, a pistol gripped in his hand. He pointed the barrel of the weapon to the heavy man's chest.

Fear swept through my core. I prayed my coat would muffle the sound of my pounding heart, though the twigs crackling beneath my feet threatened to betray my presence. With a mind to dart back to the speakeasy and alert the doormen to the crime, I turned around quietly, only to smack into Evan and Lyla as they appeared from around the corner.

Lyla yelped loudly enough to be heard two counties over, startling the man with the gun. He shoved his weapon into his coat and bolted to a motorcycle parked across the street. He slammed on his helmet, fired up the engine, kicked the sportbike into gear, and burned off into the night.

We raced to the limousine to find the wealthy man lowering his arms to his bulging waist.

"Are you hurt?" I asked, reaching for my phone to call the police.

"We shouldn't be here," he said, tumbling into the plush leather of the backseat as his driver emerged to open the door. A sea of ripples rolled across his expansive midsection. "It isn't safe." He removed the round glasses from his thick face and wiped his eyes, then brushed his fingers through his short gray hair and instructed the driver to shut the door.

As the driver barked at us to move, we stepped back from the curb and watched in silence as the limousine sped off, its headlights illuminating the empty road ahead.

Chapter 11

Sunday morning arrived at eight o'clock with the filtered rays from the autumn sun peeking into my bedroom through the slats in the blinds. On the sidewalk out front, a sledgehammer pounded against the concrete, though as I pulled the covers back, I realized the pounding was in my head. The cool surface of the narrow-board pine floors sent a shiver across my shoulders, a temperature that felt right for my aching temples. I considered lying flat on the floor, but opted for a cup of coffee instead.

I slipped into a pair of jeans, put on the glasses worn only in the first hours of the day, and wandered into the kitchen to fire up the coffeepot.

Comforting aromas of roasted beans filled the air as the coffee dripped and sizzled in the carafe. Into an oversized chair by the window I settled, and pulled a blanket over my shoulders while I waited for my liquid savior to finish brewing. Minutes later, the telltale sounds of the coffeepot's final spurts echoed out, and like a good soldier, I reported for duty.

A peppy knock at the door diverted my attention as I took a mug from the cupboard. I squinted through the peephole and groaned to find Evan standing at my doorstep, bright-eyed and bushy-tailed. He knocked once more, an eager tap from someone whose early-bird-gets-the-worm approach to life was irritating in even the best of circumstances.

Reluctantly I slid the lock back and let the chain fall to the side.

"Nice glasses," he said. "Borrow those from your Aunt Tilly?"

I grumbled. "A jab is not the best way to ingratiate yourself with someone you've rousted before their morning cup of Joe."

"Find a pea under your mattress last night?"

"Just a shrew scratching at my door first thing this morning."

"It's not often I find myself likened to a shrew." He walked into my living room. "Where's your television?"

"I don't own a television."

"Since when?"

"Since I cut the cord last month. You should know this. You've raided my refrigerator twice since then."

"We'll have to watch the news from my apartment. Something shocking happened overnight."

"I'll read about it online later today."

"This can't wait."

Too groggy to resist his orders, I caved. "Let me grab a cup of coffee before we go."

"I have a pot brewing downstairs."

Warm aromas of French roast greeted me as I followed Evan into his apartment and headed to the kitchen. Dark and bitter, the first boiling sips of coffee singed my tongue.

Evan flipped on the television and turned up the volume as I joined him in the living room.

With heavy makeup and poofed-up hair, a female newscaster stood before a Tudor Revival mansion in the ritziest part of town. Uniformed officers busied themselves in the background while a flock of rubber-neckers angled themselves in the corner of the lens.

"I'm standing before the home of Benjamin Arshile, CEO of Arshile Design Partners, where police are investigating an armed robbery that occurred overnight," the newscaster announced. A digital box in the corner of the screen displayed the headshot of a portly man with short gray hair and round glasses. "Police say at around three o'clock in the morning, two men, armed and wearing masks, entered the Arshile residence through an unlocked window and stole a valuable painting while holding Mr. Arshile at gunpoint. According to police, Mr. Arshile was home alone and was not hurt during the incident. Anyone with information is asked to contact the police. Steven, back to you."

As the camera panned over to the news station, the polished anchors shared in a halfhearted sentiment of concern that felt empty in contrast to their pearly smiles. The television grin is a requirement of the job, I've heard, because the news is typically bad, and no one wants to see a foundation-caked anchor dissolve into a puddle when—according to reports from concerned citizens—an eagle wraps its talons around a kitten and makes a meal of its prey.

"Home invasion stories freak me out," I said. "Once upon a time, no one locked their doors and the honor system governed sidewalk fruit stands. Nowadays, one must sleep with a switchblade under their pillow to feel safe. What's happening to our society?" I looked at the pool of rocket fuel steaming in my mug. "Have anything Irish for this?"

"I didn't drag you down here for a hair-of-the-dog lamentation about the woes of our society," said Evan. "Did you recognize the picture of the victim?"

"The newscaster's frozen frown lines distracted me. Someday

scientists will realize injectable facial fillers are seeping into the bloodstream and oxidizing people from the inside out."

"Everyone will revolt in the streets when that day comes, but we have more important matters to discuss. The victim of the home invasion bears a striking resemblance to the wealthy man whose mugging we interrupted last night."

I choked on my coffee. "Seriously?"

Evan gestured to the television, just as the broadcast cut to commercial. A giant red Vita Bone filled the screen while a hungry Labrador howled in the background. Fido learned to shake today, and it was time to reward him with some delicious gnawing and crunching. Evan flipped to another channel, where the freight train of advertising rolled across the screen, followed by the weather forecast and the financial news. Then the coverage of the Arshile robbery resumed.

My jaw dropped as the picture of Benjamin Arshile appeared on the screen.

"It's him, isn't it?" asked Evan. "This is the man who was mugged outside 18 Laws."

"I need another cup of coffee to process this." I covered the distance between the living room and the kitchen in five seconds flat. Then I returned with a steaming mug and plopped down in Evan's swivel chair, careful not to disturb the loose pens and unopened envelopes cluttering his desk as I kicked my feet up. "Has Lyla seen this?"

"Not yet." He pulled his phone from his pocket and punched in her number. "Put on some pants and get down here." He hung up and tossed his phone on the coffee table.

"Since when did you view pants as a positive?" I asked.

"I've turned over a new leaf. Lyla will be down in five."

"Better make a fresh pot of coffee. She gets finicky about drinking the last quarter in the carafe."

Evan headed for the kitchen. "Picky, picky."

As he busied himself with the coffee pot, I gazed out the window to find the gluttonous autumn clouds choking out the sun. I closed my eyes and transported myself to the sandy beaches of Brazil, where the feathers of the native birds mimicked a Pantone color wheel. As I imagined myself sipping a fruity cocktail from a coconut shell, unnerving thoughts seeped in—thoughts of the home invasion robbery at Benjamin Arshile's estate, a crime that occurred on the heels of a man who resembled him getting mugged outside 18 Laws Saturday night.

Mugged by a motorcycle thug, to be exact.

I opened my eyes as memories of the thug from the Titan Gallery rushed back to me like river water spilling from a broken dam. I hustled into the kitchen to share my epiphany with Evan.

A limp knock at the door signaling Lyla's arrival distracted me.

"Is that coffee?" she asked with a yawn as I let her in.

"I'll get you a mug."

"Go heavy on the Irish."

"No Irish."

"I'll pass." She ambled into the living room like a lazy-boned sloth and slumped into the couch, grimacing at the firmness of the cushions.

Evan nestled in beside her. "If your delicate hip bones aren't up to the task—"

"The couch is fine. What's the big news, have your succulents sprouted new leaves?"

"My succulents bit the dust a week ago. Do you know who Benjamin Arshile is?"

Her ears perked up. "Of course. His design firm is Absent Thought's main competitor. The man has a reputation for being a real shark—an eat-his-young type who leaves his rivals cowering in the copy room. Why do you ask?"

"Two masked men robbed Benjamin Arshile at gunpoint in his mansion overnight," I said, recapping the thin details of the crime as a commercial for carpet cleaner blasted from the screen, a man with a cheeseball grin pouring ink on a white carpet while readying a neon spray bottle labeled *Carpet Zowie*.

"Those cleaning solvents never work," Lyla complained as the noisy racket diverted her attention.

I snapped my fingers. "Forget the solvents. Did you recognize the mugging victim from 18 Laws as Benjamin Arshile?"

"I couldn't say. I've never met Arshile in person. I've only heard the partners at Absent Thought deride him in private for being an unmitigated jerk. Where is this question coming from?"

"We think Arshile may have been the victim of both crimes—the mugging and the home invasion."

She straightened up. "What are the odds the same guy gets held up at gunpoint twice in one night, half those of a cougar attack? Even a ruthless man like Arshile doesn't have that kind of luck." She eyed my steaming mug of coffee.

"Clean mugs are in the cupboard," I said.

"I just want a sip."

I handed her the mug.

She took a long gulp and returned it half-empty. "If Arshile was the victim of both crimes, that makes the timing suspicious. What do you make of it?"

"Could have been unfinished business," I said. "On Friday night, a motorcycle thug stormed into the Titan Gallery and threatened Domino. What if the mugging we witnessed at 18 Laws the following night was an escalation of those threats?"

"Why rob Arshile in his home later that night if the point was to make a scene at Domino's speakeasy?"

"It was a crime of opportunity. After realizing Arshile wasn't well-protected, which would have been obvious based on the way his driver cowered behind the steering wheel, the thug circled back and followed him home for a big score—a valuable painting."

"His driver's gutless reaction doesn't make sense," said Evan. "Why didn't he honk his horn, trigger the panic alarm, or flash his high beams?"

"The news said there were two intruders involved in the home invasion," said Lyla. "If the thug from the gallery was one of them, who was the other?"

"His accomplice of choice," I said.

She flipped the hood of her sweatshirt over her head. "It was dark outside the speakeasy that night. Are you sure you got a good enough look at the mugger to conclude he and the thug from the gallery were the same man?"

"Not entirely, but why would a random mugger think there'd be anyone around the Meland Hotel worth mugging? Aside from the speakeasy hidden in the old hotel's basement, the neighborhood is abandoned."

She considered my remarks. "You have a point. If one were in the business of sidewalk muggings, they would focus on locations with a higher probability of paying off."

"Pick any steakhouse in the financial district with meat cuts in the window and you're looking at prime mugging candidates," I said. "Once the high-rolling investment bankers who haunt those establishments saturate themselves in expensive martinis, their diluted senses make them an easier target than an injured pigeon."

"Mugging investment bankers is a terrible idea. Do you know how scrappy men in pinstripes can be? I'd rather take my chances looting the dinner tray of an arboreal predator." She yawned and leaned back in the couch cushions. "What did the news report about the mugging?"

"Nothing yet."

"Do police have any suspects in the home invasion?"

"If they do, they aren't saying."

"Do they think it was premeditated?"

"No information on that, either."

"Then what is there to discuss?" She looked at Evan. "And why are you grinning?"

"Because this could be a game-changer for my career." He stood from the couch and paced around the living room. "If I can boost the drama in my story about 18 Laws by introducing an element of danger, my editor will eat it up like bumbleberry pie." He halted his footsteps. "But we need details only the victim can provide. How did the mugging unfold? How did the victim feel having a gun pointed at his chest? What did his assailant look like up close?" He clasped his hands. "If Arshile was the victim, he'll have the answers. We need to contact him to find out."

"Count me in," I said. If Evan had the notion to question the advertising maven in search of details for his article, I had the notion to accompany him for my own nosy reasons.

"We also need to figure out the best way to approach the man. He'll call the cops if we show up at his doorstep dressed like Girl Scouts looking to interrogate him."

"Hold on, did you say *interrogate*?" asked Lyla, fixating on the word. "As in cuff the man, drag him into custody, and question him in a depressing cinderblock cell painted with the words *No Touching* while the guard outside picks bits of Mars Bars from his teeth?" She pushed her tongue out. "Do you know how infrequently they wash those chairs?"

"We'll introduce ourselves as the kind folk who thwarted the mugging last night, and cross our fingers he knows what we're talking about," I said. "If Arshile proves to be the victim of both crimes, we'll tell him we wish to offer our condolences."

Lyla rolled her eyes. "Offer your condolences? Real convincing."

"You have a better idea?"

"Yes, leave the guy alone. He's knees deep in a police investigation."

"Doesn't mean he can't answer a few questions," said Evan. He lifted his phone from the table and scrolled through his contacts. "My buddy who works at a law firm owes me a favor for watching his kid's turtle while he fumigated his house. I'll have him pull Arshile's contact information from the LexisNexis database. We can call him this afternoon to arrange a meeting for next week."

"I prefer mornings," I said, slurping the last tepid sips from my mug. I set it on Evan's desk, leaving a coffee ring on a flyer advertising two-for-one deals at the local sub shop.

"You kids have fun with that," said Lyla, sinking deeper into the cushions to check her eyelids for leaks. "Call someone else when you need to get bailed out."

Chapter 12

Droplets of mist speckled the windshield of my boxy Swedish coupe as I navigated the rain-soaked roads winding through Benjamin Arshile's posh neighborhood. Affluence abounded in the land of the wealthy, and I couldn't help but feel out of place. It wouldn't have taken much to convince me the spying eyeballs of territorial housewives were watching me from behind the pleats of their linen curtains. If a band of crazed butlers brandishing pitchforks had rushed from their quarters to chase me from their masters' turf, I would have informed them their tableau was old as dirt.

Buckled into the passenger seat with the heater vents blowing warm air through his fingers, Evan called out the turns while critiquing the condition of my wiper blades. "Your windshield looks like a shower door. How can you see?"

I disengaged the power locks. "You're welcome to walk."

"And ruin my new kicks?" He reached across me to flip on the wipers. "Much better."

Convincing the CEO of Arshile Design Partners to accept a

meeting with us had been an easier feat than anticipated. Upon receiving our call—Evan delivering his lines masterfully—the advertising maven had confirmed he was the victim of both crimes. He showed appreciation for our desire to check in on him, and with minimal inquiries as to how we obtained his contact details, suggested we meet at his estate Monday morning.

Manicured lawns, verdant and trimmed to the height of a Ballybunion dream, lined the stone walkway leading to Arshile's Tudor Revival mansion. Steep and gabled, the roofline featured dormers peeking out like eyes from a pine marten in the boughs of an evergreen tree. Elaborate herringbone bricks accented the half-timbered façade while multi-paned windows spanned the main floor, a copper awning capping the largest of the bunch. Flower pots spilling over with red geraniums and a stone arch marked the entryway. When penning the tale of *Hansel and Gretel*, it was the mansion of Benjamin Arshile the Brothers Grimm almost certainly had in mind. I glanced at my feet for a trail of breadcrumbs, but found a garden slug inching along in a trail of slime instead.

Melodic chimes swept through the entryway as we pressed the doorbell and listened with storybook wonder.

I ran my hands down the front of my twill skirt to iron the creases, imagining what our meeting with Arshile would have in store for us. I wondered, would the bad reputation Lyla made no bones about describing reveal itself when we met with the man on his home turf?

Gray-haired, heavyset, and dressed for a morning of swinging his golf clubs on the front nine at the country club, Arshile invited us to enter. After exchanging pleasantries, we followed him through a grand foyer, where contemporary paintings flanked a mahogany-framed mirror resembling that from Mosè Bianchi's *Woman in Front of a Mirror*.

Arshile adjusted his round glasses and led us into a handsome study with stately bookcases, lavish furnishings, and elements of fly-fishing tucked throughout—a fly rod here, a tackle box there. A commanding pair of Wayne Thiebaud paintings from the artist's *Cake Slices* series depicting giant slices of birthday cake in pastel hues hung prominently from the wall. The images invoked memories of my first day on the job at the modern art museum, when the curator had been giddy over an acquisition of a painting by the same artist depicting a trio of gumball machines. Both men, I felt, had good taste.

Arshile offered us a morning dram of scotch from a crystal decanter as he poured one for himself. "Microbiologists say germs will wipe out humanity, but I believe scotch will be my demise."

We passed on the liquor and settled into a richly upholstered salon sofa with silk tassels. "Your home is lovely," I said, making conversation as I combed my fingers through the tassels. "The Wayne Thiebaud paintings are fantastic."

Arshile sat in a wingback chair across from us, the fabric cushion grunting beneath his weight. He sipped from his scotch, surrendering himself to the smooth taste of the barrel-aged spirit. "My ex-wife picked out the paintings of the cake slices, but I kept them in the divorce. They remind me of the day I learned the meaning of the Dutch proverb *sharks eat smaller fish*."

"A day for the history books?"

"In a manner of speaking. It was during my first gig in advertising at an unproven firm. I quickly discovered the place was a sinking ship, though the ignorant dunces at the helm refused to consider my ideas for turning things around." He sipped from his scotch. "One afternoon, a partner from the firm called me into a stuffy conference room with leftover slices of cake from the receptionist's birthday—the cheap frosting melting onto the flimsy paper plates—and delivered a message on management's behalf: *Shut the hell up.*" He huffed. "The cherry on top was the news my salary would be cut."

"The price of having an opinion," said Evan.

"Yes, though I had the last laugh. Two months later, I leaked news of the firm's impending implosion to the press, and opened the doors to Arshile Design Partners shortly thereafter, poaching every one of their clients." He grinned with coffee-stained teeth.

At a loss for words, I found myself wondering if all big kahunas had such an antidote up their sleeve—the first time a superior muzzled them, they kicked them in the shins. "When did you decide to pursue advertising?" I asked.

Arshile adjusted his trousers for comfort. "Are you familiar with marshmallow crème? It's the sticky white spread my generation smeared on their Wonder Bread sandwiches growing up—peanut butter on one slice, marshmallow crème on the other." He smiled at the thought of the sugary treat. "In 1960, an advertising agency coined the term *fluffernutter* to increase the marketability of the sandwich. Kraft released an ad for their marshmallow product soon after, featuring a freckle-faced boy with a goofy grin. Sales increased. Cavities did, also. And when the genius of it all set in, I knew advertising would be my path."

I was mesmerized. "That's an inspiring story. If only we all had a similar tale—"

Arshile belted out a grating laugh. "Hilarious! You actually believed a jar of marshmallow crème was the impetus to my lifetime of success?" His pudgy waist jiggled beneath his polo shirt with the turbulence of the lower Congo River.

The sting of gullibility made me feel ten inches tall, but I laughed to disguise my embarrassment.

Evan swooped in to change the subject. "We were shocked to learn about the robbery at your estate. How are you doing?"

"Not well," said Arshile. "Over the years, I've battled executives, bruised up negotiators, and left decision-makers licking their wounds. But I froze when I stared down the barrel of that criminal's gun and watched helplessly as his accomplice ripped a valuable painting from my wall." He sighed, the impact of loss worn on his sleeve triggering memories of the art thefts I investigated during my short-lived occupation in the field of art recovery and insurance investigations. Every victim had displayed similar anguish, including the forger whose deceptions cost me my job.

"What can you tell us about the painting?" asked Evan.

"It was the prize of my collection, painted by a darling of the New York art scene. The piece was from the artist's *Spin Marbles* series in which splashes of color were spun across the canvas like the colorful marbles of my youth." He sighed again. "The painting set me back two hundred grand, though the greater value was my sentimental attachment to the piece. In the image, I found warm recollections of the happier days of my youth playing marbles with the other children in primary school."

"We're sorry for your loss," I said, feeling a sense of sympathy for the man.

"The alarm company was here yesterday to update my system to the most cutting-edge configuration on the market. I'm having a gate installed at the driveway this afternoon, along with security cameras positioned around the property."

"You didn't have cameras at the time of the theft?"

"Foolishly I thought living in an exclusive neighborhood made me immune to crime." He reshuffled in his seat. "Going forward, I must be vigilant about locking my windows and doors. It was through a kitchen window left ajar the thieves entered my home. As the Dutch say, *When the gate is open, the pigs will run into the corn.*"

"Do police think the timing between the mugging at the speakeasy and the robbery in your home is suspicious?"

"I'm afraid I cannot discuss the details of the investigation with you. I've been gagged."

"What's your personal take?"

"I've entertained more theories than you can count." He stood and walked to the window, drew back the curtains, and gazed at the robins pecking for worms in the grass. A fly buzzed along the sill. "Anyway, when I received your call, I assumed you were seeking a reward." He retrieved his checkbook.

"We're not here for a reward," said Evan.

"Everyone wants a reward, young man. That is the American way."

"As are government handouts and reality television, but those aren't the reason we've called this meeting, either."

"You want a favor?"

"We want to know more about the mugging at 18 Laws—the fear you must have felt as you looked your assailant in the eyes, his gun held to your chest. How did the crime unfold?"

Arshile placed his checkbook on the desk. "I had just come around the front of the building to meet my driver when I heard a man near the hood of the limousine snapping his fingers, saying, *Come over here.* When I followed his voice, the criminal emerged from the darkness with his weapon drawn and demanded my wallet. He threatened to…" His voice trailed off.

"Did you work with a sketch artist?" I asked after allowing him a moment to collect himself.

"It was no use. The mugger's face was a blank. His pistol pointed at my chest had distracted me."

"Do you recall if his hair was blond?"

"I couldn't tell in the darkness of the night, though I believe it was tied into a knot at the nape of his neck."

"Any identifying marks, like an octopus tattoo on his throat?"

"Maybe he had a tattoo. Maybe he didn't. I'm just not sure."

"What you experienced sounds like the weapon-focus effect," said Evan. "It's an unfortunate phenomenon in which victims of crimes involving deadly weapons become too focused on the weapon to imprint the details of their assailant's appearance."

"You sound like a detective."

"I'm not. I studied it during an elected criminology course in undergrad."

"The man was a brute, I can tell you that much. His eyes were empty and cold. I felt as though he could pull the trigger and never think of it again." Fear flashed across Arshile's cheeks. He turned his face to the window to conceal it.

"Do police think the mugging was a random act?"

Arshile looked back with arms crossed. "As I explained moments ago, I cannot discuss with you the details of the investigation. I am only at liberty to share my personal thoughts, and I would expect you to respect that." He narrowed his eyes. "Unless your reasons for calling this meeting are insincere."

Guilt spread across Evan's face like a malaria germ.

I kept a neutral expression. "We have lingering questions about the crime because we walked away wishing we had done more."

Arshile uncrossed his arms. "There isn't more anyone could have done."

"Except for your driver."

"I don't pay him enough to risk his life for me."

Evan paused before changing gears. "Are you aware of other crimes occurring at the speakeasy?"

"None that I'm aware of."

"Had you been to 18 Laws before Saturday night?"

"Several times. I've been a client of the brothers since they opened the Titan Gallery a year ago."

A pendulum clock affixed to the wall released a loud gong to announce the arrival of the hour. Seeking respite in the walls, the rattled daddy longlegs had surely considered launching a protest or two.

Arshile glanced at the clock, then back to us. "Last chance to accept my reward."

"We'd rather ask you a few more questions," said Evan. "Aside from being their client, how well do you know Domino and Julian?"

Arshile's jaw tensed. "That inquiry is of a personal nature and I don't see how it's any of your business."

I patted the air in a calming gesture. "We're not here to pry into your personal matters, Mr. Arshile. If Evan seems over-zealous, it's only because he drank three cups of rocket fuel on the way over."

"I'm not so sure I believe that. You wouldn't be the first dodgy journalists looking to drum up fodder for a gossip column." Arshile ordered us to our feet. "I'm afraid this conversation is over."

I opened my mouth to launch a final Hail Mary, though found the tactic useless as Arshile marched us through the foyer on heavy footsteps. The large mirror reflected back our failure as he tossed us like stray cats into the flowerbeds.

Chapter 13

Where I come from along the brackish shores of West Seattle, ordering a cocktail on a Monday is perfectly acceptable. Nowhere is it written that cocktails with an eighty-twenty ratio of booze to mixer are only appropriate during the forty-eight-hour window spanning the weekend. If only our day jobs didn't interfere with our after-work pursuits, for it wasn't until six o'clock that we finally hailed a taxi to deliver us back to the Empire Martini Bar.

Warmth to be relished greeted us when we entered the lounge, along with the pleasing site of Dane's surfer-blond hair and slate-gray eyes. Preoccupied mixing a martini for a middle-aged accountant who had just clocked out from a long day of counting beans, the handsome bartender was slow to notice our arrival.

"What other tricks do you suppose Dane has up his sleeves?" I asked, watching him shake a vessel with the expressive hands of a symphony maestro.

"There's one way to find out," said Lyla. She loosened the top button on her cream blouse. "Work time is over and I would happily tip extra to see him pull a fluffy rabbit from his hat."

Evan settled into a stool at the bar and picked up a drink list. "What are you thinking?"

"Club soda," I said, taking a seat on the stool beside him.

He gave me a funny look.

"Club soda mixed with something spiritual that is. But I don't have all night. I've promised my snowbird parents a Skype session to check out the stubby arm the saguaro cactus at their Tucson casita sprouted."

"If you're in the mood for something creamy, I bet Dane makes a mean grasshopper martini in which a confirmed crème de menthe drinker such as yourself would luxuriate."

I stuck my tongue out. "Crème de menthe is for the birds."

"You can say that again," said Lyla, settling in beside me.

I turned in my stool to face her. "Has Absent Thought been abuzz with chatter since the robbery at Benjamin Arshile's estate?"

"It's the hot topic around the water cooler, though few have expressed sympathy other than the lady who waters the plants. Most feel Arshile had it coming to him. Even the named partners raised a glass to toast before dusting off their dancing shoes."

"Harsh."

"Only slightly. They were recently stung by an unfair legal run-in with Arshile Design Partners."

Dane arrived and drummed his fingers on the bar as he attempted to place our faces. Lyla's blue eyes seemed to jog his memory. "I wondered if I might see you three again. Trust me to mix up something spectacular?" He accepted our nods as consent and prepared a colorful trio of martinis: Sanguinello Valentine, a blood orange martini with vodka, triple sec, and pink champagne; Framboesa Libertação, a romantic nod to the French martini with Chambord, vodka, pineapple, and prosecco; and Greek Osmosis, an ouzo-based concoction with the sharp flavors of anise and coriander, softened by a merciful dash of peach schnapps.

I selected the Framboesa Libertação hued like a ripened plum in the dog days of summer.

Lyla swiped it away and buzzed in my ear. "I wanted that martini."

"What are you doing, handsy?"

"Order and progress are meant to be shared." She licked the rim to mark her territory, then passed me the tangy Sanguinello Valentine to replace it.

Dane returned the liquor bottles to the shelf. "What's the latest?" It was a simple question, the sort one might ask when encountering a neighbor on the sidewalk while retrieving their morning paper.

I felt it unnecessary to beat around the bush. "Upon our arrival at 18 Laws Saturday night, the owners, Domino and Julian, had their doormen lock us in the VIP room like guinea fowl from chickens on the range."

"How do you know the first thing about guinea fowl?" Lyla asked me, a question I could only answer with a shrug. Sometimes weird nuggets stuck like that, brain cells better saved for the operation of the fickle heater in my Swedish coupe the sacrifice.

Dane showed little reaction. "The bottle of Pappy's was a decent consolation prize. You know how much that stuff costs?"

"You've heard the news?"

"Domino read me the riot act when he called the next day to ask if I gave you the directions."

"That's why we're here." I sipped from my citrusy martini, thoughts of the British mariners and their eighteenth-century seagoing pursuits flashing through my mind. So many fewer lives those seamen would have lost to scurvy had they kept a vial of that tincture on hand. "Why were we sequestered?"

Creases formed across Dane's forehead as he contemplated a response.

Evan leaned into my ear. "Tell Lyla to put her hair down and do that thing girls do to their cheeks to make them blush."

I turned to Lyla and whispered Evan's orders.

She tugged the rubber band from her hair and pinched her cheeks to don a rosy glow. She considered undoing another button on her blouse, though hesitated when she noticed the wandering eyes of two older men seated across the bar. In a coaxing manner, she looked back to Dane and said, "Come on, Dane. Do your country proud and answer our questions."

He hemmed and hawed. "Domino would sentence me to the gallows if he caught me revealing information about 18 Laws." His eyes wandered down Lyla's chest. "Then again, I can tell you've opened a couple buttons on your blouse, so I feel like I should give in."

Lyla looked down at her blouse to find another button popped open on its own, revealing a peek at her lacy particulars. She chose to leave it untended, a strategic decision for which Evan and I would applaud her later in the night.

Dane leaned forward and lowered his voice. "When you three came in here Friday night, gushing about the gala at the Titan Gallery, boasting about the painting of the toreador—" he pointed to Lyla "—this one calling herself a lady, I sized you up as strong prospects. I didn't know you'd crashed the event at the gallery and concocted the whole lady bit on a lark. It makes sense, in hindsight. I didn't get why a noble lady would pick up her own dry cleaning." He pulled a proud bottle of Macallan 25 from the shelf, selected a petite tulip-shaped glass, and inspected the rim for water spots.

Enchanted by the sight of the high-end Scotch whisky, Evan dropped the subject of the speakeasy like a basket of bad eggs.

"If Macallan is a perk of your employment, I'll seethe with envy until I get hired here myself."

"If Macallan were a perk, I'd bankrupt this place."

"You just like to fondle the bottle?"

"A regular who drinks this stuff will be here soon." Dane set the bottle on the bar and arranged the glass beside it. Ready, aim, fire. "How'd you solve the directions, anyway? The hint I provided about M90 was too vague to be useful."

"Resourcefulness, intelligence, keen powers of observation," said Evan, speaking casually as though listing the ingredients in a loaf of bread. He patted me on the head. "Annabel could launch a stagecoach carrying bricks of plutonium into space. Her brain capacity is that immense."

I removed his hand to smooth my hair. "My skull is weakening under the pressure of my brilliance as we speak, but that's a topic for another time. What do you mean we were strong prospects?"

Dane fidgeted.

"Why not tell us? Once you're baking your skin cells in the sweet, parching sunshine of southern California, 18 Laws will be a distant memory." I kicked back in my stool. "As relevant to your life as the lunar cycle is to the oysters on special at the chophouse down the street."

Lyla spoke up with unnecessary clarification. "Prior to meeting their untimely fate, those oysters cared a great deal about the lunar cycle. I once researched the matter, and what I learned is that oysters feed and actuate their valves according to the tides—"

"Thank you for the biology lesson."

"She's right," said Dane.

"Please don't coddle her."

"It's hard not to."

Lyla grinned.

Dane pressed forward. "When I slipped you three the lead on the speakeasy Friday night, I figured you'd get stumped and call the number on the directions for help. It connects to the brothers' answering service. I thought you'd impress them when they called back to vet you, and I'd get paid my finder's fee." He handed Lyla a cocktail napkin to clean a dribble of martini from her chin. "It's too bad you didn't pan out. I already spent the thousand bucks."

A frazzled girl with bloodshot eyes and a tailored business shirt that lost its crisp lines hours ago stumbled into the martini bar in a state of dishevel. Two breaths away from either falling on her face or leaping across the bar to help herself to a bottle of Leopolds, she ordered the stiffest martini on the menu as Dane excused himself to serve her.

"There's more to the story than Dane is telling us," said Evan.

"How can we convince him to sing?" asked Lyla.

"Pound your martini and wave him over with come-hither fingers for a refill."

"I'm enjoying my martini at a leisurely pace. Pound yours."

"It tastes like fermented foods. I'm planning to dump it into Annabel's glass when she looks the other way."

"What do you have against fermented foods?" I asked.

"They taste like a strange salve of anchovy paste and seltzer water used for cleaning the inner plumage of a pelican."

Lyla rolled her eyes. "You had one bad experience with an expired bottle of kombucha six months ago and now the entire fermentation trend is dead to you?"

"Just cowboy up and pound your drink."

"Fine." Lyla gulped the purple liquid in her glass.

"Round two?" Dane asked, catching sight of her wiggling fingers.

She squeaked out a hiccup from the prosecco bubbles.

Evan took the reins. "Why won't you give us the full picture?"

"Why do you care? You aren't the brothers' target clientele. Life goes on."

"We need the mental stimulation. Documentary television is no longer educational, and the mystery paperbacks have all diverged to the same predictable plot." Evan motioned to me. "Plus, Annabel vacuumed up two game board pieces from *Clue* last week."

"Miss Scarlet and Colonel Mustard are choking on dust bunnies deep within the folds," I added.

"We can make it worth your while," said Evan.

Dane raised an eyebrow.

"We're prepared to offer you Lyla's hand in marriage. She may have some bite to her, but she'll keep your closets organized and your dishwasher running like a dream."

"Don't you need the consent of the bride?"

"The merry maiden will be fine with it."

Dane considered the offer. "I like you three. You're a shade of crazy, but I like you." He glanced around the bar, checking for eavesdropping ears. "Here's what I'll tell you. Domino is the brains of the business—the guts, the finances, the strategy—and Julian with his Teasie Weasie bouffant is the face."

"We figured out they play different roles," I said.

"Did you figure out why they resurrected the speakeasy?"

"To make money off selling premium booze."

"Wrong. The brothers don't care about the bar business. They run 18 Laws as a networking tool, a way to woo their clients into spending money at their gallery. And it works well for them—the invitation to an exclusive speakeasy to which few are granted access makes their clients want to oil the hinges on their pocketbooks and spend, spend, spend." He mimed pulling the handle on the till of an old-fashioned register as if to say *ka-ching!*

"Since you found the speakeasy without calling the number, the brothers didn't know you'd be there until Domino caught you ogling his bartender."

"We didn't ogle him," said Lyla. "At least, not conspicuously."

"When Domino recognized you three from the gallery, he was furious. The speakeasy is meant to be ultra elite, yet there you were, watering down the exclusivity."

"If only we'd pledged allegiance to capitalism," said Evan. He swallowed the last sips of his martini and placed his empty glass on the bar.

"Locking you in the VIP room was overkill, but Domino can be irrational when it comes to his reputation." Dane clapped his hands together. "And that's all there is to it. When can we arrange for the interview with the food writer from the *San Diego Beacon*?"

"About that…"

Dane's shoulders slumped. "You don't know the food writer at the *San Diego Beacon*?"

"No such man exists. Domino seems well-connected, though. Surely he can put you in touch with—"

"I have no intention of telling Domino I'm leaving. He won't find out until I've crossed the state line into Oregon and found the last working pay phone along I-5 from which I'll leave him a vague message with no indication of my whereabouts."

"Why so secretive?" I asked, certain I'd satisfied my annual quota of blood orange liqueur as I drank the last tart sips.

"Domino is prone to suspicion. The last thing I need is him tracking me down in my new area code, demanding to know why I skipped town."

"You can't be serious."

"Serious as the IRS knocking at your door." He rapped his knuckles on the bar. "Domino isn't the kind of man you want to get sideways with, nor is Julian, for that matter. Leave the subject of 18 Laws alone. Let the mystique live on in your memories. Maybe if you win the lottery, it'll be different next time." He cleared our glasses. "Another round?"

I glanced at my watch. "The cacti in Tucson are calling. Time to go."

Dane printed the tab, rolled it into a ball, and tossed it in the waste bin. "Your drinks are on the house. Consider it a peace offering. Just promise me you'll keep everything I said about the brothers under wraps."

Chapter 14

Hours later, my phone rang to life with a synthesized jingle that sounded like a frisky woodpecker tapping out Morse code on a medieval harp. I startled awake, flipped on my bedside lamp, and glanced at the clock. "It's midnight, Lyla. Why are you calling so late?"

Her voice was anxious. "My driver's license is missing."

"Why is this an emergency? You lose stuff all the time and eventually it turns up. Don't run any red lights until then."

"I never lose my belongings."

"Except for the pricey waffle iron from Holland that grew legs and liberated itself from your apartment last month?"

Her voice was sheepish. "I blame a tribe of sticky-fingered Pygmies from Ancient Egypt."

I rubbed my eyes. "Are you sure your license didn't slip between the driver's seat and the gearbox in your car? I saw the missing Irish crown jewels nestled down there last week."

"Already checked there."

"What about your pockets?"

"Checked there, too."

"Your refrigerator?"

"There, too. It's like the lost Minoan civilization of licenses."

I flipped off the lamp, blanketing my bedroom in darkness. "I don't know what to say. Go to the DMV tomorrow and pay the thirty clams to replace it."

"It's not that simple. I think it fell from my handbag when I tripped outside the speakeasy Saturday night. I had removed it from my wallet in anticipation of the doormen checking our IDs. When they let us in without asking, I forgot to put it back."

"This isn't like the time you told me naval historians had uncovered the lost waterproof maps from Leif Erikson's journey to America, only for me to later learn from Evan that he'd planted that kernel in your ear to see if you'd fall for it?"

"I knew he wasn't being serious. I was playing along."

"Keep telling yourself that." I yawned. "If your license fell from your handbag when you tripped, you would have found it when Evan helped you pick up your stuff."

"Not if it landed in the ivy. We didn't check there."

"If it landed in the ivy, a burrowing rodent has already taken it back to its den."

"We don't know that for sure, and in light of Dane's ominous warnings about Domino and Julian, the thought of my license floating around the grounds of their speakeasy makes me uneasy. It has my address on it, along with my height and weight."

"What do you want me to do?" I asked.

"I need you to go with me to 18 Laws tomorrow to find it."

"What if the brothers are there?"

"Tomorrow is Tuesday. No one will be around." She was insistent. "Evan and I will pick you up from the museum at five. Don't be late."

"You've already spoken with Evan?"

"He hasn't written his article about 18 Laws yet, and he's chomping at the bit to take pictures of the Meland Hotel from outside."

"I thought you were opposed to Evan's article. Are you changing your tune?"

"I'm warming to the idea. The thought of the barista from the coffee shop around the corner—the guy who has piercings the size of coffee coasters in his ears—kicking his feet up at the bar makes me giddy."

"If Evan is going with you tomorrow, why am I needed?"

"Someone needs to play lookout."

"Lookout for whom? You just said no one would be around."

"This is a dangerous part of town governed by questionable individuals, and we have no business being there unarmed unless we're three deep." She paused. "I'm prepared to bribe you. I know how much you love those pretentiously organic granolas, and I know they make you weak in the knees: diced figs, pitted cherries, chopped nuts, baked oats. Flax."

I felt myself caving. "How do you intend to produce said granola?"

"My boss at Absent Thought is traveling to Portland to pitch a fairy-tale granola company on Wednesday. Her trunk will overflow with granola when she returns."

"What makes you think she'll hand over the loot?"

"She won't eat diced figs."

"What other way is there to eat figs?"

"Sliced into quarters."

"That's entirely too much fig for one bite."

"Which is your opinion, Annabel. Can I count on you for tomorrow?"

"Let me sleep on it."

"I'll take that as a yes." *Click.*

Chapter 15

The exhilaration of returning to a far-off destination is nothing short of intoxicating. The anticipation of the return is a thrill, yet tender at the same time. Memories bring back fondness, and fondness brings back joy so palpable—so tangible on one's tongue—that the taste that awaits them upon their return is like the wholesome sweetness of homemade apple pie on a hot summer Sunday.

Returning to 18 Laws in search of Lyla's missing license felt nothing at all like this. If only Evan hadn't cancelled at the last minute, handcuffed to his desk by his demanding editor intent on throwing him into the flames of a frivolous fire drill. And if only Lyla hadn't been so impatient as to deny his plea to postpone our escapade until the next day when he could accompany us.

"I refuse to delay another night," she said, jerking the wheel as she steered between the lanes of traffic. "It's now or never."

"Slow down," I said. "This isn't the Daytona 500."

"Slow driving is for the elderly."

I rolled down my window to breathe in the urban air and

watch the dim rays of the late-day sun glow from within a narrow slit in the clouds as the burning orb slid toward the horizon. "We still have time to turn this car around and reroute to the DMV. The line for a replacement license will be long, but I'll buy you an ice cream sandwich from the vending machine while we wait."

"I don't like ice cream sandwiches," she said, a bold-faced lie. "Besides, I refuse to allow the crooks at the DMV to rip my face off with a thirty-dollar replacement fee. It's not like the thing is made of crocodile skin."

"It's just thirty dollars."

"Do you realize what thirty dollars can buy?"

I entertained the question. "Fifteen pounds of peaches, four jugs of maple syrup, lentils for a lifetime—"

"I'd rather have the maple syrup."

I shook off her complaints and turned my attention to the deteriorating scenery outside. "Are you sure you know where you're going?"

She tapped her eyebrow. "The directions are all right here." It was a gesture in which I took little solace, the artificial sense of security one I'd seen before. If the past were any indication of the future, we'd end up sputtering to a stop in the middle of the freeway, two hours in the wrong direction, gas tank wheezing for fuel as Lyla gave me a headache yammering on about kidnapper vans. But as she navigated the car onto Logan Street—the crumbling yellow brick road leading us back to the decaying industrial district—I realized she had her bearings straight.

"It's official, folks," she said. "We're not in Kansas anymore."

I sent Evan a text to tell him we'd arrived. "Evan says we should go incognito and park a block down from the Meland Hotel," I said, reading his response aloud. "Isn't going incognito a celebrity trend from the eighties?"

"It doesn't matter," said Lyla. "It's sound advice."

We parked a block away, climbed from her car, and stared down the empty road. A bottomless silence settled over us, the playful chortles of children skipping rope muted long ago. Lyla pressed the button on the key fob to lock her car and we hurried to the vacant hotel on foot. Near the decrepit front porch, we paused to peer around the corner of the building, where shadows were collecting in a thick curtain.

Bent at the waist and craning our necks, we behaved like beachcombers searching for treasures in the sand as we scoured the trail of bricks for Lyla's missing license. From the ground I wrangled a stick to comb through the vines, my implement crude and imperfect. Critters rustled beneath the leaves as I poked through them, their homes and hiding places disturbed.

Lyla gasped. "Put that stick down. The mouse-borne illnesses you're stirring up are a six-month sentence to soft foods and antivirals."

"Toughen up, Lyla."

"Have you no idea what the Choclo virus can do to one's intestines?"

I rolled my eyes. "Your gumption is shriveling like a prune."

She huffed and took a final sweep of the path. "Maybe you're right about the burrowing rodent. Is your offer for an ice cream sandwich still on the table?"

"What about the pictures you promised Evan?"

"Now you remind me?" She pulled her phone from her coat and swiped her finger across the screen to unlock it. A battery icon displaying a skinny red bar flashed and then the device shut off. "Oops," she said. "I'll tell Evan the nightcrawlers wriggling from their subterranean dens in search of rotting plant matter for dinner forced us to abort our mission."

"That excuse will never work."

"Then use your phone. It takes better pictures than mine."

"It's not the phone, Lyla. It's the photographer." I riffled around in my handbag in search of the device, but as my fingers wrapped around the portable power cord to find only a loose gum wrapper attached to the other end, a vision of my phone left behind in Lyla's car smacked me across the forehead. "I left my phone in your car. Give me the keys."

Lyla swatted my hand as I reached for her pocket. "This is the universe telling us to leave."

"You read too much into things. Every minor inconvenience encountered in life isn't necessarily symbolic of—"

Lyla planted her hand on my mouth. "Did you hear that?"

I paused to listen to the breeze. "Hear what?"

"It sounded like a motorcycle off in the distance." She pointed her finger in the air. "There it is again."

I winced as the sound became audible, first as a faint whinny that grew into a piercing squeal as a motorcycle burned down the street in front of the hotel like a bolt of lightning splitting a turbulent sky. Disturbing memories of Arshile's mugger rushed back to me, joined by the nagging suspicion he was the same thug who had stormed into the Titan Gallery and taken me hostage.

As the motorcycle took another screaming lap, we flattened ourselves against the exterior wall like tinned sardines.

"He knows we're here," said Lyla, pinching my skin through the folds of my coat. "He's trying to root us out."

"Be rational," I said. "How would anyone know we're here?"

"My car is the only vehicle within ten blocks and it's too clean to be mistaken as abandoned. I ran it through the car wash this morning after spilling a carton of eggnog on the hood."

"What were you doing with eggnog? I thought that stuff reminded you of the amniotic fluid into which frog spawns are hatched."

"The receptionist at Absent Thought tasked me with buying a

creamy beverage for our holiday party. It's harder to find eggnog in November than you think." She slid her hand down my sleeve to interlace our fingers and nodded in the direction of her car. "On the count of three?"

Screeching like the meanest chainsaw on the planet, the motorcycle took a final lap before turning into the alley. Its engine softened to a purr as it came to a stop behind the hotel.

"What's going on in the alley?" I whispered, tugging at Lyla's arm as a dangerous curiosity crept over me.

"This doesn't concern us," she said. "We need to leave."

"Don't you want to see if something nefarious is unfolding back there?"

"Are you insane? The man on that motorcycle is likely armed, and our odds of outrunning his bullets should he find us lurking in the shadows and decide to take aim are thin. Once the pin hits the primer and ignites the propellant, the bullet will zip down the chamber at a muzzle velocity of 830 feet per second, faster than either of us can run."

"What fun would life be without a little calculated risk?" I hurried off on tiptoes.

"Annabel Riley, get back here this instant!"

I spun around and raised my finger to my lips: *Shh!*

Exasperated, Lyla hurried up behind me, mouthing the words *reckless* and *beheading*. The second of which made no sense, but I didn't stop to clarify.

When she caught up, she yanked my stick away and tossed it to the ground, freeing me of the *obvious encumbrance*. It was the sort of foolish action typically saved for the movies, where the short-sighted protagonist tosses their only semblance of a weapon as the antagonist nears; a blunder on par with that same protagonist dashing upstairs to hide in the shower from an intruder who's just smashed in through the kitchen window.

We peered around the corner toward the alley, where a broad-shouldered man in black motorcycle leathers zipped from his ankles to his chin straddled the idling sportbike, his buckled boots resting on the pavement. The visor of his helmet was flipped open, though the features of his face were visible only in contours.

Lyla whispered into my ear. "Is that Arshile's mugger?"

"I can't tell but it seems suspicious."

"Do you recognize the motorcycle?"

"All motorcycles look the same to me."

"What is he doing here?"

"I don't know, Lyla. You want to go ask him?"

"Maybe he's here to case the joint."

"The guy is planning to rob 18 Laws, and we happen to be here when the *case the joint* phase of the crime goes down?"

"Tuesday evening at sundown is the perfect time."

From within his leather coat, the brutish man retrieved a box of cigarettes and set one between his lips. He pulled out a lighter, rolled his finger over the flint wheel to generate a spark, and sucked in deeply. He held the smoke in his lungs, then exhaled a cloud of benzene and carbon monoxide.

Deep and throaty, the rumble of a heavy diesel engine laboring down the alley made known the presence of a nondescript delivery truck that puttered along until stopping behind the Meland Hotel.

Dressed in plain clothes and work boots, a bulky kid no older than twenty stepped from the driver's seat and shuffled a baseball cap on his head. He exchanged nods with the goulash on the sportbike, then headed for the rear of the truck to roll open the tailgate.

As if performing an assigned duty, he removed a steel dolly from the truck and situated it on the pavement, then lifted out a wooden crate—narrow and rectangular—and balanced it atop the dolly. With steady hands, he pushed his load to the wrought-iron fence separating the alley from the hotel, the small rubber wheels bumping along the uneven pavement. He lifted the latch on the gate, pushed the dolly through the opening, and navigated the ribbon of bricks connecting the alley to the hotel.

"What do we have here?" I asked, feeling intrigued as black symbols stenciled into the narrow crate became visible: arrows pointing upward with the words *Fragile Contents*. Thoughts of the *Spin Marbles* painting ripped from Arshile's wall during the armed robbery at his estate days earlier flashed through my mind as I registered the symbols and the dimensions of the crate. The suspicious timing between that crime and the mugging at 18 Laws had nagged at me, and the scene unfolding before us was the bellows stoking the flames.

From a canopy of evergreen branches tangled overhead, a duet of chipmunks chattered loudly as they scrutinized our primitive investigative abilities. In their opinion, any sleuths worth their salt would have taken photographs by now.

"I need to get my phone from your car to take pictures," I said to Lyla, fishing the keys from her pocket. "Wait here." Gripping the key fob between my fingers, I hurried to the front of the building, rounded the corner, and hustled down the sidewalk to her car.

Lyla appeared from behind me and grabbed the keys. She rushed to the driver's door and banged her knees on the steering column as she slid into her seat.

"What are you doing?" I asked, aghast.

"I'm getting us the hell out of here." She put the key in the ignition and fired up the engine. "Sometimes you have more tenacity than sense, and I cannot in good conscience support your careless determination."

I shook my head with disbelief. "Have you gone mad?"

"Madness is a mental state we blew past ten minutes ago. The camera flash would betray our presence, and I guarantee you that thug on his motorcycle could outrun us. I prefer to keep my vehicle free of bullet holes. The warranty expired three years ago." She pulled her door shut. "Get in before I leave you behind."

Chapter 16

"What do you mean all motorcycles look the same to you?" Evan quizzed me as the three of us gathered for a meal later that evening at Le Baguette, the affordable slice of the French countryside located a stone's throw from our apartment building in a brick storefront the size of a scrabble tile. To call the café small was to call a soapbox derby car a bit of a squeeze, though what it lacked in size, it made up for with character: provincial tables and chairs, antique apothecary tins, Eiffel Tower statuettes, a worn chalkboard displaying the specials of the day.

"We can't all be gearheads like you," I said, twisting the cap off my bottle of Orangina. Mandarin aromas wafted out.

"On the night of the mugging, Arshile's assailant sped off on a supercharged Ninja that purred like a fighter jet," said Evan. He sank his teeth into his *saucisson* sandwich, a delicious opus of crusty baguette, cured sausage, Emmental cheese, and Dijon mustard. "It's the sportbike of choice for those intent on breaking the sound barrier without strapping a skin-roasting jet pack to their back."

Lyla stuffed a forkful of salad greens in her mouth. "Wouldn't Macho be jealous if he could hear you now?"

"Macho knew his place in the world. The question we should be asking is why neither of you took pictures of the suspicious delivery at the speakeasy tonight."

"The danger of the situation transcended the reward."

"Which was Lyla's assessment," I said.

"The enormity of the situation wasn't lost upon me. I simply preferred not to be found lifeless in a ditch because you had to use the camera flash."

"Despite the lack of photographic evidence, the delivery tonight is fishy," I said, sucking a ribbon of fig jam from between the layers of ham and Gruyere in my *jambon fromage*. "Consider the timeline. A motorcycle thug stormed into the Titan Gallery Friday night and threatened Domino. The following night, a man of similar appearance mugged Benjamin Arshile in front of Domino's speakeasy. Hours later, Arshile was robbed in his mansion, a valuable painting the loot. Fast forward to tonight, and we just witnessed a motorcycle thug overseeing the delivery of a crate to the speakeasy." I wiped flakes of baguette from my mouth. "Who wouldn't find those events suspicious?"

"My brother wouldn't," said Evan. "But that's only because he's jaded from working in commercial real estate."

"Wouldn't he wonder why we're being so snoopy?" asked Lyla between bites of olive and artichoke from her *pain bagnat*. "Reasonable people would have contacted the police by now."

"He'd wonder if you're single, too."

"What would you tell him?"

"I'd say you have more strange bedfellows in your life than you can count."

She leaned across the table to smack his arm.

"I'd be doing you a favor. For all his strengths, my brother is the consummate bachelor. The day he settles down is the day the moon actually turns into Swiss cheese."

"I mean how would you explain our persistent nosiness? Rather than concerning ourselves with the delivery, we could be sipping mai tais, dancing the calypso, and showing the world what it means to live."

"Are you kidding me?" I interrupted, slurping from the tangy orange liquid in my bottle. "In what version of reality would I elect to mind my own business when matters of fine art and the theft thereof are on the line? Snooping around is in my DNA."

"Not to mention, you have two left feet," said Evan.

I chafed at the observation.

The swinging doors for the kitchen swooshed open as servers passed through them, balancing plates piled high with sandwiches and salads.

Lyla changed the subject with a frown. "I don't like seeing into the kitchen while I eat." She slid her plate across the table toward mine and picked up her napkin. "The last thing I need is to see some rogue chef of the *bork, bork, bork* variety whack the tail off a prairie dog and place the disrupted appendage between two slices of baguette."

I threw my napkin on the table and switched seats with her. "You're an oddity of nature. Everyone knows man declared prairie dog tail inedible many years before the Dark Ages."

Evan devoured a slice of shaved ham from his sandwich. "Prairie dog tail? I hear it tastes like—"

"Don't you dare say chicken."

"I was going to say tofu. It's the new white meat."

I took another bite of my sandwich and pressed forward. "In my estimation, the crate delivered to the speakeasy was the right size for the contemporary painting stolen from Benjamin Arshile. I researched the pieces in the artist's *Spin Marbles* series while Lyla and I were driving back from 18 Laws." I brushed a waterfall of baguette crumbles from my lap. "If the crate contained Arshile's stolen painting, it means the brothers were involved in the theft. There's no way some thug would have access to their speakeasy without their knowledge."

"The thug lingered in the alley while the delivery went down," said Lyla. "Only the kid who arrived in the delivery truck accessed the building."

"Are we certain the speakeasy was the crate's destination?" asked Evan. "There must be dozens of spider-webbed nooks and crannies in the walls of the vacant Meland Hotel."

The songbird server who delivered our sandwiches returned to check on us. Her golden hair was tied into a bun, her apron smudged with white handprints from the flour-dusted baguettes. "How are your meals?" she asked in the delicate warble of a grosbeak dining on sunflower seeds.

"Magnificent," said Lyla. "Your chef has perfected the baguette—crusty on the outside, soft on the inside. There's always that moment when I take the first bite that I ask myself, is today the day I lose a tooth?"

The girl smiled. "Anything else I can get you three?"

A server carrying a buttery apple tart emitting the aromas of cinnamon and vanilla passed by our table en route to a couple gripping their forks like the Hammer of Thor.

"What is that?" I asked, salivating.

"A traditional French apple pastry called *pompe aux pomme du Périgord*."

"We'll take an order with three forks."

"Excellent choice." She glided away to arrange for the dessert.

Evan nibbled at the ring of citrus on his plate. "From the perspective of one who ambitions to be an investigative journalist, the fact of the delivery is too suspicious to ignore." He tapped his fork on the table by my plate. "I know you feel the same way."

"I'm already three steps ahead of you," I said. "What if this is bigger than the theft from Benjamin Arshile?" I swallowed the last bites of my sandwich and kicked back in my chair. "What if the thefts from the entrepreneur and the socialite are connected?"

"One criminal, three crimes?"

I nodded.

"You sound like you spent the morning straightening the creases on your tinfoil hat," said Lyla.

"Tinfoil hats are for people who think the government is watching them," I said. "Not sane-minded individuals posing reasonable questions based on a balanced synthesis of the facts."

"The government *is* watching them. It's all over the news."

I ignored her observation. "The brothers are well-connected businessmen and the art world is their playground. What if their connections extend into the criminal underworld, to men like the motorcycle thug who will steal paintings from local collectors on their behalf?"

"For what reason?" asked Evan.

"To increase profits for the Titan Gallery by selling stolen paintings on the black market."

"The value of a stolen painting would only be a fraction of what it's worth in a gallery," said Lyla. "Would there be enough meat left on the bone to make it worth the risk of getting caught?"

"Paintings worth a couple hundred grand each have a lot of wiggle room," I said.

"According to your curator, Tate's painting was only valued at four thousand dollars."

"Maybe the thief made a mistake—stole the wrong painting from her conservatory."

Evan rolled up his sleeves. "This would explain why the motorcycle thug stormed into the Titan Gallery and threatened

Domino Friday night. Maybe Domino was tardy in paying him his cut from the black market sales."

The server swooped in to collect our plates. "Your dessert will be out shortly. Care for a cappuccino?"

I folded my napkin and laid it on the table. "We'll pass on the coffees and take dessert to go."

"Dessert to go?" asked Lyla with suspicion as the server left to make the arrangements. "What is this, a ploy to avoid sharing a scrumptious pastry with Evan and me? Don't think we've forgotten about the cannoli incident from three months ago."

"I have no idea what you're referring to."

"You don't remember when we ordered a plate of cannoli from the Italian joint around the corner, and you devoured three of the five cannoli while Evan and I were distracted examining the checkered pattern on the tablecloth to which you had drawn our attention?"

"Oh, that cannoli incident."

"You still owe us two cannoli each."

"Forget the cannoli. We have research to conduct and time is of the essence."

"Research about what? Historians have already solved the mystery of the Nazca lines."

"We need to look into the pillaged elite and the brothers who may have pillaged them. I'll toss and turn throughout the night if we don't." I handed Evan a credit card to split the tab as the server returned to deliver the flaky apple pastry nestled inside a plastic to-go container. I said to him, "I assume you know all the secret journalism tricks for digging into peoples' personal lives."

He handed the server our credit cards. "It's scary what a few strategic mouse clicks can unearth. Remember the pale-skinned mortgage broker with a future of sunburns and freckles Lyla went out with last month?"

"You mean the guy who babbled about interest rates?"

"Thanks to my research, we uncovered his mound of unpaid parking tickets and head-in-the-sand stance on climate change."

"Dodged a bullet," said Lyla. She slipped on her raincoat and tucked the dessert beneath her arm. "Thanks for dinner, by the way."

"Can you carry the apple tart home and up to my apartment without dropping it?" I asked. "I don't own any Carpet Zowie."

Lyla responded with a surprising insistence. "We will not eat this dessert in your apartment, Annabel. The tines on your forks are hazardously sharp and I prefer to keep my uvula attached. A clear speaking voice is necessary for my big meeting at Absent Thought tomorrow morning. My alarm is set for six."

"Ouch," said Evan. "Even the roosters won't be up yet."

"The big cheeses at the hardware company in Pennsylvania we're pitching will."

He shook his head. "If you don't rein in the hours, the linen pattern on your cubicle wall is going to burn itself into your brain, leaving us with nothing but the shell of an overeducated coconut."

"It's a regrettable state of affairs, but someone must be responsible for stroking the egos of corporate executives," said Lyla. "I'm pricing out baby wipes and jars of strained peas for the CEO of an artisanal cheese company who's proving to be the neediest of the bunch."

"Give him a firm smack on the rump to show him who's boss." Evan signed the tab for both of us and slid into his wool mackinaw coat. "We'll eat the apple puff and conduct our research from my apartment."

"You have three clean forks?" I asked.

"No, but I have three clean spoons and a butter knife."

Chapter 17

If a well-oiled machine is the secret to big business, then a happy stomach is the secret to finding facts. This I know, because once the final morsels of the apple pastry were licked clean from our forks, our research efforts quickly commenced. It was a proper team effort, one for which a row of strapping sailors hauling in a hefty mooring line would be proud, minus the manual labor and muscular structure. And as the hour hand ticked and tocked its way around the black-and-white face of Evan's Swiss railway clock, a series of patterns emerged.

Exhilarated, I spun circles in Evan's swivel chair, using my feet as propellers. Each revolution turned me faster than the last as the unoiled mechanisms squeaked and whined. "We're onto something big. I can feel it."

Lyla grabbed the chair by its arms. "Watching you spin in that chair is like watching someone pace around the living room with their socks dragging on the carpet." She collected the empty to-go container with our used spoons deposited inside and headed to the kitchen. "It's almost eleven. Gotta go." She tossed the spoons in the sink and rinsed out the to-go container for recycling. "Fill me in on everything tomorrow."

As she let herself out, I kicked my feet up on Evan's desk, knocking a stack of business cards to the floor. I left them for Evan to pick up and retrieved the lined notepad scribbled with our findings. "Let's recap what we've learned."

Evan flipped off the lights, save the antique banker's lamp with green glass shade illuminating his desk.

"What's with the lights? Are gondoliers with violins cued up in the bathroom to serenade us, and it's your responsibility to set the mood?"

"Your big brown eyes were looking bloodshot." He settled into the firm cushions of his streamlined leather couch and gestured to the notepad. "Start with the entrepreneur Byron Quimby."

"This guy has an impressive knack for piddling away the hard-earned money of his business-minded kinfolk," I said, studying our notes. "Since cashing in on a massive inheritance fifteen years ago, he's sunk a ton of money into every silly business venture one could possibly think up." I flicked my finger against the page. "The Dead Sea Scrolls look like a grocery list in comparison."

Evan handed me a pillow from the couch to slide behind my back. "Let's hear it."

"Two years ago, Byron Quimby developed a pocket-sized weather forecasting instrument called the *faddleboom* he promised would give Doppler radar a run for its money. After spending five million bucks on research and development, he abruptly dropped the idea when an embarrassing story printed in the *Seattle Business Journal* slammed the invention as a glorified thermometer. Quimby responded by launching a libel suit against the journalist."

"No one taught him to take criticism in stride?"

"Guess not. The following year, he unveiled a pricey series

of animal-whispering courses he touted as the secret to under-standing the root cause of conflict within the animal kingdom."

"The guy calls himself an animal whisperer?" Evan asked with laughter.

"Appears so. When experts in the field called his methods into question, he defended his gift for whispering by claiming he could prove the aggressive outbursts from a western gorilla at the Cleveland Zoo were the result of an upset tummy over a meal of bananas that didn't sit right. The experts laughed until their sides hurt."

"Or until the lawsuits were filed?"

"You got it. Quimby lobbed slander suits against them all."

"Nice of him to clog up the legal system."

"Now he's working on a hot dog cart supply chain business he says will revolutionize the way the world thinks about tubed meats."

"He's eliminating nitrites?"

"Wishful thinking. He's focusing on logistics—connecting the hot dog vendors who sell the wieners on the sidewalk to the suppliers who provide the buns and meats and toppings."

Evan scratched his head. "Aren't they already connected?"

"I assume so."

"I've heard enough. Let's move on to the wealthy socialite."

"Lady Evelyn Tate," I said, flipping the page. "Hailing from a small town in North Kentucky, Evelyn Tate—named Pattie Mae Sprunkle on her birth certificate—stumbled into a massive windfall several years ago when the numbers on her lottery ticket lined up. Leaving the Bluegrass State in her rearview mirror, along with her southern drawl and deep fryer, Tate headed west, where she acquired a new persona. She chiseled her nose, veneered her teeth, swapped her overalls for runway trends, and purchased an estate in Benjamin Arshile's neighborhood. Then she bribed her way into the exclusive Widemoor Country Club." I looked up from the page. "Obviously the *Lady* part of her name is a misnomer. A hamster has more royalty in its blood."

"An imposter hiding in plain sight," said Evan.

"A quick study, too. It didn't take long for Tate to amass a premium art collection and host elegant soirees to show it off to her hoity-toity acquaintances." I set the notepad on the desk. "Her fondant-frosted *petits fours* were apparently out of this world."

Evan licked his lips. "Tate's true identity would get her kicked out of the ranks of the elite should it ever be uncovered. Must be painstaking work to guard that secret."

"I applaud your internet search skills to have uncovered such a tasty morsel."

He beamed.

"Tate's enemies would kill for such delicious ammunition, her neighbors being first in line. Earlier this year, she pissed them off royally when she hired a day laborer to chop down a mature western oak thriving on her neighbor's property."

"Why would she do such a thing?"

"The squeaky voices of the children playing on the tree swing disturbed her meditation."

"No one likes the neighborhood antagonist."

"Antagonists of any sort aren't particularly well liked, which means all three of the victims had enemies." I counted on my fingers. "Tate destroyed her neighbor's property, Quimby lobbed baseless lawsuits against his critics, and Arshile behaved like a shark in his business dealings." I stood from the swivel chair and headed into the kitchen for a glass of water.

"You could also say their wealth defined them," said Evan. "Quimby's inheritance funded his ridiculous business ventures, Tate's windfall financed her silk-stocking rebirth, and Arshile's trappings inflated his ego to Mount Rushmore proportions."

I returned with a full glass and took a long drink. "Promise me if you ever hit the jackpot, you won't change your name to something snooty like Thaddeus. Or have your initials stitched into your cuffs."

"I'd have to play the lottery to win, and I haven't bought a ticket since that dark day last year when my editor sent me on a mission to interview a car wash owner about the salmon spawn."

"Car wash owners have an opinion about the salmon spawn?"

"I wasn't there long enough to find out. When I told the guy I was a journalist, he chased me off his property with a garden hose." He helped himself to a sip from my glass. "It was almost as humiliating as the time my editor sent me to the waterfront park near Lyla's office to interview a random sampling of dog walkers, stroller pushers, and seagulls."

"Humiliating because the seagulls deposited a holy offering at your feet?"

"Worse. A gluttonous squirrel that had gorged itself on rotten Halloween pumpkins expelled its stomach contents all over my backpack."

"Yikes. What was the angle?"

"Ninety degrees, give or take. The squirrel was perched in a tree and I was walking beneath it."

"The angle of the story, Evan."

"Oh. Conflict abounds as human decency and avian decency deteriorate."

"The clash of the century?"

"It makes the Boston Tea Party look like a game of hop-scotch." He chuckled. "Anyway, this is good stuff. What did we learn about Domino and Julian, aside from the fact that they've done a remarkable job avoiding the spotlight?"

"Not much." I picked up the notepad and flipped the page. "About a year ago, the brothers arrived in Seattle and cut the ribbon for the Titan Gallery. Prior to that, they spent two years in Santa Barbara running a high-end gallery, an endeavor that was preceded by a decade of traipsing around the Eastern Seaboard, running ritzy galleries along the way."

"That's the life, isn't it?"

"I prefer to put down roots."

Evan laid flat on his couch and stretched his legs out. "We need to figure out if the brothers knew the victims before the art thefts occurred. When we met with Arshile at his estate, he said he'd been to 18 Laws several times before the night he was robbed. What about Quimby and Tate?"

"Call your lawyer friend in the morning and see if he'll pull the contact information for those two from LexisNexis. We'll give them a call and ask them about their relationship with the brothers."

"What makes you think they'll talk to a couple strangers?"

"We'll massage the truth and say we have a lead on the whereabouts of their stolen paintings."

"We *might* have a lead," said Evan.

I shrugged. "As Lyla would say, splitting hairs."

Chapter 18

The hot dog entrepreneur named Byron Quimby was at Le Baguette early, slurping from the ceramic cappuccino mug gripped between his hands as a plume of steam rose from the surface like a swirl of mist from a mountain lake.

Evan and I arrived at the French café on time at six o'clock on Thursday evening and joined the man at a table near the window. The darkened evening outside allowed the lights of the café to mirror back our reflections in the glass.

We gestured for the songbird server to order two foamy lattes while Quimby, sporting a smirk and receding hairline, took an appraising look around the café, where contented customers were nibbling baguette sandwiches or getting cozy with a steaming espresso and slice of *tarte tatin*. As his gaze landed upon a shelf of whimsical Eiffel Tower statuettes, he furrowed his brow, as if doubting the accuracy of the touristy reproductions.

"This place is quaint," he said with an uppity air. He blew upon the hot liquid in his mug. "Problem is, Americans don't want quaint anymore. It makes them feel like they're buying raffle tickets to win the blue-ribbon custard pie from the county fair. What this place needs is vision." He sipped from his mug and gestured to the masonry wall with the chalkboard. "Take that wall, for example. No one wants to see exposed brick. It conjures up images of tending to the pipes in a medieval boiler room. If the decision were mine, I'd cover it up with a thick coat of avocado paint."

I trembled at the thought of that terrible paint color, one of the more offensive decorating trends from the past seven centuries.

"Then I'd address this provincial furniture. Trust me, unless you're eating meat scraps off the floor of a 4-H goat barn, distressed wood is a goner. Retro is the way of the future— checkerboard floor tiles, doo-wop on the jukebox, 1950s dinette sets with polished chrome and cherry vinyl." A layer of foam formed a mustache along his upper lip as he took another sip from his cappuccino. He looked like a child drinking from his holiday hot chocolate; missing only were the puffy humps of marshmallow and the stomping of the feet when Mother tells him to wipe his mouth.

"With all due respect," said Evan, "the 1950s ice cream parlor you're describing would cramp the French café vibe."

"You feel that way because you lack vision. As we speak, a group of small-minded Americans is gathered around a butter churn in the micro-town of Lemmingsville, USA, debating the conspiratorial placement of the dinosaur bones. They believe the Earth is flat. They don't have vision, either."

The door to the café swung open and a frazzled Lyla entered on a gust of wind that fluttered the edges of the menus resting on the tables. Unaware of the insult uttered by the hot dog entrepreneur, she exchanged friendly greetings with him, then laid her coat over the neighboring chair and settled in beside him.

"Forgive me for running late," she said. "The partners at Absent Thought are pitching a vegan yoga apparel company tomorrow and a series of changes came down at the eleventh hour."

Quimby yawned with boredom. "I had the vision for a vegan yoga apparel company three years ago."

"Why didn't you patent the idea?"

"Procuring digestible fibers was too costly."

Lyla was momentarily silent. "You realize no one actually eats the pants, right?"

With smudged apron tied at her waist and golden hair swept up into a bun, the songbird server arrived at our table with two foamy lattes. She placed the mugs before Evan and me, then accepted Lyla's order for an Americano.

I blew upon the steam rising from my mug. "Mr. Quimby, we know you're a busy man—"

He raised his hand. "*Mr. Quimby* is too formal."

"Of course. Byron, is it?"

"The only people allowed to call me Byron are my wife, my gardener, and the kid at the dry cleaner who lifted the floor wax stain from my trousers." He lowered his hand, leaving the topic of an appropriate name unresolved. "I was optimistic to receive your message regarding my stolen paintings. Your call was the first I've received that hasn't struck me as a scam. Since I announced the reward three months ago, the outpouring of interest has been nothing but a bottomless pit of hustlers. My attorney has been tireless in his investigations of each." He sipped from his cappuccino. "I'll never forget the first call we received from a woman with a phony German accent claiming to be an underworld antiquities dealer. She said she'd spotted my paintings in a shipping crate down by the docks and would provide their location once I delivered a bag of unmarked hundreds."

I dribbled coffee on the table. "Sounds like a scam."

"My attorney tracked her down two days later. Turned out, she needed money for implants."

"Desperation at its finest."

"Then came the fictitious prince of Nigeria claiming to have purchased the paintings at a flea market in Enugu. He threatened to burn them if I didn't wire the reward money into his overseas bank account. Two weeks later, the same guy called back, claiming to be a voodoo priest from the bayou who'd seen a vision of the paintings during a cleansing ritual. I don't think we ever returned that call, come to think of it."

"If your attorney has been chasing down leads on your behalf, why are you meeting with us yourself?" asked Evan.

"It's a matter of practicality. My attorney recently suffered a traumatic divorce and is healing his wounds on a nude beach in Aruba."

I choked on my coffee, memories of the man in the black fedora at 18 Laws bemoaning his loss of a giant Swingline stapler installation revisiting me. The man had shared a similar account of a divorced attorney with the baby-faced bartender, and it seemed an unlikely coincidence. "Is Aruba a popular destination for divorcés?" I asked.

"Beats me. Your timing is pinpoint, though. I leave town tomorrow."

"Business or pleasure?" asked Lyla, progressing the conversation before I had a chance to dig deeper on the attorney.

"I'm conducting market research for a hot dog cart supply chain business I have in the works."

"Heading east?" I asked, envisioning the surplus of hot dog carts lining the streets of New York, the soft buns and pickled relish swaddling the water-warmed frankfurters.

"I believe Farmington is southeast."

I scratched my head. "Farmington, New Mexico?"

Quimby nodded.

"Are there many hot dog carts in New Mexico?"

"Some, though I'll schedule a trip to New York in the coming weeks. The Big Apple, I've learned, is the hot dog cart capital of the contiguous US."

Or the *continuous* US, unless Alaska had burst onto the hot dog cart scene with a tear of tubed-meat fury. This thought I kept to myself.

"I read in the *Seattle Business Journal* you preferred to self-fund your ventures," said Evan, recalling the information learned during our research.

"Typically I do. It keeps the lines clear and the terms in my favor. But this venture is too sweet to keep to myself." Quimby rubbed his hands together with anticipation. "I'll begin courting investors when I return from Farmington in a few days. This'll be the biggest transformation for the hot dog cart industry since the invention of corrosion-resistant metals."

Evan resettled in his chair and sipped from his mug. "It sounds like you have it all figured out—investors chomping at the bit to bankroll the deal, promising returns on the horizon, a revolutionary idea to wow the masses…" As Evan's forced flattery rolled off his tongue, Quimby happily sopped it up.

"Now I need those prattling reporters from the business journal to appreciate the potential of this idea," he said, sipping from his mug. "Don't believe anything you read about me in the papers. Journalists are only concerned with ratings. While they're sitting in their cubicles taking shots at my business ventures— snacking on Corn Nuts and biting their fingernails because they forgot to set the trash bin to the curb and the shrimp shells from Monday night's stir-fry are starting to reek like the long, strange trip through a fishmonger's sinus cavity—I'm over here revolutionizing the world one hot dog at a time."

Astonished by the grandiosity of the man's self-assessment, Lyla struggled to stifle her laughter.

I kicked her under the table.

She composed herself and responded with solidarity. "Everyone wants to be a critic."

"Everyone wants to be a critic until they experience the sting of a lawsuit smacking them upside the head," said Quimby.

"The aphorism of attracting more bees with honey than vinegar a worthless one in your mind?"

"I don't believe I asked for your opinion."

Lyla shrunk in her seat. "My mistake."

"My attorney will hear about this."

"Please don't sue us."

"My attorney is my de facto psychiatrist." The clarification was odd and left without explanation as Quimby took another drink from his cappuccino. "I have Bikram yoga in thirty minutes. Let's get down to business."

"I imagine you heard the recent news of the armed robbery at the estate of Benjamin Arshile in which a valuable contemporary painting was stolen," I said.

"Of course. I read the paper daily."

"Then you will also recall a local socialite who was robbed last month, a priceless painting lifted from her conservatory while she hosted a private party."

"Sounds familiar. What does this have to do with me?"

I took a long, warming sip from my mug. "Common threads between those thefts and yours suggest all three crimes could be related. We'd like to ask you a few questions to help us figure out if we're on the right track."

Quimby crossed his arms. "Whenever someone approaches

me wanting to ask me a few questions, three things come to mind: nosy neighbors, snooping journalists, and wily private investigators."

"All of whom likely deserve a door in the face."

"You don't?"

"Our intentions are sincere."

Quimby hesitated. "What do you want to know?"

"Are you familiar with the Titan Gallery?"

"I know it well. I came close to purchasing a pricey installation of a life-sized Swingline stapler from the gallery quite recently."

I grinned. Asked and answered.

"The owners of the Titan Gallery are good businessmen. They offered to arrange for a commissioned piece from the artist, but my interest has waned."

"You're referring to Domino and Julian?"

"That's right. You're a patron of the gallery?"

"Only in spirit."

"After our surrealist paintings were stolen, my wife and I purchased two pieces from the gallery's *Decaying Flora* series to hang in our foyer in their place."

"Expensive, I assume?"

"At sixty grand each, the new paintings weren't cheap, but the images are stunning—a field of clover demolished by cutworms, a swarm of locusts devouring crops." He grinned with pride. "Worth every penny."

"Sounds like it," I said with a cringe. "Since acquiring these paintings, have you installed security cameras?"

"Cameras were installed around our estate as a first order of business in the wake of the burglary."

"Why didn't you have cameras before then?"

"I'm a busy man. It fell through the cracks."

I pondered the brief explanation. "Were you a client of the Titan Gallery before the theft of your surrealist paintings?"

"Well before then," said Quimby. "Soon after Domino and Julian opened the Titan Gallery, my wife and I purchased an oil painting of a gutted trout floating belly up in a swimming pool."

I choked on my latte. "Delightful."

"We later acquired a painting of a watermelon from the gallery's *Melons* series during their spring exhibition. The artist painted the series as an ode to her previous life working as head chef at a snout-to-table restaurant in the SoHo neighborhood of Manhattan. Her claim to fame was the marriage of melons, organ meats, and Siberian squash, which she served atop a bed of nettle greens."

I turned my head away from the table to cough.

Evan assumed the reins. "We heard through the grapevine you might increase the reward for the return of your stolen paintings."

"My wife and I are desperate for their return," said Quimby. "We purchased the paintings while on honeymoon in Europe many years ago. They mean more to us than any other piece in our collection." He lifted the cuff of his casual button-up to glance at his watch. "I don't want to be late for Bikram. If the threads you're looking into lead to the return of our paintings, the reward money is yours."

Lyla plopped her mug on the table. "How can you endure an hour of hot yoga after drinking a cappuccino? Boiling coffee and foamy milk hardly seem the appropriate aperitif for an hour of suffering in a hundred-and-five-degree sweat box."

I kicked her under the table. "That question is of a personal nature and is therefore none of our business."

Quimby was unbothered. "The only people who will suffer in Bikram tonight are those who lay their yoga mat too close to mine. Coffee clears the body through the pores, a fact few realize until the heat in the studio intensifies."

Lyla and I exchanged glances. Coffee clears through the pores? That can't be right.

Insistent on paying, Quimby offered the server two tens when she returned to drop off the tab. He stood from his chair, slid into a corduroy blazer, and headed for the exit with a brief farewell.

I wrapped a thick scarf around my neck and pushed back from the table. "Is it just me, or was his departure abrupt?"

"Abrupt," said Evan. "I'm not sure it matters, though. Other than the part where he compared me to a small-minded lemming, Quimby told us everything we need to know."

"Small-minded lemming?" asked Lyla, swallowing the last sips from her Americano as the server collected our empty mugs.

"Don't ask." He rolled his eyes. "What matters is that we've confirmed Domino and Julian knew Quimby before the theft of his surrealist paintings."

"We've also uncovered another common thread amongst the victims," I added. "Quimby said the stolen paintings meant more to him and his wife than any other piece in their collection. It's the same story for Arshile and Tate."

"Curious coincidence or something more?" asked Lyla. She tied her hair into a low pony tail and pulled the hood of her raincoat over her head.

"I don't know, but I intend to find out."

"So what's next?"

Evan stood from the table. "In the morning, I'll call Tate's assistant to arrange a meeting with the showy goose. With any luck, we'll establish a link between her and the brothers before the weekend is over."

"Do you intend to call Tate's assistant before or after you finish churning butter with your fellow non-visionaries in good ol' Lemmingsville, USA?" I asked, donning my coat with fuzzy lining.

"After, of course. That cream isn't going to paddle itself."

Chapter 19

Ambrosial flowerbeds blooming to life with violet pansies and peach petunias lined the paved roadway meandering toward the gated entrance of the exclusive Widemoor Country Club. Lush fairways flanked the peaceful lane, the tended greens spongy from showers that fell overnight. Mature maples and Oregon ash formed a thinning canopy as fallen leaves gathered at their trunks. From the thicket of their branches, warbling songbirds sang their morning chorus while bright-and-early golfers swung their clubs on the course below, singing a frustrated song of their own as their misbehaving golf balls rolled into the rough.

The previous morning, Evan had attempted to arrange a meeting with the imposter socialite, Evelyn Tate, though with little success. For reasons unclear to anyone, he had introduced himself as Theo Tolstoy, a strange choice of alias the girl spotted as a phony, likely because of its obvious similarity to Leo Tolstoy, the author of *War and Peace*. The ruse, however, was not detected as quickly as one might think, and before the absurdity of the name occurred to her, Tate's assistant revealed the socialite's plans to attend the Ladies of Larkspur brunch at the Widemoor Country Club the following morning.

Named in honor of the official flower of the country club, the Ladies of Larkspur brunch was a Saturday morning staple of bored dames sipping bottomless mimosas while discussing lip injections and the best attorneys to break a prenuptial agreement.

Evan had called the social columnist at the *Seattle Courier* to score an invitation to the ritzy club, though to our dismay, learned he was still hiding out in the Seychelles, a fact that left us with no choice but to hobble together a plan to sneak in. While Lyla waited in her car outside the club gates, Evan and I would trick the guard into letting us pass. We would then locate Tate in the clubhouse where the brunch was being hosted, and separate her from her flock for a brief round of questioning.

Lyla had recalled seeing swag from a charity golf tournament in the supply closet at Absent Thought—a pair of branded golf visors and two polo shirts the color of creamy citrus desserts. Snoozing away merrily beside the mop and broom for the past nine months, the items had patiently waited their turn to be called from the bench. Evan and I would wear the attire to blend in.

"The fit of this shirt is ridiculous," Evan whined as we climbed from Lyla's car and walked to the stone carriage house marking the entrance to the club. He tugged at his collar like a fussy baby in a pair of claustrophobic footie pajamas. "What is this, a boy's medium?"

"Stop messing with your collar," I said. "You're going to draw attention to us."

"Once our mission is complete, this shirt and your beloved copy of *The Communist Manifesto* will roast in a flame of fury."

"Nowhere on my shelf will you find *The Communist Manifesto*. You're just being grumpy." I shivered as a trail of goose bumps snaked up my bare legs and across my uncovered arms, a warm outer layer left behind in Lyla's car. "Please cure this malady of mood before we arrive at the clubhouse. You need to be in the right frame of mind to charm Tate into divulging the details of her private life."

"Don't worry, Annabel. I know how to work it. While you locate Tate in the banquet room, I'll wait in the clubhouse bar and order two glasses of fine champagne." He thought for a moment. "Unless champagne is overkill. Should I order Tate a glass of Chardonnay instead? She may fancy herself a socialite, but she's still a country bumpkin at heart. Someone had to teach her not to put ice cubes in her wine glass."

Irritated by his departure from the plan, I smacked him on the back. "Schemes of deception should never be changed in the eleventh hour, a fact to which any criminal who has outlasted his theoretical expiration date can attest. What will you say when the bartender asks for your membership number?"

"I'll wing it."

I shook my head. "Just stick to the plan and wait outside the banquet room."

We stopped several yards before the carriage house, an elegant stone structure plucked from a pastoral New England manor. Green hostas were tucked along the foundation, their waxy, perky leaves offering soft landing to the beads of moisture dripping from the gutters.

A security guard armed with walkie-talkie and membership roster monitored activity from inside the carriage house. He took his job seriously, a fact that wasn't lost upon us as we watched him step from his post to question the driver of a modest sedan with Idaho plates that had driven through the gate on a self-guided tour. With a confrontational demeanor, the guard instructed the driver to turn himself around and return from whence he came.

Taken aback, the driver rolled his window up with a huff, and turned the vehicle around in an elongated maneuver presenting with more points than a pincushion cactus in the Mojave Desert.

"We've got this," said Evan, reading my hesitation. "Hold your head high, push your chest out, and at the right moment, wave your dainty wrist in the air as though you've locked eyes with the queen bee of your social circle." He swooshed his hand around while puckering up his lips. "A pretentious squeal is effective, but only if you can pull it off without sounding like a drunken babirusa."

"We better steer clear of the pretentious squeal," I said. "You might want to lower your hand. You look like you're attempting to screw a hot potato into a light bulb socket while warming your kisser for a romantic encounter with a puffer fish."

"An overzealous security guard is all that stands between us and an interview with Evelyn Tate. Once we clear this obstacle, the rest will be smooth sailing." He swiped his palm through the air in a *smooth sailing* gesture.

"Which were the exact words uttered by the captain of the doomed *Rouse Simmons* moments before a squall the size of Manhattan slammed into the schooner's sails and sank the vessel to the murky depths of Lake Michigan."

"You've been watching too many shipwreck documentaries." Evan hooked his arm through mine like a western lad obliging the call of a barnyard do-si-do. "Now, my dear, shall we proceed to the carriage house?"

Dressed in the official attire of navy slacks, black boots, and a dark button-up with the words *Widemoor Security* stitched over the chest, the guard at the gate stopped us with an outstretched hand. "Are you members?"

Evan leaned into my ear. "Play along." He looked to the guard and delivered a cover story as contrived as the plot of a daytime soap opera. "I'm a business associate of Jones. He suggested I swing by the club for cigars in the men's lounge while my darling Phoebe attends the Ladies of Larkspur brunch."

"Which Jones are you referring to? We have several members with that name."

Evan ignored the question. "Has Jones been by to show off his flashy Lamborghini? I hear it's a bit of an extension, if you know what I mean." He winked at the guard, a gesture that made everyone uncomfortable. "How Jones intends to keep those sparkling rims from tarnishing remains to be seen. Amino acids in golf course fertilizers are barbarian. They'll munch right through those polished surfaces."

"I need to verify you're on the guest list." The guard motioned to the carriage house. "Follow me."

"Now what?" I whispered to Evan.

"We improvise." He held his hand out in a halting gesture. "This is not the time for a display of power. The lifespan of hollandaise is disgracefully short, and if this needless delay leaves my darling Phoebe staring into a buffet dish of curdled yolks and butter, your superiors will hear about it from our attorneys."

The guard stuttered. "Your attorneys?"

"Unless you wish to see the consequences they're cooking up, I suggest you allow us passage so we may wait for Jones in the clubhouse like civilized human beings."

With fleeting reluctance, the guard ushered us along.

"What happens when this fictitious Jones never arrives?" I asked as we continued to the clubhouse. "Or the real Jones arrives driving an Audi?"

Evan brushed off my concerns. "We'll be long gone by then."

Paces farther, we arrived at the clubhouse to find a commotion of golf carts puttering across the blacktop while members dressed in coordinated colors chattered airily. Luxury vehicles with pearlescent paint jobs filled the parking stalls.

We ascended the grand stairway to the clubhouse and eyed the heavy double doors flanked by giant flower pots. As we crested the stairs with a confident gait, the doors pushed open from inside. Two serious men in matching slacks and collared shirts stitched with the words *Widemoor Security* emerged and stared us down. With their walkie-talkies pressed to their lips, they uttered a series of words that looked uncomfortably similar to *trespassers* and *call the police*.

I stopped in my tracks like a set of hooves at a cattle guard. "These guys aren't looking for our autographs. The guard at the gate must have called ahead for reinforcements. What do we do now?"

Evan gripped my hand. "We run."

Chapter 20

Few elixirs this day and age are as enticing as a flight of mini-sized pint glasses filled with deeply hued stouts, lined up along a serving paddle like sharpened crayons. Irish stout, oatmeal stout, coffee stout, chocolate stout, imperial stout, milk stout… I felt like an educator conducting roll call as I took stock of the taste presentation before me. The heady beers were darker than dark, and as I gazed upon the alluring convocation, I found everyone present and accounted for.

"Stop batting your eyes at the suspects and drink up," Evan said to me. He tipped his head to the row of six-ounce pours.

Not one to disobey orders, I selected the first brew in the lineup, a rich Irish stout with a head as thick as cake batter, and took a long sip. Evan helped himself to the sweet milk stout while Lyla ordered a chalice of Belgian pilsner, paying homage to the pioneering monks who germinated barley malt from the dimly lit catacombs of their monasteries.

"Cheers to The Arms," she said, lifting her glass.

So called on account of the heraldic coat of arms painted on the doors, The Arms—the lively taproom located a few blocks from the arts district—boasted more brews on tap than stars in the galaxy and a collection of bartenders every bit as diverse.

The omniscient bartender—the man with one hand perched atop a tap handle while the other slid a royal pint glass beneath the spout and turned the spigot—knew us well by name and even better by our preferences. Flanked by his best comrades—aproned tapsters adept at pouring pints while calculating simple arithmetic in their heads—he served the thickening Saturday night crowd with cool aplomb. Orders were called, beers were poured, cash exchanged, rinse and repeat.

As thirsty customers filled in around us, Evan swallowed the milk stout in three long draws and appraised the remaining soldiers.

"Hands off the imperial stout," I said as he reached for the brew I'd been eyeing.

"Sharing with you is tricky," he said and helped himself to the coffee stout. "Our preferences always collide."

Lyla sipped from her glass. "I can't believe you two allowed the neutered security guards at the country club to derail your plans to question Tate. How could you be outsmarted like that?"

Evan was peeved. "This wasn't a case of Alexander the Great outmaneuvering his opponents in a battle of tactical prowess. It was simply bad timing."

"I don't understand why you took such a theatrical approach. Rather than introducing yourselves as prospective members, you flustered the guard with some story about a fictitious Jones, then threatened a tangle with his superiors in response to curdled hollandaise?"

I hung my head. "The threat of involving attorneys may have been overkill."

"How many times must we spin this around the axel?" asked Evan.

"Just tell me why you ran," said Lyla, signaling the inquisition wasn't over yet.

"We didn't run in the technical sense of the word. No one broke a sweat, no shin splints were endured."

"In our defense," I said, "you have no idea how dizzying a pair of buzzing walkie-talkies and sternly pointed fingers can be." I finished off the Irish stout and reached for the imperial stout, the dark liquid trembling in the glass. "Let's forgive the blooper reel and focus on crafting a new plan to speak with Tate."

Lyla stretched her hand out. "The floor is yours."

"To establish a link between Tate and the brothers, we must learn her routines—who reads her horoscope, who shrinks her head, who waxes the fur from her upper lip?"

"And who hems her gaudy dresses?" added Evan, his voice taking on the eager lilt of an ambitious gossip columnist hot on the trail of the latest prey of the paparazzi: America's favorite heartthrobs spotted sneaking a kiss a la *Lady and the Tramp* at an intimate trattoria.

"Perhaps you should try her assistant again," said Lyla. "Choose a better alias this time."

"Tate's assistant is like a mushroom-sniffing pig rooting out tubers. She'll smell our deception from a mile away." He finished off the last sips from the coffee stout and smiled with anticipation as he wrapped his fingers around the chocolate stout. "Since this is Saturday evening, 18 Laws will be open for business. The shadowy front porch of the Meland Hotel would provide the perfect vantage point for surveilling activity on the street to see if Tate arrives."

I set my empty glass on the paddle and picked up the oatmeal stout. "While the idea of surveilling the speakeasy beneath the romantic glow of a crescent moon is appealing, there may be another way. How late is the Titan Gallery open?"

Evan squinted with confusion. "Why do you ask about the gallery?"

Check, check, check... a shaggy-haired crew member from the evening act tuning their instruments in the corner murmured a sound check into the microphone. Hungry for a record deal that would never materialize, he lifted the hot microphone from its cradle and exposed his rookie status as he marched his checkered Vans past the main amplifier, creating a feedback loop with the ear-splitting squeal of a pterodactyl feeding frenzy. The crowd contorted their faces in response to the auditory assault.

I cupped my ears. "The theft from Tate's mansion occurred during a private party centered around showing off her premium art collection. While we don't know how she acquired that collection—galleries, auctions, or private arrangements—we do know she's been an avid collector since her rebirth into riches several years ago."

"Which means she's precisely the sort of collector for whom Domino and Julian would salivate," said Evan, finishing my thought.

I nodded. "If we could examine the gallery's customer files, we might find something linking Tate to the brothers by way of their gallery."

Lyla shifted in her seat. "Diverting the attention of the sales associates long enough for one of us to sneak into the gallery's office would be challenging. The slipping on a banana peel bit is too transparent, and a cola spill only requires one set of hands to clean up. Not to mention, a high-end gallery like the Titan will store their customer files electronically. This wouldn't be a matter of picking the flimsy lock on a file cabinet with a bobby pin."

"The files aren't our only source of information. Who knows

what gets left out on a desk: an address book, an appointment calendar, a stack of invitations for an upcoming exhibition." I swallowed the last sips from my glass. "As we speak, an unpaid gallery intern could be licking and sticking a bundle of envelopes announcing a retrospective show for an artist who dedicated his life to painting milkweeds while rendering beeswax in an Uruguayan village. If Tate is on the mailing list, an envelope addressed with her name could be sitting in that bundle, awaiting the morning mail run."

"What about security cameras?" Lyla pressed.

"Shouldn't be an issue," I said. "Since we aren't stealing paintings from the gallery, there will be no reason for anyone to check the security footage."

"We'd need to hobble together believable disguises," said Evan. "The sales associates will call the cops if we show up wearing Chaplin suits and Groucho glasses. Bushy eyebrows haven't been convincing since the Muppets broke the scene." He paused to think. "What about those white surgical masks normally worn by—"

"Surgeons? Even petty criminals stealing bulk straws from the local mini-mart have graduated to more sophisticated disguises. We'll blend in best dressed like normal people."

"Should we be concerned with the risk of encountering the brothers? If they catch us breaking into their office, they'll have us charged with criminal trespassing. Cuba may not extradite, but the brothers will have their own thugs on the ground."

"Since when did we agree on Cuba?" asked Lyla.

"Why wouldn't we agree on Cuba? Mojitos, beaches, classic cars…"

"The Cuba debate is irrelevant," I said. "Domino and Julian will be busy preparing for a night of schmoozing at the speakeasy." I knocked on the bar for luck. "Our primary obstacle will be the pushy sales associates. They'll be relentless in their ambitions to secure a sale."

"Worst case scenario, we'll distract them with a charming monkey-with-cymbals dance," said Evan.

"Why did you look at me when you said that?"

"You're the most charming monkey I know."

"While that may be true, we have an issue with the cymbals and pants."

"The red velvet pants? We can have the waist taken out." He chuckled and pulled his phone from his pocket to check the gallery's hours.

"In order to formulate a winning strategy, we must visualize what we're up against," said Lyla. She wrapped her fingers around a stack of matchbooks and removed several wooden matches. "Given the size of the gallery, I estimate two sales associates will be on staff tonight, possibly two and a half, if Julian has taken in a stray guppy and set the creature to swimming in a fishbowl with the sort of accommodations meant for a wealthy man's mistress." She held up two matches and snapped a third in half. "These three matches represent the sales associates and the guppy." She lined up the matches on the bar and held up three more. "These matches represent the three of us." She set the matches on the bar, two of them incidentally landing on top of one another.

"Should the two matches I presume to represent Evan and you be stacked on top of each other like that?" I asked, smirking.

Evan slipped his phone into his pocket. "If we're relying on me to play the role of Lothario, then it appears she's stacked them just right." He dusted off his collar as Lyla flipped him an eye roll. "No time to hash out the particulars, though. According to the hours posted on the Titan Gallery's website, they're set to close in thirty minutes." He gestured for the bartender's attention.

With bobbed rings pierced through his ears, the bartender slid over and eyed the matchsticks. "Readying your warriors to storm the castle?"

"No time to explain," said Evan. "We'll take the tab."

"Since when did you three rush out like sirens to a fire before the band played their first set?" He gestured to the evening act applying their finishing touches—the guitarist slipping the leather strap for his Les Paul guitar across his chest while the vocalist took the final swigs of his high-AVB quadrupel.

"Our presence is required elsewhere."

"If you got more important places to be, it better involve the foxy mixologist from the gastropub down the street."

"A gentleman never tells."

"Good man." He flipped us the shaka sign and ran the tab.

Chapter 21

In the window of the Titan Gallery hung a massive portrait of Marie Antoinette. The image was eerie like the horror-flick stare of a mummy peering out from a candlelit canvas in an Überwald castle. Her powdered hair was swept up in a pomaded pouffe, her pale lips reflecting the hauntingly fiendish grin of one who had returned from another realm to carry out a devilish act in which only the undead could find humor.

I paused to stare into the disapproving eyes of the ill-fated dame, and prepared to ask her (should the opportunity arise) about the quality of cooking in Varennes: "Was the Quiche Lorraine to your liking?"

Evan drew open the heavy glass doors and ushered us into the gallery, where two female sales associates dressed in dark skirt suits with colorful silk blouses sat behind a rectangular desk situated atop an ikat-patterned rug in the center of the room. Arranged before the desk, a quartet of stiff Danish chairs invited no one to take seat. The gallery was calm and absent customers, the smell of fresh wall paint lingered in the air.

Lyla wandered to a giant installation composed of weird anthropomorphic objects ranging from a gelatinous ballistics dummy to the cross-sectioned anatomy model from a high school science class. Unaware of the thin line between artist and mental patient that only the most discerning collector could distinguish, she uttered the word *creepy* beneath her breath. Little did she know, the artist was one sale away from buying a Porsche, and the sales associates were eager to make that sale happen.

With pencil-thin frame and ankle-torquing heels, the taller associate stood from the desk and hurried over to Lyla. "Do you have any questions about the piece?"

"Yes," said Lyla, studying the suspended objects that resembled the ingredients for a low-budget horror movie. "In which psychiatric ward did the artist spend his formative years?"

The girl's hazel eyes bugged out.

"Only kidding. I find the piece waggish and inventive."

"How does it make you feel, emotionally?"

"Antsy. Like a nightmare is brewing."

The girl frowned. "The gelatinous material of the ballistics dummy is meant to represent the tactile qualities of human flesh while the layers of dermis represent the shedding of cells. In contrast, we have the plastic composite of the removable organs from the anatomy model representing the hardened emotions of a jaded society."

Lyla nodded with disinterest.

"Do you see the omission?"

"A television production crew waiting to reveal the location of the hidden cameras."

The girl shook her head. "Missing are the his-and-hers crash-test dummies."

"Crash-test dummies are gender specific?"

The girl seemed unsure. "Despite their humanoid form the

dummies would lead viewers to conclude our society is sympathetic to the impact of capitalism on our marginalized citizens. But we are not sympathetic. We would rather throw their broken bones and fragmented mental faculties into the sea. Hence the name: *Death of a Plutocrat.*"

Patience depleted, Lyla flashed me a look that said, *Make it quick.*

Evan stopped before a painting of a young boy in subdued frocks holding a limp rubber chicken. In a startling trick of dimensions, the boy appeared to climb from a gold-leafed frame, pointing to two words painted at the base: *Escaping Epigonism.* It was a modern take on a trompe l'oeil masterpiece, and as the subtle satire set in, Evan laughed aloud.

Registering the sound, the second sales associate leapt to her feet and hurried her patent leather ballerina flats in his direction. Freshly plucked from an internship program, she giggled as Evan offered a coy smile. He introduced himself as the ambassador of Tuvalu with an abundance of high-functioning brain cells, and she introduced herself as Bianca.

With the attention of the associates diverted, I put graceful motion to my feet and glided like a prima ballerina from the Ballets Russes to the desk in the center of the gallery. My limbs felt lithe, my movements fluid, until I collided with the same steel sculpture of a dead banana tree that assaulted my shins the night of the gala. I yelped as the impact agitated the bruise, then collected myself and pressed forward.

Stacked brochures and a lipstick-ringed coffee mug emitting the mild aromas of Colombian roast rested on the desktop beside a glass vase spilling over with blue hydrangeas. The computer beside the vase displayed a nondescript screensaver. I gave the mouse a jiggle, though was thwarted by an empty password box.

I turned my attention to the desk drawers. Nestled amongst

an assortment of pens and pencils, a multi-pack of paperclips questioned its place in the top drawer while in the drawer beneath it, an outdated phone book gasped for air. In the bottom drawer, sitting atop a box of business cards, a white envelope displayed the handwritten words: *Humor Submission for The New Yorker*. With a fleeting sense of pity, I left the envelope and its unfulfilled dreams to fester, and abandoned my fruitless search of the desk.

I made my way to the hallway at the rear of the gallery. A ribbon of perspiration wet my brow as I spied a security camera, and I pulled a curtain of hair across my face. My tongue felt parched. A lump caught in my throat, the sort one might feel when encountering a federal agent intent on picking apart the specifics of a false alibi.

Painted the color of Edelweiss blooms, the corridor walls were flanked by two doors: one for the unisex bathroom, the other for the office. I pressed my ear against the office door to listen for signs of life on the other side. From within resonated a faint tapping. I closed my eyes to place it—fingers tapping on a typewriter, a heel tapping on the floor, the ruthless hand of Arshile's mugger tapping on his cold, cruel handgun.

"Dammit," I said, raising up. I glanced back to the gallery space, where Evan and Lyla, counting on me to get things done, were engaged in forced conversations with the pesky sales associates. Unwilling to disappoint them, I placed my ear against the door for a second time and listened to the consistent, rhythmic sound. A series of rational explanations began to take shape—an air-conditioning unit on the fritz, a ceiling fan with a tangled cord, a row of pickle jars unsealing at regular intervals.

It must be the pickle jars.

I gripped the door handle and pulled hard.

It refused to budge.

A fortune cookie aphorism about knocking when uninvited

came to mind, but I dismissed the idea and conceded defeat. As I stepped from the hallway to consider my options, a hideous painting of a wilted dandelion hanging from the back wall caught my eye. A novel idea occurred to me. I rushed back to the main gallery space and approached Evan from his periphery as he and Bianca stared with blank faces at the painting of a deconstructed cardboard box filled with plastic doll heads.

Evan gave up on the painting and said to the young associate, "Do you like sushi?"

"As long as it isn't covered in fish eggs," I said, making my presence known.

Evan glared at me. "That question wasn't meant for you."

Bianca turned around. "Can I help you?"

"The painting of the dandelion on the back wall fascinates me," I said. "Though, I'm certain this gentleman from Tuvalu and I will fight like Cro-Magnons when it comes to deciding who takes it home. Have you another piece by the artist in inventory?"

Bianca thought for a moment. "I believe we still have *Dinner for Kings*, a glorious oil painting of yellow pansies being chewed to death by spider mites. It would look lovely in a dining room." She motioned to the office. "Come with me."

Lyla excused herself from the suffocating sales associate to join Evan and me as we marched like insects behind Bianca toward the office. With breath held, we watched the girl insert a key into the lock, then deflated when she retracted it.

"I apologize ten times over," she said. "I forgot we lent the painting to another collector who wished to see the piece in his mansion before committing to the purchase. I'll show you an image of the painting on my computer in case he opts not to buy it."

I sighed. So close, yet so far… No. I couldn't finish that thought. I wasn't in the mood for a cliché.

Bianca's auburn curls bounced on her shoulders as she guided us to the desk in the center of the gallery. We settled into the Danish chairs arranged before it, cursing the lumps of coal digging into our backs. Bianca sat behind the desk, typed the password to unlock the computer, and swiveled the screen to face us. She navigated to a folder labeled *Decaying Flora*.

"Wait—" I said as the newly revealed background image caught my eye. It was a high-resolution photograph of two men and a woman dressed in formal attire, posed beneath the mammoth painting of a stick figure balancing a triangle of melon on its head. Attired in a scarlet cocktail dress that matched the rosy hue of merriment cast across her cheeks, the artist smiled passionately for the camera, her lips parted to reveal a sparkling row of teeth. To her right, a black-haired man with intense sapphire eyes gazed into the lens while to her left, a dazzling man with a glossy bouffant blew a kiss. And lurking in the far edge of the frame, a stone-faced thug with long blond hair and octopus tentacles tattooed on his throat stared at the trio with a steely expression.

I gasped and motioned to the screen. "Who is the guy with the octopus tattoo?"

"You mean Sapo? He's a nobody. He used to work security for our evening events and helped Julian deliver paintings to our clients' homes after hours. Domino fired him shortly after this picture was taken."

"When was that?"

"Right after our spring exhibition."

"What led to his termination?"

Bianca hesitated. She clicked her fingernails on the desk.

Evan leaned in close and buttered her up with a flirtatious wink.

Persuaded by his charm, she pressed forward. "Domino and

Sapo had a big dispute the last night of our spring exhibition."

"A dispute about what?" he asked.

"Their voices were muffled behind the office door, but I gathered Domino was telling Sapo he couldn't work security for the gallery anymore because he made our customers uneasy. I wasn't surprised. Sapo always had this criminal way about him, like he was about to knock-off a convenience store. Plus, he smoked." She crinkled her nose. "Sapo got worked up, saying Domino stole his idea, whatever that meant. Domino warned Sapo that if he didn't remember his place in the world, he'd be fired. Ultimately that's what happened."

I glanced at Lyla to find her jaw dropping in a bottomless *wow*.

"You think one of your customers complained about Sapo?" I asked.

"Domino wouldn't hesitate to take action if they did. He cherishes his customers. He'd bend over backward for them."

"When was the last time you saw Sapo?"

"I haven't seen him since our spring exhibition. After the argument, he never worked security for the gallery again, though he continued to help Julian with art deliveries until Domino officially fired him a couple weeks later."

"You weren't here the night of the gala when Sapo stormed in and threatened Domino in front of everyone?"

Bianca contemplated the question. "I was in Vancouver visiting family, but I heard about the ordeal. Domino said Sapo was here looking for money. Apparently he pretended to take some uninvited gawker off the street hostage."

I chafed at the label but chose to keep my identity secret. "Domino told his guests Sapo's intrusion was a case of mistaken identity."

"Of course he did. Domino didn't want his customers to be afraid. Sapo just wanted money."

I scratched my head. "That doesn't add up. When Domino offered Sapo two hundred dollars to get lost, Sapo refused it. He said he couldn't be bought off with table scraps."

Bianca swept her fingertips across her clavicle. "All I know is what Domino told me: it was a matter related to money that Sapo handled inappropriately." She tugged at her auburn locks, her loose lips growing looser. "You know Sapo isn't even his real name? It's a nickname Domino gave him when they were young on account of Sapo's blond hair. The term *sapo* refers to a bleaching agent of tree ash and goat fat the Roman women put in their hair to dye it blonde." She brushed her fingers through her hair to demonstrate. "I'd have gotten in trouble for saying that sort of thing, but I guess their family was different than mine."

I sat up straight. "What do you mean *their family*?"

Bianca motioned to the screen. "I mean Domino, Julian, and Sapo. They're brothers."

Chapter 22

We lifted our jaws from the floor as Bianca raised her finger to her lips. "I shouldn't be discussing Domino's personal matters. Let's keep this between us." She used the mouse to access the folder labeled *Decaying Flora* and clicked upon the first icon in the list. "This is the painting I mentioned, *Dinner for Kings*. What do you think?"

"Breathtaking," said Evan, wincing at the masticated pansies. "I may weep a single tear. Please don't judge me."

Bianca clapped. "I knew you'd love it. Let's put your contact information into our customer database so I can notify you if the painting becomes available." She navigated to the gallery's electronic address book.

Leery of leaving behind a trace of our presence, Evan said, "I'll take your business card instead."

Bianca selected a card from the stack situated by the keyboard and pressed it into Evan's palm. "Call next week."

Dressed in the traditional regalia of leather sporran, tartan kilt, and black ghillie brogues, a Scotsman of impressive stature lumbered into the gallery and filled the room with a thick Scottish accent. "I'am lookin' fer Domino."

From behind a steel sculpture of a fern plant with miniature plane propellers for fronds, the sales associate once conjoined to Lyla's hip materialized. "Can I help you, sir?"

"Domino said he had a paintin' fer me to pick up, but he isn't answerin' his telephone."

Flummoxed by his heavy accent and large size, the girl stared up at him speechlessly like a garden ant staring into the hungry beak of its feathered predator.

"Are ye gonna say somethin' or stand thar starin' at me?"

She squeaked out a reply. "Domino didn't mention a painting awaiting customer pickup. I'll call Julian."

"Julian isn't helpful, either. All his eggs are double yoakit. What good is a man like that a'gonna do fer me?"

Bianca jumped to her feet and clamored over to the towering Scotsman. "Welcome back from the Northern Isles, Mr. Napier. What a marvelous kilt." She cringed from the man's grip strength as they exchanged handshakes.

"I stopped in Canmore fer the Highland games and baught meself this kilt. What do ye think?"

"It's a handsome look for you."

"Thank ye. As ah was sayin' to the lockjaw, Domino has a paintin' fer me, but ah cannot reach him."

Bianca tapped her chin. "Domino brought a painting in on consignment yesterday, but he hasn't cataloged the piece yet. It's still sealed in its crate." She gestured to the office at the back of the gallery. "Follow me, Mr. Napier. We'll see if Domino left a note."

We stood from our chairs to issue Bianca an empty promise to call the following week as she guided the kilted man through the gallery. Evan shook her hand, a friendly if not lengthy shake.

Lyla and I followed suit in a more abbreviated manner.

As the Scotsman and the two sales associates disappeared into the office, I bolted to the other side of the desk and swiveled the screen around. "Bianca left the gallery's address book open. If we can locate an entry for Tate, we'll know a connection between her and the brothers exists."

"Better make it quick," said Lyla. "The freedom of motion afforded to that Scotsman by his kilt will give him an unfair advantage should he chase us down the sidewalk on Bianca's command."

I typed furiously on the keyboard, then straightened up as an entry for Evelyn Tate filled the screen, along with a designation that read: *VIP Client.* "Here it is," I said, pointing to the screen. "Tate is a customer of the Titan Gallery."

"Hallelujah," said Lyla. "Let's split before we get caught."

"There's one more thing I must check first." I set my fingers back to the keyboard. "Keep an eye on the office and whistle out like an Eastern bluebird atop a telephone wire if the Scotsman and the sales associates emerge."

"I cannot guarantee my ability to replicate such a specific bird call."

"I've got this," said Evan, fixing his eyes on the rear of the gallery.

As my fingers danced along the keyboard, a rush of exhilaration washed over me. I glanced over my shoulder, then back to the screen as the information appeared. "Looks like Arshile and Quimby are also customers of the Titan Gallery," I said, tapping the screen. "Both men have VIP designations." I closed the address book and hopped out from behind the desk. "Another common thread amongst the victims has been uncovered. I say we head back to The Arms to discuss tonight's developments over a round of pints."

"Before we go, I must visit the contemporary rendition of Edvard Munch's *The Scream* hanging across the gallery," said Evan, motioning toward the far wall. "The piece appears to be reproduced with construction paper and finger paints."

"We don't have time for this," I said, following him to the painting, where carmine reds and burning yellows were draped across a sinuous sky while shadowy swirls of ochre green and navy blue accented a road and a river in the distance. A blurry figure stood alone in the foreground, gripping its hollow cheeks, its mouth open wide in a scream. Trumpeted from the mouth in a cartoon bubble were the words *Laundry Room Renegade*, because even in satire, the image was clichéd.

I snapped my fingers before Evan's face. "You've seen it. Let's go."

On quick feet we scrambled to the heavy glass doors and prepared to dump out onto the sidewalk like a freight train jumping its tracks. As I laced my fingers around the handle, the door pushed open from outside.

Attired in a dark linen suit and charcoal Homburg hat that gave him the appearance of a relic from the roaring twenties, a middle-aged man entered the gallery with the confident gait of one who owned the place.

Because he owned the place.

I gulped. "Domino."

He stopped in his tracks as recognition of our faces set in. "What the hell are you doing in my gallery?"

I was at a loss for words. "That's a great question. It's like, why do people look for love in the wrong place?"

Domino's lips flattened. "We agreed you three would vanish yourselves from my existence, yet here you are, sneaking around my gallery unsupervised with guilty expressions on your faces? I demand you leave at once."

"We have every right to be here," said Lyla. "You can't refuse us service."

"This is my gallery. I can do whatever I please. Anyone can see you have no intention of making a purchase—your clothes are department store and your shoes aren't shined."

Offended, Lyla planted her hands on her hips. "Your snobbish assessment is patently wrong, and you've just cost yourself the sale of that sagging dandelion hanging from your back wall. It's clearly the handiwork of a delirious drunk slapping pigments on a canvas. Good luck finding another buyer to take it off your hands."

Domino scoffed. "Don't kid yourself, Lyla Finch. I know exactly who you are."

She froze. "You know my name?"

Chapter 23

Domino registered the fear in Lyla's eyes. He sneered. "I know all about you, Lyla Finch—your height, your age, your address. Tell me, how does apartment living treat you?"

The color drained from Lyla's face.

I stepped forward with newfound confidence. "If you found Lyla's driver's license, it would have been nice of you to return it. That thing cost her thirty dollars to replace."

Ire flashed across Domino's cheeks like a tower of storm clouds hulking in a giant anvil, a response that emboldened me to say more.

"You figured out who Lyla is? Congratulations. We've figured out who you are, too."

Domino cracked a mocking laugh. "You think so?"

From the back of the gallery, the voice of the Scotsman boomed out as his footsteps thumped upon the hardwood floors. Pinned upon his kilt, a grouse claw trembled from the swishing movement of the pleats over his knees. "Is tha' the voice of Domino ah hear?"

Domino peeled his attention away from us and softened like a kitten with a ball of yarn. "Mr. Napier, what a pleasure to see you. I rushed over the moment I received your messages."

"Ye said ye had a paintin' fer me, but the lasses were unable to find it."

Bianca materialized from the office and hurried across the gallery with relief in her eyes. "Domino, thank goodness you're here. We couldn't find a painting on hold for Mr. Napier, and we were hesitant to unseal the crate you brought in on consignment."

"Your judgment is appreciated," said Domino. "I'll take it from here." He pointed to us with a stern finger. "Please see these three out."

"We'll see ourselves to the door," I said, certain the threatening glare he hurled me would cause the most hardened of criminals to quake in their boots.

The stars in the distant sky flickered in the unusually cloudless night as we emerged onto the sidewalk and left the unwelcoming walls of the Titan Gallery behind. We put forward motion to our feet, The Arms our destination.

"Guess it wasn't a burrowing rodent that took your license after all," I said to Lyla.

She sighed. "I shouldn't have ripped the note from the mailbox at our apartment building ordering tenants not to prop open the doors. Domino can easily find his way in."

"You can stay at my place for the next few days. The couch pulls out into a bed and I have a spare set of flannel sheets. Extra pillows, too."

"I'll take you up on that." She sneezed. "Why was Domino so hostile toward us?"

"He must have found out we were asking around about him."

"Who would've told him—Arshile or Quimby?"

"Or Dane," said Evan.

"Dane? No way. He would never betray our confidence."

"Either way, we must continue digging into the brothers."

I kicked through a sodden pile of maple leaves, rustling up the damp, soggy aromas of decaying plant matter. It wasn't a bad smell, really. "Hell of a bombshell Bianca dropped on us tonight."

Evan nodded. "My knees buckled when she revealed Sapo's identity."

"We ought to do something neighborly to thank her for that tidbit—send her a gift of bath salts or a pony."

"She'd like the pony."

"How does news of the dispute between Domino and Sapo affect our theories about the crimes?" asked Lyla.

I pondered the question. "It's tempting to conclude Sapo robbed the gallery's clients to get even with Domino for firing him, but the theft from the first victim, Byron Quimby, didn't occur until a couple months after Sapo was terminated. Wouldn't Sapo have acted sooner if he were hungry for revenge?"

"It would be helpful if we knew what the dispute that led to Sapo's termination was about," said Evan.

"We know what it was about. Bianca explained that Domino told Sapo he couldn't work at the gallery anymore because he made their customers uneasy."

"That was her guess. Their argument could have been about something else entirely."

"Meaning?"

"Maybe Sapo developed a taste for fine art while working at the gallery. He couldn't afford anything on his security guard salary, though, so he asked Domino for the family discount. When Domino denied his request, Sapo hatched a plan to cherry-pick the art collections of Domino's customers."

Lyla tripped over her heels. "Tap the brakes, will you? The joints in my feet are protesting from this fleet-footed pace."

"Says the girl with giraffe legs?" I asked. "You should have no problem keeping up."

"I refuse to apologize for my blessings. And it's the neck that makes giraffes tall, not the legs." She slowed the pace and looked to Evan. "Your scenario would explain why it was the least expensive painting from Tate's collection that was stolen. Sapo didn't know which of her paintings were valuable. He just knew which one he liked the most when he saw the pieces hanging in her conservatory."

"There's a problem with that theory," I said. "Each theft had an element of complexity that would have required intimate knowledge of his victims to pull off. How would Sapo have possessed that information?" I covered my ears as a fire engine rushed down the street with sirens blaring. "He would've had to know his victims' addresses, their social engagements, their vacation plans, and how to enter their homes."

Evan allowed the information to marinate. "Sapo couldn't have known the specifics unless someone fed it to him."

"Someone like Domino or Julian," I said. "I think Sapo and Domino reconciled, and along with Julian, they've been working together to pull off the art thefts." I bent down to rescue a quarter from the pavement and flipped the meter feed between my fingers. "It would explain Domino's behavior tonight."

"But it doesn't explain the theft from Tate," said Lyla. "Domino is an expert. He would've known the abstract landscape wasn't valuable."

"Maybe the value was irrelevant."

"How do you figure?"

I tossed her the quarter. "If the brothers had a client with a specific taste for abstract landscapes by obscure Scottish artists, they could secure that client's ongoing loyalty by connecting him with Tate's painting."

"What are the odds the brothers have such a client?"

"Quite good. We just watched a Scotsman with an obvious love for his motherland enter the Titan Gallery in search of a painting Domino had on hold for him."

"You think the Scotsman was there to buy Tate's painting?" asked Evan.

"The only piece the sales associates could locate was sealed inside a crate, the contents of which only Domino had seen. I don't know about you two, but if I were using my gallery to resell stolen paintings, I wouldn't let my employees in on it."

As Evan and Lyla processed the suggestion in silence, we crossed the intersection with the red hand flashing. A truculent teen with the mouth of a sailor rolled by us on a skateboard, cursing the world for dealing him a bad hand. Shouting a string of expletives, he swatted the quarter from Lyla's fingers, then pumped his foot on the concrete to skate away. She shrugged off the loss and stuck her hands in her pockets.

"All three of the victims had a VIP designation in the gallery's address book," she said. "It's hard to imagine Domino, a man Bianca described as willing to bend over backward for his clients, would rob the most prized of the bunch."

"What other explanation could there be?" I asked, fanning a winged insect hovering near my eyebrow.

"I can think of at least one." She flicked the insect as it floated over to inspect her eardrum. "What if these aren't crimes against the gallery's customers, but rather, crimes for them."

"Insurance fraud?"

"Think about it. If the victims were complicit, the crimes would be easy to pull off. Quimby could furnish the brothers with the code to his alarm and a key to his house, Tate could add the brothers to the guest list for her expo peinture, and Arshile could leave his kitchen window unlocked. All three could then look the other way while the brothers had Sapo remove the paintings from their homes. The victims could then file the insurance claims, collect on the losses, and retrieve their paintings once the dust settled."

"That would explain the delivery you two witnessed Tuesday evening," said Evan. "The speakeasy would be the perfect place to store the paintings in the interim."

A metro bus with prankish tires splashed through a greasy lagoon formed in the curb lane as we took a right at the next block. I jumped to the side to avoid the disgusting shower. "The insurance fraud angle has an interesting spice, but none of the victims were desperate for money," I said. "Why else would someone commit insurance fraud?"

"Our research didn't validate the victims' financial solvency," said Evan. "We assume Quimby is flush because he inherited a massive trust fund, but he's been frittering away his inheritance at an unprecedented rate." A section of sidewalk heaved up from a thriving tree root formed an uneven ledge. Evan took a tall step to clear it. "While Tate may have held the winning ticket to a record-breaking lottery, she's been blowing through her jackpot with reckless abandon. Ill-prepared for the windfall, she could have found herself on the fast track to bankruptcy court."

"In that scenario, wouldn't Tate have chosen a more valuable painting from her collection? What good does four grand do for someone facing bankruptcy."

"A smaller insurance claim draws less scrutiny."

"Arshile doesn't fit the narrative. He built his dynasty from the ground up, a feat for which financial prudence would have been a key ingredient."

"Arshile may be a successful advertising giant, but he recently divorced a woman with caviar tastes. She could've made out like a bandit in the settlement."

I contemplated his suggestion. "Arshile Design Partners is a major player in the advertising industry. Even if the man took a personal financial hit from the divorce, he'd still have his business to fall back on."

"Unless Arshile's business isn't as solvent as he'd like the world to believe. Earlier this year, the *Seattle Business Journal* published a story about an investment shop downtown abruptly closing its doors when the coffers ran dry. No one other than the owner saw it coming. Who's to say Arshile's firm isn't headed for a similar fate?"

Lyla tripped over a crack in the pavement as we crossed the next intersection. "While I find this conversation riveting, my internal compass tells me The Arms is still three blocks away. With the cracks in the concrete threatening to test the tensile strength of my heels, I suggest we take a taxi the rest of the way." She pointed to a yellow cruiser parked at the curb, just as a pair of stranded daredevils darted across the busy street like spring-launched marbles in a pinball machine. With a final mournful glance tossed to their lifeless Datsun spewing smoke from its long-toothed engine, they clamored into the backseat.

"Tough break," I said. "We're almost there."

At the next corner, we took a left and spied our destination at the end of the block. Silence fell over us. Thoughts of the art thefts, the victims, and the brothers revolved through my mind like a roll of sixteen-millimeter celluloid film winding around its reels, the edges cracking and crinkling.

The bouncer posted outside The Arms checked our IDs and stamped our wrists, the blue ink smudging on contact.

Punchy sounds from the nickel strings of the band's electric guitars reverberated in my ears as we weaved through the crowd inside. Evan took our coats and laid them over an empty stool. "As much as we pivot the possible explanations for the crimes we're still staring into a whirlpool of unanswered questions."

"Questions that need answers," I said, appraising the wall of tap handles. I locked eyes with a blackstrap porter from a microbrewery in Utah. "As stumped detectives in the movies would do, we must return to the beginning and revisit the first victim we interviewed."

"Benjamin Arshile? He'll never agree to it. He labeled us gossipmongers and kicked us to the curb."

"He labeled *you* a gossipmonger, Evan."

"What are you saying, send Lyla instead?"

"Not happening," she said. "The partners at Absent Thought would lop my head off if they knew I was corresponding with the enemy. Not to mention, I'm flying to Portland tomorrow to visit my parents. I won't return until Thursday."

"I'll take the meeting myself," I said. "Twice the man got a laugh at my expense, which means he thinks I'm gullible."

"How does that persuade him to meet with you?" asked Evan.

"I'll tell him you duped me into believing our first meeting with him was for altruistic reasons. Then I'll apologize for the intrusive turn that meeting took, and offer to provide tips for navigating the laborious insurance investigations process. He needn't know my experience in the field was fleeting." I gestured for the bartender's attention and ordered the porter. "Text me his contact information. I'll call him in the morning."

Chapter 24

Layers of stratus clouds swaddled the city of Seattle on the afternoon of my second meeting with Benjamin Arshile. Puffy folds formed in the sky as a light mist fell and wet my windshield. Soggy smells of damp tree bark and a whisper of must saturated the air. It was a day to be savored.

Much deception proved necessary to convince the advertising maven to accept a second meeting. His first instinct upon receiving my call had been to treat me like a telephone solicitor pitching a fake vacation package to Bermuda and slam the phone down, but he had held the line long enough for me to make my case. In the end, Arshile bought my story like a Cajun chef buying littleneck clams, and suggested we meet at his estate after work on Thursday for round two.

Propped open at the end of the driveway, a security gate with galvanized steel slats awaited my arrival. I paused to examine the camera mounted beside it before heading to Arshile's mansion on foot.

Unexpected aromas of toasted vanilla beans greeted me at the doorstep and I breathed in deeply of the scent, envisioning the shark-minded advertising giant robed in a frilly apron with batter-dripping spatula gripped in his hand. Perhaps he'd taken to whipping up pastries to put his nerves at ease, and perhaps sharing those confections had helped him find peace. I hoped that to be true as I felt my stomach rumble.

The stony-faced man who answered the door looked nothing like Benjamin Arshile. His jaw was chiseled, his shoulders square, his hair buzzed to the scalp. Beneath his earlobe dangled a curly earphone cord, the handgun holstered next to his ribs forming a pooch in the fabric of his black suit. In the brusque voice of one whose resume included a stopover at Quantico, he demanded my name, and I answered the question confidently, as though the answer was one I'd known my entire life.

The man uttered a strand of words into a tiny microphone planted in his cuff as I entered the residence, then hovered at my side, the air passing through his nostrils the only sound to be heard. Unable to tolerate the silence, I broke it with the most worn-out topic of small talk known to man: the weather.

"I hear the forecasters are calling for another week of rain," I said. "The California transplants must be going stir-crazy."

The man was silent.

"Massachusetts is gearing up for its first big nor'easter of the year. Boy, those shutters will be shaking."

Still silent.

I shifted my weight from my left foot to my right. "Say, does that earpiece pinch the inner cartilage of your ear? I feel like men such as yourself frequently press their ears in the movies, and I've often wondered if discomfort is the reason. I'll admit, though, I'm basing that observation entirely on Hollywood's portrayal of a government secret service agent. It's naïve to assume the whole pressing of the ear bit is anything more than a cliché."

The man pressed his finger to his ear. It strangely felt like a Kodak moment. "Are you carrying any weapons or recording devices?"

"Aside from the Russian KGB wire taped to my chest?" I clucked.

"Raise your arms to the side and spread your legs shoulder width apart!"

Zero to fifty. I reluctantly assumed the position.

From across the foyer, Arshile's voice bellowed out. "Buy her a drink first, Percy." He thumped into the room, carrying a silver tray piled high with biscotti. "Yes, I baked biscotti, and no, I will not allow you to hold it against me if it tastes like modeling clay."

Thick curtains filtered out the daylight in the darkened study as the man ushered me into the room. He flipped on the lights, laid the tray of biscotti on the coffee table, and tossed his apron sloppily beside it. I settled into the salon sofa and gazed at the paintings of the cake slices. Memories from my first meeting with the man flooded back to me—his self-important tales and laughter at my expense. I wondered what fresh tricks Arshile would have up his sleeve, and if I should have come prepared with hijinks of my own.

Arshile sat in the wingback chair across from me, the fabric cushions groaning beneath his weight. He motioned to the tray. "Have one. I insist."

"I hear baking is a tremendous hobby," I said, selecting the least burnt from the tray.

"Little else has been comforting these days. A round on the links sends my blood pressure through the roof, and an after-noon in the garden puts my histamine receptors into overdrive."

I placed the treat in my mouth and took a bite. A waterfall of crumbles tumbled into my lap, and I instinctively brushed them to the floor, shuffling my shoes across the fine Persian rug to grind away the evidence.

Sidetracked licking his fingers as he plopped a biscotti in his mouth, Arshile failed to notice. "What do you think?" he asked.

"The flavor is exquisite."

"And the texture?"

"Heavenly." As I uttered the insincere compliment, a sticky raisin fell from my mouth and landed in the cracks of the sofa. With fingers barely fitting between the cushions, I pawed at the morsel, though pushed it deeper into the abyss.

Arshile cocked his head. "Young lady, are you familiar with the Palais du Louvre?"

"The Louvre Palace? Yes."

"You will be humbled to know the sofa upon which you sit was once the centerpiece of the Palais du Louvre grand salon in seventeenth-century France. It was from that very perch the marquise de Rambouillet commanded her literary salons."

As the weight of the man's narrative began to sink in, I flicked frantically at the raisin, which had stuck itself to the fabric.

"Historians say the marquise penned the poem inspiring the famous French cabaret *Le Chat Noir* while sitting on that very sofa." As his words hung in the air, I extracted the meat of the raisin, leaving its sheathing squished into the upholstery fibers. Arshile frowned. "Have you anything to say for yourself?"

"I apologize for the raisin," I said. "I'll pay to have your sofa cleaned—"

Arshile smacked his thigh and blurted out laughter. "Young lady, you are far too trusting for this world of scoundrels. That story about the marquise is pure fiction and you're welcome to rub your muddy feet into the cushions if you like." He looked at me like I was born yesterday, stirring up irksome memories of his fluffernutter sandwich story.

"Real hilarious," I said, concealing my irritation.

Arshile helped himself to another biscotti and chomped the treat. "My ex-wife purchased the sofa from a design boutique in Toulouse. The proprietor sniffed her out as a rich man's trophy and sold her that pile of wood and upholstery for the cost of a Lear jet." He rubbed his belly and released a final spurt of laughter. "Many afternoons that leech of a woman whiled away on that gaudy sofa, complaining about the size of her pores. I intend to dump the thing on a street corner in Chinatown." He adjusted his glasses. "What folly that brainless woman brought upon herself. Had she read the fine print in our prenuptial agreement, she would have understood the ramifications of having an affair with the pool boy on the grounds of the estate. In the divorce, she made out with nothing more than a sack of coal. I hear she's back to waiting tables at the crusty seafood shack by the waterfront to make ends meet." Arshile shoved another biscotti in his mouth. "Meanwhile, I kept my empire intact."

"I know which seafood shack you're referring to," I said. "They make the best crab cakes west of the Potomac."

"I've never been a crab man myself." Arshile beckoned his personal secret service agent. "Percy is retired Green Beret. He's a devil behind the sights of a sniper rifle and adept in close combat. He could snap you in half like a chopstick." Arshile flicked his fingers in a snapping motion to demonstrate. "Now, young lady, I will need you to submit to a pat down before we can proceed." He gestured for me to stand as Percy moved closer. "Modern recording devices are the size of a peanut shell, so this could get personal."

"I thought you deemed the pat down unnecessary in the foyer," I said, rising to my feet with hesitation. "My comment about the KGB wire was a joke that failed to land—"

"Hysterical!" Arshile exclaimed, belting out another grating laugh. "You can't buy tickets to a comedy show this entertaining. Young lady, you look as though you've sucked a lemon through a straw." He slapped his midsection, the onrush of laughter leaving his deeply buried abdominals aching.

With blushed cheeks, I slumped into the sofa.

Arshile waved Percy away and gobbled another biscotti from the tray. "As I mentioned over the phone, I agreed to meet with you because you promised your intentions are sincere." A large crumb migrated from the corner of his mouth and stuck to his cheek. "I'm willing to forgive our last encounter, so long as you keep that gossipmonger as far away from me as Mercury is from Mars. Money may be good in the rumor mill business, but it's not the honorable way to build one's fortune. Those who traffic in hearsay are as dubious as the rash spreading across the back of my neck."

I cringed. "I apologize for your rash, Mr. Arshile."

"Merely a stress reaction to the recent events. Sure to clear up within the week."

The pendulum clock affixed to the wall released a loud gong as the hammer struck the bells to announce the arrival of the hour.

"I'm expecting an important delivery at quarter past the hour, and no, it isn't the brick of Normandy butter I'm having flown in from France."

I couldn't help but seek clarification. "Normandy butter?"

"Farmers in Normandy feed their cows a special diet that results in a higher butterfat content than conventional butter." He wiped his mouth, liberating the crumb attached to his cheek. "Are you curious about my delivery?"

"I'm resisting the urge to be nosy."

"Go ahead, take a guess."

"A partridge in a pear tree?"

"Wrong season, young lady. I've upgraded my domestic staff."

I popped another biscotti in my mouth. "The postage couldn't have been cheap. What motivated the change?"

"Some might call it a fit of paranoia, though a change was overdue. The house was in shambles. The dahlias were wilting, the saltimbocca was salty, and a moth had bored a hole in my hunting jacket." Disgust crossed his face. "Unlike my old staff, my new staff will live in their quarters full time. The privilege of walking around unspectated in whatever state of undress I please is one I am relinquishing." He furrowed his brow. "Old habits are hard to break. Percy and I had an encounter last night that left him blushing from cheek to cheek." Arshile raised his voice and shouted to the Green Beret posted in the foyer. "Haven't we, Percy?" He looked back to me. "Percy didn't expect to find my bare posterior poking out from behind the refrigerator door in the middle of the night, but I had baked a batch of vanilla custard earlier in the evening—"

"How is the investigation going?" I asked, changing the subject before a mental image set in. "Do detectives have any leads in the case?"

"As I explained the last time we met, I cannot discuss the details of the investigation. Please understand the position I'm in."

"Can you say whether you intend to post a reward?"

"If I do, you can read about it in the papers." He walked to his desk and returned with a photograph displaying the portrait of a man with fleshy cheeks, heavy eyelids, and fuzzy hair. Cut off at the shoulders, the image left just in view the flaps of a black suit and the white collar of the pressed shirt beneath it. "My latest acquisition."

"Should I recognize this face?" I asked, studying the image.

"That, young lady, is the magnificent writer Alexandre Dumas. His portrait has been reimagined by an artist from Manhattan in a frenzy of tiny right-triangles on a canvas the size of a tractor tire." His fleshy cheeks bulged as he grinned. "If you're familiar with *The Count of Monte Cristo,* you'll appreciate why I've selected this piece for my private quarters."

"I'm familiar with the novel, though I'm embarrassed to admit I've forgotten much of the storyline."

Arshile bent down to select another biscotti, the buttons on his trousers wheezing. "I urge you to procure a copy of the title."

"I'll check the used bookstore on lower Queen Anne."

"Specify that you are looking for *The Count of Monte Cristo.* Otherwise, the bookseller will steer you toward the romances. You seem like the type."

"I've never read a romance in my life. The covers alone are enough to make me gag."

"The *Marie Antoinette Romances,* young lady. Dumas penned those, as well."

I sat up straight, recalling the massive portrait of Marie Antoinette hanging in the window of the Titan Gallery. "Did you acquire your painting of Dumas from the Titan Gallery?"

"The artist was featured in the gallery's autumn exhibition," said Arshile. "His contemporary portraits are centered around Dumas and the characters from his literature. The owners of the gallery have exceptional taste."

"Domino and Julian," I said.

"Principled men, those two."

"That may be up for debate."

"How so?"

"I have news about the brothers. You might want to sit down."

Arshile returned to his seat, his trousers tightening around his thighs. "What sort of news?"

"I have reason to believe the man who mugged you outside 18 Laws is the brother of Domino and Julian, a man who goes by the name Sapo." I paused to gauge Arshile's reaction, but struggled to interpret the blank face staring back at me. "I suspect Sapo was also involved in the armed robbery at your mansion later that night."

Arshile picked a sliver of almond from his teeth. "Young lady, I'm not sure what your angle is, but your suggestion that Domino and Julian are in any way related to the coward behind those crimes is preposterous." He stood from his chair and approached the window. Daylight peeked in through the thick curtains as he drew them back. A dead fly rustled on the sill. "Was your offer to assist with the insurance process merely a ruse to stir up fodder for a rotten buzz column? Have you, like others, concluded I deserved this?"

I suspired with frustration. Television detectives made it look so easy.

Arshile signaled for his Green Beret. "Percy, show this young lady to the door and close the gate behind her."

I waved my hands in a halting gesture. "This news may come as a shock, but I assure you I'm telling the truth. If you don't believe me, you can see for yourself. A photograph on the main computer at the Titan Gallery shows Domino and Julian posed for a picture with an artist from their spring exhibition. Sapo is lurking in the edge of the frame. Once you lay eyes on the image, you'll see I'm right."

Arshile halted Percy with a sigh. A very heavy sigh. The ghostly snailfish of the Mariana Trench would feel the ripples—fifty jumbo jets of pressure perforated by a single breath. "I suppose you're going to beat this out of me."

Chapter 25

Arshile clenched his jaw and spoke in a voice that was low but stern. "Young lady, if you divulge anything from this discussion to anyone outside this room, I will have the police charge you with hampering the investigation."

"I understand," I said, envisioning the detailed conversation in which Evan and I would engage the second I climbed into my car. My phone was in my handbag, the battery charged. Evan was on standby, waiting for my call.

"The detectives working my case already know who Sapo is. They're investigating him in connection with the mugging at the speakeasy, as well as the armed robbery in my home."

I drew in a startled breath. "Do they suspect Sapo was involved in the thefts from Byron Quimby and Evelyn Tate, also?"

Arshile urged me to lower my voice. "I cannot comment on that."

"Do they think Domino and Julian were involved in the crimes?"

"I cannot comment on that, either."

"What can you comment on?"

"Nothing else, and I implore you to stop playing detective. If there are further connections to investigate or other culprits to consider, the investigators will flush that out. They're experienced in their craft. Let them do their job." He cleared his throat. "As the Italians say, *Let every fox take care of his own tail.*"

Percy stuck his head around the door. "Sir, I've received word your driver will arrive soon with your staff in caravan."

Arshile glanced at the clock. "They're late."

"Your driver said he needed to make a stop along the way."

"Is the lottery drawing tonight?"

"I believe so."

Arshile grit his teeth. "Have everyone park outside in the roundabout."

Percy whispered into the mouthpiece planted near his cuff, then resumed his post in the foyer.

Arshile looked to me. "My driver is a gambling addict. Like clockwork, he loses his shirt at the blackjack tables, then squanders whatever pennies remain on the lottery." He shook his head. "Only fools play the lottery, and it is only the most royal of the fools who ever wins."

"You must be keen to replace him," I said.

"My driver? No, I could never fire him."

"Why not? He did nothing to scare off your assailant when you were mugged at the speakeasy. Shouldn't that be a basic requirement of the job?"

"The man has been with me since the beginning of time. He knows my routines, understands discretion, and is the only person on Earth who will tolerate me." Arshile collected the platter of biscotti and tossed the apron over his arm. "Now, if you'll excuse me, I must be going."

As he guided me out the study, a newspaper resting atop

his desk caught my eye. I tapped on the headline. "Says here, Byron Quimby has upped the reward for the return of his stolen paintings."

Arshile lifted the newspaper and skimmed the details. "This announcement will bring that poor fool nothing but an onslaught of swindlers angling to separate him from his inheritance."

"What makes you think so?"

"If the paintings were still out there, they would have been returned by now. No one would allow a reward that sizeable to go unclaimed."

Percy intercepted us as we entered the foyer. His voice was punctuated by a strange urgency, as if we'd all engaged in a high-stakes game of *Operation,* and someone was about to go for the liver. "An unexpected delivery with a return address of New Orleans was left on the doorstep, sir. I've brought the package inside and triggered the gates to close so I can question the driver of the delivery truck."

Arshile patted the air. "I'm expecting the package. Let the man be on his way."

Edges tattered from the long journey, a cardboard box the size of a birthday cake rested on the entry table. The shipping label identified the sender as a costume supply store on Esplanade Avenue. Uncertain of its contents, I surmised the box contained a fresh pair of sheep's clothing.

As the door to the mansion closed behind me, I zipped up my coat and stepped over a helpless roly-poly bug flipped on its back. If Lyla were with me, she'd flick it into the bushes and wipe her fingers on my sleeve.

I placed a call to Evan as I walked down the driveway. It rang to voicemail. The message I left was brief, interrupted by the arrival of Arshile's caravan of domestic staff, led by his driver—his long-standing lieutenant. The scene felt weird, like a circus act rolling into town, the clowns and contortionists unaware of the migraines that awaited them. Saltimbocca was meant to be salty. I wished them luck beneath my breath.

~

Minutes later, my cell phone rang to life. Garbled and heavy with static, the voice on the other end crackled through the phone.

"Where are you, Evan?" I asked, squeezing the phone between my shoulder and my cheek as I drove away. "It sounds like you're running a tooth drill in an aquarium tank."

The static cleared. "I'm in the car. What's the good word?"

I flipped on the wipers as the heavy rain clouds devoured the sucker hole of sunshine overhead. "I've parted ways with Arshile."

Evan's voice was eager. "And?"

"Twice he made a gull of me. Are modern recording devices really the size of a peanut shell?"

"How should I know? Tell me you didn't fall for his fluffer-nutter sandwich story again."

"Please. A mollusk would know better than to take that bait twice."

"Was it beneficial that I sat this one out?"

"Arshile likened your existence to a stress-induced rash, so I'd say yes, it was beneficial."

"Did you defend my honor?"

"I figured his assessment had merit." I chuckled. "Before I could speak up, he moved on to the subject of his upcoming deliveries."

"Let me guess. A marble statue of Poseidon and the vertebrae of a constrictor snake?"

"Try a brick of French butter and a bevy of new staff."

The phone went silent.

"Are you there?"

"Reception in this part of town must be spotty. It sounded like you said a brick of French butter."

"You heard me right. Arshile has taken to baking sweetened confections to calm his nerves."

Evan howled. "You're a riot."

"The man greeted me with a platter of biscotti and a gingham apron tied around his waist."

"Let me guess, aside from that apron he wore only argyle socks?"

I rolled my eyes as his laughter grew. "Care to pull yourself together?"

He exhaled. "Yes, please continue."

"More important than the factual butter delivery is the news the man has fired everyone but his driver in a fit of paranoia."

"What sort of paranoia—aliens built the Hippodrome or the chef and the maid are in cahoots?"

"Maybe both." I slowed to a stop at a red light.

Evan's voice faded to static. "Spp... phhz... bbr... kllp..."

"Call me back when you have reception."

The static cleared. "Someone ought to address the inadequate cellular transmission in our city's tunnels."

"Write a letter to your senator."

"Thanks, Annabel. I'll be sure to sign your name to it."

"Do that and I'll hand-deliver your GPS coordinates to Arshile's secret service agent. Did I mention the man has hired a Green Beret named Percy who has a knack for glowering rudely and flopping at small talk?"

"Hiring a security guard of that caliber suggests the man is more shaken up than we realized."

"Percy sure as hell wasn't hired for his companionship. He had the unaffectionate qualities of a mealy tomato."

"If I were in Arshile's shoes, I'd stack the ranks with military personnel. No one expects the shirtless hunk holding a pool skimmer to be a Special Forces operative."

"Funny you should mention the pool boy." I tapped my fingers on the steering wheel, waiting for the light to change. "While licking biscotti crumbs from his fingers, Arshile shared a gleeful account of the big fat goose egg his ex-wife's affair with the pool boy earned her in the divorce."

"An affair with the pool boy is a worn-out cliché."

"Now is not the time to judge her extramarital choices. Before joining in holy matrimony, she and Arshile entered into a prenup that contained language regarding infidelity. According to Arshile, his ex-wife walked away from the divorce with nothing but a lump of coal." I pressed the gas as the light changed.

"The man is financially sound?"

"Appears so. Our theory of insurance fraud grew wings and flew the coop."

At the next intersection, I hung a right and found myself stuck behind a metro bus pulled to the curb to collect its load of passengers. A beefy pickup truck with a cattle grill and oversized LED lights screeched to a stop behind me and laid on the horn.

"Stop honking at little old ladies," said Evan.

"The blaring sound to which you're referring is coming from the urban cattle rancher crawling up my rear bumper." I scowled into my rearview mirror. "Apparently the virtue of patience is a dissolving concept. Even the crocodiles in the Everglades are ordering takeout."

"Enough with the crocodiles. Tell me more about your meeting with Arshile."

I changed lanes to steer around the bus. "The man told me

detectives are already investigating Sapo in connection with the mugging and the home invasion."

Evan was incredulous. "How did the police put the pieces together so quickly?"

"Arshile didn't say how or when they got onto Sapo's scent, but I assume they've done this before."

"Have they brought him in for questioning?"

"It doesn't sound like it. I suspect Sapo would hop the next smuggler's skiff to Cuba if he found out."

Evan sighed. "This doesn't bode well for us. We'll only benefit from blowing the lid off a crime ring involving Domino and Julian if we do so before every news outlet in the city reports pictures of the police carting the brothers off in handcuffs."

"We don't know how much of the puzzle has been solved. Arshile wouldn't discuss whether or not the police thought Sapo was involved in the other thefts, nor would he say if Domino and Julian were also suspects. Maybe they're nowhere near making an arrest."

"Let's hope that's the case. How did you convince Arshile to share this information with you at such a fragile point in the investigation?"

"A natural segue presented itself when Arshile showed me the photograph of a contemporary painting of Alexandre Dumas he acquired from the Titan Gallery's autumn exhibition. He said if I were familiar with *The Count of Monte Cristo*, I'd appreciate why he chose the painting for his private quarters. I had to admit the storyline was a distant memory. I could likely recite the seminal works from a roster of dead Irish poets before I could tell you who in that story was cursed and who sought love unrequited."

"Have you actually read *The Count of Monte Cristo*?"

"I'm not sure. Hence my offer on the dead Irish poets."

"Name one dead Irish poet other than Oscar Wilde."

I paused.

"Just one."

From some cobwebbed corner, a name came to mind: "Flann Mainistrech."

"Now you're being pretentious."

With a cherry paint job and speedometer topping out in the territory of a rocket engine, a sleek German convertible slowed to a stop beside me as the light turned red. "If you could see the jaw-dropping sports car idling one lane over, you would salivate into the phone," I said, listening to Evan ooh and ahh as I described the vehicle.

"Take a picture for posterity?"

"What is the posterity in this situation? It's not like one of us has joined our founding fathers in signing the Constitution or landed *Apollo 11* on the moon. In thirty-three seconds or less, that convertible will speed off into the sunset."

"Just take the picture."

I rolled my window down. "The things I do for you."

Unaware of my spying eyes, the man behind the wheel of the sports car lowered his visor and gazed into the mirror, feathering his silky bouffant, which was ruffled from romping about town with the convertible down. For half a second I studied the man, then gasped as his identity set in. "While I would give you three guesses as to whom the captain of this glorious machine beside me might be, I lack the patience to await your response."

"You're going to spoil the surprise?"

"Yes. It's Julian."

"Julian?" Evan exclaimed. "Did he see you?"

"He was too busy marveling at his reflection to notice me. A stork could have laid a diapered baby on the gearbox."

"You must follow him."

"What?"

"He could lead you to a secret war room, where the plots for future art thefts are being formulated."

I glanced at my gas gauge. "I'm sitting on less than a quarter tank."

"Is the gas light on?"

"Not yet."

"Then I implore you to follow him."

"What is it with people imploring me to do things today? Arshile implored me to stop looking into the thefts, and now you're imploring me to follow Julian on this escapade of unknown destination. My car hasn't been bathed since the summer equinox and I'm pretty sure my left headlight is out."

"A dirty car plays in your favor and you don't need your headlights during the day."

As the stoplight turned green, Julian's convertible sped off into accelerative bliss. A switch flipped in my mind. I signaled to change lanes, filed in behind him, and pressed the gas to take chase.

Chapter 26

"Listen to me, Annabel. Pursuit driving is a specialized skill," Evan said with an excitement that was audible through the phone. "You must follow my instructions carefully. Ready?"

"Yes, go, go," I said, sailing past a row of urban storefronts at fifteen over.

"Maintain at least a full car length of distance between your car and Julian's at all times. If you spook him, he'll hit the gas and leave you choking on his fumes."

"Got it," I said, following half a car length behind as Julian blew through the intersection.

"If he signals for a turn, follow him, but do not use your signal. And if you find yourself entering a controlled slide as you approach a roundabout, the emergency brake is your friend."

"We don't have any roundabouts in this part of town."

"Any two-way stop with a yield sign counts."

"What shall I do if a police helicopter hovers over my hood, pull into a fast-food chain and feign a fried-food emergency?"

"I'll let you be the judge of that."

"Your faith is appreciated." The sports car accelerated and I pressed the gas to keep pace. "Should my reward for engaging in this pursuit arrive in the form of a speeding ticket and five points off my driving record, I shall demand you shower me with gifts of frankincense and myrrh."

"I can pull strings to make that happen."

"Fantastic. I must disconnect now. This task requires two hands. I will call you later when I feel like it."

"Don't leave me hanging," Evan exclaimed, the last words I heard as I tossed my phone into the passenger seat.

As I rushed through intersections with the cherry convertible locked in my sights, I wondered if the five o'clock news would feature a ratings-grabbing story about a chase between a supersonic sports car and a boxy Swedish coupe in need of a wash.

A plumber's van with a stack of ladders mounted precariously to the roof veered in front of me and rolled to a premature stop as Julian sped through a yellow light. I slammed on the brakes and honked, then anxiously counted down forty-five seconds until the light turned green. I swerved around the van and caught sight of a flash of red zooming through oncoming traffic as Julian took a sharp left. I hit the accelerator and followed in his tracks, swerving past a mail truck and between two sedans.

Four blocks farther, I spotted the racy tail of the convertible slip into a cobblestone alley near the waterfront. I pulled into a parallel spot at the corner of the block, cut the engine, and hoofed it down the pavers on foot.

Historic brick buildings in varying states of disrepair lined the dingy alley while greasy spills pooled between the pavers. Trash from a banged-up dumpster laid scattered at the receptacle's feet, the putrid smells of last week's chicken bones wafting from beneath the lid. Halfway down the alley, Julian's convertible came into view, parked beneath the fire escape ladder of a shabby brick building with a door signed *Loft 242*. Julian was nowhere in sight.

I approached the vehicle and hovered over the cockpit to peer inside. Folded on the dash were a pair of calfskin driving gloves while draped across the passenger seat was a designer houndstooth coat. Resting on the supple leather beneath the coat was a manila folder stuffed with documents begging to be rummaged through. My eyes lit up at the sight. I contemplated reaching my hand into the car to lift out the folder, though a scraggy voice distracted me from behind. I spun around to find a gray-haired hobo wandering aimlessly down the alley, a cardboard beggar's sign pinched beneath his arm.

"Purrrty car," he stammered, indifferent to my presence as he shuffled to the convertible and dropped his dirty, crumpled sign atop the shiny hood. Fearful of a spectacular show of alarm bells should he grab the handle next, I extracted a five-dollar bill from my wallet and fluttered it before his eyes. "I hear the lottery is paying big these days. Go buy yourself a ticket."

"Purrrty coat," said the man. He stepped around me to scrunch his fingers around the collar of the houndstooth coat, the garment screaming for rescue.

I shoved the cash in his face. "I said you should take this money and buy yourself a lottery ticket."

With one arm squeezed into a sleeve of the coat, the man turned his focus to the driving gloves, pulling them from the dash to stick his hands inside. The fit was poor and he flung them to the ground in frustration.

"Just take this money and go," I said, waving the bill urgently.

Finally aware of my presence, he yanked the cash from my fingers and ambled away, the coat dragging like a ragamuffin doll along the dirty cobblestones behind him.

I turned my eyes back to the manila folder. I thought, two

types of people exist in this world—those who get away with things, and those who do not. With that truism in mind, I lifted the folder from the convertible. It put up little fight as I thumbed through its contents.

The first pages displayed the words *Customer Database* printed along the top while a list of alphabetized names with contact details filled each sheet as computer-printed rows. Highlighted in yellow, several names stood out as important to the preparer, though the reason was unclear.

To gain clarity, I scanned the names and turned the pages, soon locating entries for Arshile, Quimby, and Tate. Electrified, I set the list aside and flipped through the remaining documents, careful not to dislodge the paperclips. I perused the contents, quickly identifying the files as a series of insurance appraisals printed on Titan Gallery letterhead. High-resolution images of the paintings stolen from the three victims stared up at me from the pages.

From a tangled lattice of electrical wires overhead, a bunch of feral pigeons babbled and hummed as they urged me to photograph the documents. Evan, biting his nails with anticipation, would applaud the foresight.

With the stuffed folder tucked beneath my arm, I reached into my handbag to retrieve my phone, though grumbled to recall having left it behind in my car. Frustrated, I yanked my hand from my bag, jarring the folder and causing the insurance appraisals to spill into the cockpit as a jumbled mess. An exclamation of alarm leapt from my lips. I pawed desperately at the documents in a bumbling action that diverted my attention from the door to Loft 242 swinging open.

Chapter 27

My heart sprang from my chest as the sound of Julian's flowery voice issuing a farewell to an unidentified host rang out from behind the door. With a panicked flip of my wrist, I sent the empty folder sailing before turning to race for cover behind a smelly dumpster with a sticky orange syrup dripping down the side. I crouched down low, breathed through my mouth, and peered around the receptacle.

Julian bleated with disgust as he spotted the ratty beggar's sign resting atop the hood of his cherry convertible. "What is this vile piece of garbage?" He threw it to the ground like a soiled diaper and wiped his fingers across his pants, then rushed around the vehicle to stare at the mess of documents cluttering the passenger seat. "What happened to my files? And my overcoat?" With a horrified gasp, he hurried to the driver's seat, fired up the engine, and sped down the alley, his racy tires driving over the calfskin gloves marooned upon the cobblestones.

As the sports car disappeared around the corner, a postcard fluttered from the cockpit and danced along the pavers until coming to a rest upon a sloppy mush of cardboard. I hustled over to retrieve it.

Dampened with slop, the postcard crinkled at the edges as I lifted it from the muck and turned it over in my hands. I scanned the contents. My eyes lit up. Eager to notify Evan of my discovery, I rushed back to my car, laid it in the passenger seat, and initiated the call.

Evan answered on the first ring. "It's been forty minutes, Annabel. Where have you been?"

"No need for alarm," I said. "My ribs are intact." I placed the key in the ignition and pulled away from the curb. "Through a series of covert maneuvers, I tailed Julian to a cobblestone alley near the waterfront, where he slipped inside a building called Loft 242. Have you heard of the place?"

"Loft 242 is an event space for private parties. I've heard it's super swanky. Our social columnist from the *Seattle Courier* attended a soiree hosted at the loft by a tech billionaire earlier in the year. What was Julian doing there?"

"I don't know. I narrowly escaped getting caught rummaging through his convertible while he met with someone inside. You won't believe what I found." I provided him with a fast-paced rundown of the materials stuffed inside the manila folder.

"You're saying the Titan Gallery prepared the insurance appraisals for the stolen paintings?" asked Evan. "Coincidence?"

"Galleries often provide insurance appraisals for their clients, even if the pieces were purchased elsewhere," I said. "I can't think of any reason Julian would be driving around town with those appraisals, though. The victims' insurers would already have copies." A distracted soccer mom in a luxury SUV boasting the white window decals of a stick-figure family swerved in front of me to avoid collision with a minty green scooter as the stoplight changed to red. The postcard slid off the passenger seat and landed on the floorboard as I hit the brakes. "It's getting western out here. How far from your apartment are you?"

"I'll be there in ten minutes, barring any traffic jams. I won't be home long, though. Lyla twisted my arm into picking her up from the airport in the heat of rush hour. I expect the drive will be as relaxing as navigating a pedal-powered rickshaw through the cow-filled streets of Bangalore. You're welcome to join me."

"While I appreciate the offer to serve as company to your misery, what kind of friend would I be if I robbed you of that character-building experience?" The light turned green and I pressed the gas. "I'll meet you at your place in fifteen. We have arrangements to make."

~

Evan greeted me with a bowl of carrot sticks as I pushed through the unlocked door to his apartment. "Is this a hint about my waistline?"

"Your waistline is fine. Positively Rubenesque." He flashed me a rascally smirk. "Lyla left the bag of pretzels open before she left for Portland and the salt crystals dried out."

I followed him into the kitchen. "As a matter of science, salt crystals are always dry. What really happened to the pretzels?"

"The dog ate them, just like my homework." He removed two pint glasses from the cupboard, selected a bomber of hoppy IPA from the fridge, and unearthed the bottle opener from the drawer where the napkins and orphaned measuring spoons lived.

I took a pint glass and filled it from the sink. "Water is fine."

"Suit yourself." He returned the IPA to the refrigerator, pulled the cork from a half-empty bottle of Barolo, and poured a splash into his glass. Then he topped it off with seltzer water and a squeeze of lime.

"What are you drinking?"

"Poor man's sangria. Care to try it?"

"I'm good."

Mustard yellow and older than me and Evan combined, a vacuum that could have rolled from the Jetsons' broom closet stood in the center of the living room, its cord trailing off to a socket in the wall. Evan pushed it out of the way as I followed behind him and set the bowl of carrot sticks on the coffee table. I settled into the stiff cushions of his streamlined sofa and popped a carrot stick in my mouth. "How old are these carrots?" I asked, my tongue protesting the texture. "They taste like the fluorocarbons in your refrigerator."

Evan sat in his swivel chair and drank from his sangria. "Stop being picky. You sound like Lyla."

I sampled another one and regretted the mistake. "Is there anything edible in this place?"

"Didn't you polish off a tray of biscotti an hour ago?"

"I'll have you know I consumed no more than two biscotti that I can recall, and my insulin levels are now crashing down from the outer reaches of our galaxy."

Evan rummaged around the top of his desk and picked up a half-eaten bag of ginger snaps. Crumbles fell into his lap as he removed a cookie from the bag and squeezed it. "The ginger snaps have seen better days. There's a tub of hummus in the fridge, along with a hodgepodge of useless picnic condiments. Fair warning, the mayo is starting to liquefy."

I gagged. "What do you subsist on?"

"Leaves and berries foraged in the wild."

"It's time we find you a Susie Homemaker."

"Know anyone good?" He spun around in his chair and sipped from his glass. "My age parameters are flexible, but I'm finicky about cooking oils."

"Stop spinning, Evan. You're making me antsy."

"It's just the way I think."

"I miss the days when flipping through the pages of *Candide* was your method for thinking." I walked to his bookcase and pulled his tattered copy from the shelf. "This book is all you need to ruminate on any topic of consequence." I flopped the book on his desk, pushing aside a thick booklet patterned in yellow and black diagonal stripes. The title caught my eye and I lifted it for closer examination. "Your college CliffsNotes for *The Count of Monte Cristo*?"

"After I challenged you on the dead Irish poets, I figured you might grill me on the vengeance-filled storyline."

I snapped my fingers. "Sir Walter Scott."

"No dice. Sir Walter Scott hailed from Edinburgh." Evan tossed the booklet on the floor. "You mentioned over the phone we have arrangements to make. Should I gather references for hit men and dummy up fake passports?"

"Not yet." I took from my handbag the postcard and pressed the corners between my thumb and forefinger. "What are your plans for Saturday night?"

"First date with a well-read blonde from Tallahassee I met at the coffee shop around the block. She's lactose intolerant, but I can forgive that on account of her perky—"

"Reschedule." I handed him the elegant cardstock and drew his attention to the gilded border and gothic black font.

His eyes illuminated as he read the contents aloud in bits and pieces: "The Titan Gallery cordially invites you to attend a private masquerade ball to celebrate our clients… a magical night of fine champagne, gourmet hors d'oeuvres, unusual performers… costumes are encouraged…" He looked up. "Do you realize what this means?"

"It means the brothers and their VIP clients will all be in one location for the ball Saturday night, and we hold in our hands a legitimate invitation."

Evan beamed. "This could be our chance to get the answers we need to solve the art thefts before the detective bloodhounds beat us to it. How did you score this?"

"It fluttered from Julian's convertible as he sped down the alley behind Loft 242. I have a hunch Benjamin Arshile will be there. A package from a costume supply store in New Orleans was delivered to his doorstep. I imagine it contained a mask."

"You think Byron Quimby and Evelyn Tate will be there, also?"

"They're VIP clients, aren't they?"

"Quimby said he was heading to New Mexico to conduct market research."

"There can't be much to learn about the hot dog cart industry in Farmington. I suspect he'll be back by Saturday."

Evan jumped from his swivel chair, clutched my hands, and swirled me in a circle. "Concealed by a sparkling façade of sequins and ostrich feathers, we could infiltrate Domino's elite inner circle and question whomever we please. People are bound to talk; they'll think we're one of them." He pressed his chest against my back and strutted us across the living room, humming "Gypsy Tango."

"I kept the Colombina mask I wore in New Orleans three years ago," I said, "and there's an unopened tube of red lipstick in my purse. Do you have yours?"

"I don't own lipstick."

"Your Phantom mask, Evan."

"Unless the sticky-fingered Pygmies Lyla claims stole her Dutch blender have slid beneath the crack in my door to abduct it, my Phantom mask should be floating around my apartment." He twirled us in a graceful figure eight that turned clumsy fast as his feet entangled with the vacuum cord. Together we lost balance and tumbled to the floor, missing a rough landing on the pine boards by inches.

I pushed myself up and smiled at Evan lying supine on the floor. I said, "Lyla kept her Mardis Gras mask, too. I saw the silver cockerel feathers peeking out from the bottom of her sock drawer when I helped her get organized last month."

"Lyla will be a problem. The fateful night on Bourbon Street when she knocked the stilt walker off his poles haunts her to this day. When she sees the reference to unusual performers on the invitation—" He stopped mid-sentence. "Can we pull this off just the two of us?"

I shook my head. "We need Lyla to help us keep tabs on the brothers."

He rubbed his hand across the back of his neck. "I suppose it's time I dust off my directionless dinghy speech to convince her."

"You mean the speech where the crab yanked from the North Atlantic by the profit-seeking trollers pity your journalism career and its lack of direction and oars?" I didn't wait for him to answer. "That clunky speech has never been persuasive. We'll hide the invitation until we get there."

Chapter 28

The metal strings of the violin quivered with the haunting notes of Dmitri Shostakovich's *First Concerto* as the violinist, draped in the elaborate fabrics of Venetian costume, rolled her resin-tipped bow across the arc of steel ribbons. Harlequin greeters with bulbous Arlecchino masks stood sentry before the double doors, drawing them open once the bronzed young man in black tuxedo accepted our glittering invitation.

Arabesque tunes played by a lively ensemble of grand piano and string quartet filled the lavishly decorated room, where long silk streamers spanned the distance of the ceilings and waxed candles glowed from brass candelabras. Mirrors in gilded frames hung alongside velvet curtains looped over stout rods. Freshly buffed, the parquet floors sparkled with a basket-weave pattern that tricked the eye.

From the tray of a server wearing a filigreed feline mask, we selected a glass of champagne and appraised the scene before us: the undulating sea of tulle, taffeta, and tussore; the maze of feathers, crystals, and papier-mâché.

As if on cue, a second server swooped in to present us with a tray of bruschetta blanketed in heirloom tomatoes, basil leaves, and fresh mozzarella. I cooed with delight and helped myself to a taste, careful not to spill on my black sequined dress.

"You'll be picking strands of basil from your teeth for days," said Lyla, the thick plumage of silver cockerel feathers fanned out from the braided edge of her mask bouncing as she shook her head in disapproval.

I devoured the appetizer in three bites and pretended to wipe my hands on her shimmery dress. "A strand of basil never hurt anyone." I licked my fingertips clean and traced them along the edge of my midnight mask accented with dark ostrich feathers and satin rosettes to check the tightness of the knot tied behind my head.

"Here, let me help you." Lyla swiveled me around to adjust the satin ribbon.

"This magnificent evening deserves to be commemorated," said Evan, stroking the smooth, contoured cheek of his white Phantom mask. He reached into his suit coat and retrieved his cell phone, snapping a series of photographs as Lyla and I flashed flirty grins. "It is imperative that we avoid using our real names tonight," he said. "Even when speaking with each other."

"Agreed," said Lyla. "With everyone disguised in costume, it will be impossible to know who's standing over our shoulder."

I relaxed my smile as Evan captured the final picture. I said, "We must figure out what Domino and Julian are wearing so we can keep an eye on them. I suspect they'll go big on a night like this—"

My words were interrupted by a gasp spreading through the elegant crowd as the lights cut out. A spotlight shone to life and illuminated a circle on the stage into which stepped a tall man costumed in ruffled pantaloons, lacy neck whisk, and balloonish funnel sleeves. Glossy and coiffed, his bouffant formed a gentle wave across the forehead of his flesh-hued Frombolatore mask.

"It appears Julian has chosen the costume of a seventeenth-century ladies' man," I said, motioning to the stage.

With the microphone pressed to his lips, he welcomed the gallery's prized clientele in a gooey voice. Applause rang out, sparking the man to shimmy his shoulders from side to side, his pillowy sleeves swooshing around his arms as he blew a round of kisses to the audience.

"Oh, brother," said Lyla. "Watching Julian blow kisses to his party guests is like watching a gladiator blow kisses to his opponent as they enter the arena to destroy each other." She pressed her lips to her palm and tossed the imaginary smooches to the ceiling.

From the back of the room, a booming voice with a thick Scottish accent broke Julian's prelude. "E'nuf of this goosin'. Where's Domino?"

The audience parted like the Red Sea to reveal a towering Scotsman adorned in tartan kilt, knee-high hose, short tuxedo coat, and brown leather Zanni mask with a long, curved nose that extended down to his chin.

Startled by the interruption, Julian stood silent before addressing the audience as one. "Ladies and gentlemen, let's hear a round of applause for our patron from the Northern Isles, Mr. Napier." Upon his command, the audience clapped, then quieted as Julian patted the air. "Domino will arrive soon. Until then, enjoy the champagne and hors d'oeuvres." The lights turned on to a romantic glow as he exited the stage.

Lyla spotted the kilted man and grabbed my wrist. The gesture was abrupt and slopped champagne over the rim of my glass.

I shook the droplets from my hand. "Gentle, Lyla."

"That's the Scotsman from the Titan Gallery," she said.

Evan offered me the violet handkerchief from his lapel. "This could be our chance to determine if the painting he collected from the gallery was the abstract landscape stolen from Evelyn Tate's conservatory. We must engage him in conversation to find out."

"If the Scotsman bought Tate's stolen painting, the last thing he'll do is sing like a sparrow with chops to three strangers," said Lyla.

"Oh, ye of little faith. You should know by now my repertoire for this sort of thing runs deep." He chugged his champagne and sauntered off. "Watch and learn."

"This should be entertaining," said Lyla. "Between you and me, I don't know how he does it."

"Evan's a journalist," I said. "He's practiced in the art of getting people to open up."

"No, I mean I don't know how the Scotsman wears those itchy kilts. Animal fibers are notorious for rubbing at the dermis in the most unpleasant of ways." She ran a fingernail along her skin. "What does he wear beneath that kilt to minimize the irritation, a linen loincloth?"

"I don't know, Lyla. You want to go ask him?"

"No need. He likely has the legs of a woolly mammoth beneath those pleats and can wear whatever he pleases." She paused. "Or nothing at all, if the mood is right—"

I planted my hand on her mouth. "Please stop talking."

She peeled off my fingers and gasped to find a smudge from her burgundy lipstick blotted inside my palm. "You've smeared my flawless makeup."

"Calm down, muffin. With that flock of feathers fanned out over your head, no one will notice a rub in your lipstick."

She fluffed the glistening feathers, a tuft of plumage catching on her beaded bracelet. It ripped free and floated to her feet.

I looked at the feather and smirked. "Molting season has arrived."

She bent down to retrieve the feather. "I must fix these catastrophes at once. Where is the powder room?"

"Over there—" I pointed to a softly lit hallway with signage for the lavatories.

"I shall return in two minutes. Go nowhere." She hurried away on her tall stilettos.

I turned my attention back to Evan and the Scotsman, whose voices were drowned out by the chattering partygoers. With a mind to join them, I put forward motion to my feet, just as a procession of electrified stilt walkers dressed in flowing fabrics marched through my path. They stomped their poles to the Arabesque music while a man in crimson tuxedo and Pantalone mask ornamented with bushy eyebrows and forked beard clapped his hands like a jolly gent of comedy.

Entranced by the performance, a crowd gathered around and blocked my line of sight. I pushed my way through them, though startled to find nothing on the other side but a pair of young gents in checkered masks. Confused, I stood on my toes and scanned the crowd. Just as I caught sight of Evan in his Phantom mask shuffling through the congregation, the lights cut out for a second time, filling the room with darkness, save a single beam of light twinkling onstage.

Thick plumes of smoke puffed across the platform as the pianist punched out the ominous notes of "Moonlight Sonata." Intrigued, the audience began to wheeze, their breath heavy with anticipation as Domino materialized. Dressed in a black tuxedo and rust-colored Diablo mask with horns an inch in length, he issued a warm greeting, then disappeared into the haze as a second puff of smoke erupted. The deep chords of the bass clef faded into silence.

As the lights warmed up, I set off to search the perimeter for Evan and the kilted man. When I neared the stage, thoughts of the brothers positioned nearby compelled me to change course and cut through the dance floor, where elegant couples twirled in rhythmic bliss.

As if plucked from the funeral procession of *Amadeus*, two cloaked men in black tricorn hats and white Bauta masks materialized behind me. Rattled by images of Domino dispatching his thugs, camouflaged in costume, I rushed off to escape them—ducking between the dancers and weaving through the mingling partygoers.

As I raced toward the hallway where the ladies' room offered safe harbor, I cast a glance over my shoulder and shrieked to find the men hot on my heels. Their voices became audible as they closed the gap.

"I told you we'd find her," they chanted. "We're going to get paid."

My calf muscles flexed as I picked up the pace to make a break for the hallway. As I neared the corridor, a martini-sipping patrician chomping down on a blue-cheese-stuffed olive stepped into my path. I shifted on my heels to alter my trajectory, though slipped on the polished parquet floors. Flapping my arms for balance, I regained my footing, just as the voices of the masked men grew louder behind me. With a fearful gasp, I grit my teeth, spun around, and made my body rigid for impact.

Chapter 29

"Duck, duck, goose!"

The words rang out as the men in tricorn hats and Bauta masks split in half to race around me. Confused, I swiveled around to watch them stop inches behind a young girl with long blonde curls, red sequined gown, and iridescent volto mask. They poked her sides and tugged her curls.

She squealed. "How did you know it was *meee?*"

"No one else this side of the train tracks holds their flute of champagne by the rim," the men said in chorus. "The bet was a thousand dollars, girlie. Pay up."

Made speechless by the product of irrational thinking, I left the trio to settle their wager and headed for the ladies' room to collect Lyla.

Signed with the cartoon depiction of a Victorian female in lacy bustle, the door swung open easily and revealed inside a brightly lit powder room with oversized mirrors and a tasseled vanity bench.

"Miss cockerel feathers?" I asked, avoiding the use of Lyla's name as I passed through the empty powder room to check the stalls. An elderly lady with a featureless black mask pinched beneath her frail arm stood before the row of sinks, running her hands through a stream of water.

"Are you in here, Miss cockerel feathers?" I repeated, wiping off the smudge of Lyla's lipstick from my palm.

Receiving silence in response, I returned to the powder room and paused before the mirror to check my teeth.

A glittery woman with frosted locks entered from the party and settled into the vanity bench. Cream taffeta spilled out from beneath her embroidered skirt while red ribbons accented the décolleté corset of her Venetian costume. From within her satin clutch, she removed a tube of carmine lipstick and colored her lips.

"I'll be done momentarily, love," she said to me, her voice an unusual accent of proper British and deep South.

The unlikely mash-up halted my footsteps. I glanced in the mirror to watch her swipe a manicured fingertip across the veneered enamel of her teeth. I said, "Evelyn Tate?"

"Tonight I'm known as Corallina." She removed a powder pot from her clutch and plopped a dollop of white talcum on her chiseled nose. "A lover from the Innamorati of Commedia dell'Arte."

Stunned by the chance encounter with the imposter socialite, I fished around in my handbag for a packet of blotting papers and looked into the mirror. I pressed a tiny sheet against my chin and the apples of my cheeks, the only skin visible beneath my mask. "Your costume is lovely, Lady Tate."

She shook her finger. "Corallina."

"My apologies, Corallina, a lover from..." my voice trailed off as the name escaped me.

"The Innamorati of Commedia dell'Arte," she said again,

butchering the pronunciation. "Why must I tell everyone twice?"

"Perhaps when they hear the name Corallina, they think of a Roman salami."

Tate scrunched her nose. "Salami? I wouldn't know. I refuse to put animal fats in my temple." She puckered her lips in the mirror and assessed her hued lip line.

I couldn't resist a snarky reply. "Despite the presence of animal fats in your lipstick, I adore the shade."

"I beg your pardon?"

"Rendered animal fat is a common ingredient in lipstick."

Tate's smile shriveled.

"It's called tallow and it's a dirty secret of the cosmetics industry."

Her frown turned to laughter. "Oh, love. Has Julian put you up to this? What a trickster." She stood from the bench and fiddled with the pearl buttons climbing up her corset. "When I told him of my intention to dress the role of Corallina, I hoped he would wear the costume of my flautist, Ottavio. How handsome he would be in short pantaloons and frilly vest. Wouldn't you agree?"

"Julian has amazing swagger, but he isn't my type. I prefer guys with a little stubble on the chin."

Tate snickered. "Oh, love. I adore your spunk. Tell me your name."

Caught off guard by the question, I struggled to think of a response. "My name is…"

Tate tipped her head with impatience as the seconds ticked by.

I thought a moment longer, then floundered and broke the cardinal rule of spy-craft by telling her, "I'm Annabel."

"Pleasure to meet you, Miss Annabel." Tate extended a soft hand. I returned the gesture, delivering a confident shake. She frowned. "Oh, dear. It appears you have the grip of a wild boar."

My cheeks flushed.

"Let's try that again, shall we?" She nodded to my ogre hands.

"You bet, love." I cupped her dainty paw and shook it like a floppy spear of asparagus.

"Much better. Tell me, Miss Annabel, are you new in town? I know everyone here, and I'm certain we've never met."

"My husband and I relocated from the East Coast last month," I said, tucking my left hand behind my back to conceal the absence of a ring.

"Tremendous, love. Who is your husband?"

Who is my husband? I thought. *What is this, twenty questions?*

Tate tapped her heel as she awaited my reply.

I looked off into the distance, urging my mind to think of a clever reply.

"Surely your husband has a name," she said, growing annoyed.

"My husband's name is…" I said, stalling. "His name is…" Unable to think of anything more original than the ridiculous alias for which Evan had earned himself infamy—the same alias that ran him afoul with Tate's assistant—I answered with an ashamed sigh. "My husband's name is Theo Tolstoy. He's the mild-mannered grandson of a reclusive adhesives baron." The second the words left my lips, I longed to put the olive back in the jar.

Tate nibbled at the name. "Theo Tolstoy…" She flipped through her mental Rolodex. "Ah, yes. Your husband, Theo, and I have a bone to pick. He cheated me out of a sculpture of a moth larva during an auction last year. Quite the devil he is with a bidding paddle."

"Boy, that sounds just like my Theo," I said, seizing upon the unexpected case of mistaken identity. "Last month he offended a Samoan ambassador when he outbid the man for a lithograph—"

"Enough, love. I'm bored already. What I'm dying to know is when you plan to host your grand unveiling?"

My face was a question mark.

"Have you hired an event planner? If so, fire her. You can't trust anyone but *moi* with the arrangements." She fluttered her hands. "We'll make the event spectacular—linen napkins, bone china, seafood towers, a swimming pool of swans. Julian will manage the guest list, Domino will arrange for security, and I'll take care of the rest."

I did a mental double-take. "Domino and Julian will be involved?"

"I assure you there is no one more qualified. They've assisted with all of my private events."

"Including the expo peinture the night your painting was stolen?"

She shook her finger. "Now, now, love. You mustn't allow the theft to dissuade you from accepting their assistance. They did a marvelous job that night. The theft was a random act no one could have anticipated. Why anyone outside Dumfriesshire would even want that painting is a mystery."

"What's so special about Dumfriesshire?"

"It was the artist's hometown. He never left the area in his entire life. Can you imagine?" Tate trembled at the thought. "The artist may be a forgotten relic, but oh, how I cherished the piece." She cleared her throat and turned for the door. "Call me when you're ready to plan your event."

I followed her out and returned to the party growing livelier by the minute. Aware Domino and Julian were floating somewhere around it, I proceeded with caution and worked my way through the center of the room to locate Evan and Lyla.

Green sequins entered my line of sight as a juggler rotating a trio of crystal balls bounded into my path. His hammy smile was more than I could take, and I stepped to the left to navigate around him. Searching for applause, he stepped along with me while keeping the balls in motion. As I prepared to use my elbows, a pair of unseen hands thumped down on my shoulders from behind. An icy voice hissed into my ear. "What the hell are you doing here?"

Chapter 30

"Got you!" said Evan, whooping with laughter.

I twisted around to face him, choking down a lump the size of a golf ball. "Not funny," I said, whacking him on the chest. "I thought you were Domino."

He lifted my hands off his suit. "Careful with the lapels. It took much effort to iron them into obedience."

I selected a glass of champagne from a feline-masked server and took a calming sip. "Where did you disappear to? I've been searching everywhere for you, high and low."

"An admirer of advanced age spotted the Scotsman from across the room and made a beeline for us. It was necessary to hide." He helped himself to a glass from the tray. "The woman isn't bad-looking for her age, but the kilted man has his heart set on finding a young Scottish lass to whisk off to the fertile countryside for a proper Scottish life."

"Haggis pudding, Burns poetry, and fields of dairy sheep?"

"Aye, and the whiskey, too." He grinned and took a long drink from his glass. "Turns out, the Scotsman is the proud inheritor of several mossy acres along an idyllic coastal inlet in Solway Firth called Dumfries-something-or-other."

I grasped Evan's arm. "You mean Dumfriesshire?"

"Sounds right. Why, are you in the market for a pig farm?"

"I could never farm pigs. The squealing would drive me bonkers. Dumfriesshire is the county where the artist who painted Tate's abstract landscape hailed from. Tate told me so herself."

"When did you speak with Tate?"

"While searching the ladies' room for Lyla."

"I thought you were searching for me."

"You weren't in there, either."

"What did Tate say?"

"Well…" I proceeded to give him a quick rundown of the information learned during my brief encounter with the imposter socialite.

Evan ran his fingers across his unshaven chin. "This means the brothers had access to Tate's mansion the night of the theft."

I nodded. "They could have opened the window in Tate's conservatory, allowed Sapo to climb in, then made sure no one was watching when he lifted the abstract landscape off the wall."

"And then climbed back out undetected," Evan added. "If only we could confirm whether the brothers had access to Byron Quimby's home while he was on vacation in France. We didn't think to ask the question when we met with him at Le Baguette."

"Doesn't mean we can't ask him tonight." I sipped from the champagne fizzing in my glass. "First we need to find Lyla. I fear she may have grown disoriented and tottered into the brothers' hostile arms." I rose to my toes to scan the room, just as a bulky man with a seafood craving pushed past me like a combative fiddler crab in the throes of courtship. I tangoed sideways to catch my balance, my feet twisting in my heels. "There's no need for shoving," I said to him as he nabbed the last crab cake from a server's tray. "The caterers will be pumping out crab cakes all night."

Mouth stuffed full of crab and breadcrumbs and whatever else was buried in those fishy croquettes, the man invited me to mind my own business before sauntering off. As I turned to remind him manners were a choice, a fluff of silver cockerel feathers buoying feverishly through the crowd caught my eye. I nudged Evan and pointed at the commotion. "There's Lyla, fleeing from the men on stilts. We should intercept her before things get weird."

He smirked. "She likes it weird."

"What happened to you two?" Lyla demanded as she scurried to our side, tufts of feathers falling from her mask.

"What happened to *you*?" I asked. "You weren't in the ladies' room when I went to look for you."

"You checked the ladies' room for me? I'm touched." She eyed my champagne and reached for the glass. "Which is precisely the reason you won't mind if I help myself to a sip—"

I swatted her wrist.

"What gives?"

"A sip is never just a sip with you."

"Didn't anyone teach you the value of sharing?"

"I was already sharing with myself before you arrived."

With a champagne flute balanced on his forehead, the juggler with the hammy smile and green sequins shuffled through the congregation of partygoers in search of props. Eager to participate, a middle-aged man in a black top hat and chocolate Spaccamonti mask with scrunched skin formed of papier-mâché tossed his hat to the performer, revealing a receding hairline beneath it. Amusement gurgled in his throat as the juggler caught the hat with one hand, and with the other, the red-soled stiletto from a firecracker of a woman yipping in front of me.

As the performer rotated the objects around his limbs, the crowd filled in around us to spectate. Wobbly on her toes, the shoeless woman lost her balance and lurched backward, her arms twirling like windmills in my face. To avoid collision, I hopped to the right, grazing elbows with a man standing at my side. I turned to utter a brief apology and felt my eyes bulge from their sockets.

"Domino is standing beside me," I whimpered into Evan's ear. "We need to relocate."

We slipped from the crowd and repositioned ourselves against the wall, where a server was assessing a silk streamer fallen from the ceiling. As she rolled the crumpled streamer into a messy ball, the middle-aged man with the Spaccamonti mask retrieved his top hat from the juggler and ambled over to barrage her with a string of unsolicited opinions about the minimum degree of skill with which the decorations were hung.

"How did you fail to see Domino until he was practically standing on top of you?" Lyla asked me. She released a nervous breath.

"Given the evolutionary process opted not to install eyeballs in the side of my head?" I said.

"Regardless of your evolutionary deficiencies, that was too close for comfort." She crossed her arms. "It's time we behave with prudence—report what we've uncovered about the brothers to the police and extract ourselves before Domino catches us sneaking around his party."

"The proverbial smoking gun that proves the brothers were involved in the thefts is just within reach," I said. "We'd be insane to turn back now."

"Forget the smoking gun. The danger of this situation is far greater than we appreciate and I, for one, would prefer to show up to work on Monday with my extremities attached. Typing on a computer keyboard requires two hands." She uncrossed her arms and motioned to the exit. "This whole endeavor was ill-advised. Let's call it a night."

Evan and I shook our heads in steadfast disagreement.

Lyla was appalled. "You two are really stubborn, you know that? Most people would have thrown in the towel the moment Arshile kicked them into the flowerbeds or Quimby likened their existence to the illiterate folk who think the world is flat."

I tamped the air. "These people are the victims of crimes. They deserve justice. We owe it to them to see this through."

"You only feel that way because of what's in it for you. If it weren't for your desire to vindicate yourself for the Warhol debacle or Evan's desire to rescue his sputtering journalism career, neither of you would have taken things this far."

"That isn't fair," said Evan. "Maybe we've come to realize the victims deserve our compassion."

"You expect me to believe that?"

"Why not?"

Lyla shook her head. "What's next, invite everyone to your apartment for an Italian themed dinner party—sip from Tate's Sangiovese, share a slice of tiramisu with Quimby?"

"Brilliant idea. I'm glad you suggested it."

"You can't possibly expect me to believe you'd join the man who said you lacked vision in devouring a spongy dessert."

Evan's eye contact was unbroken. "Me, Byron Quimby, and two spoons."

Snapping his fingers to the Arabesque tunes, the man in the chocolate Spaccamonti mask left the server and approached us with a purposeful gait. His voice was muffled by the layers of his mask as he stopped before us to say, "As a matter of experience, when my ears burn it means bad press is brewing."

"Why are your ears burning?" I asked.

"You tell me." He lifted his mask to reveal his face—a face

we'd seen before, one with the surprising ability to flaunt a foamy milk mustache while dishing out groundless insults.

"Blimey!" exclaimed Evan, donning a suave British accent to conceal his identity, as if the Phantom mask hiding his features weren't enough. "Byron Quimby, in the flesh. Your ears were burning indeed, old chap. I was just singing your praises."

Old chap? Lyla mouthed to me.

I shrugged.

A glorious smile unfurled across the entrepreneur's face as the well-played flattery massaged his ego. "It's nice to meet a fan for a change. My critics outnumber you these days thanks to the ratings-hungry journalists."

"Deplorable state of affairs, isn't it? I see it in my line of business, as well." Evan patted the man's shoulder. "Say, I heard through the grapevine you were traveling to Farmington to conduct market research for your hot dog business. All went well?"

"I was forced to return early. The helium particles lingering in the air from the balloon festival in October irritated my nostril cavities."

"Wasn't the balloon festival held in Albuquerque?"

"Helium particles can travel hundreds of miles."

Evan scratched his head. "Don't they use plain old hot air for the balloons?"

"Scientists won't say. What line of business are you in?"

"Adhesives," said Evan, unaware his go-to cover story had already been wielded by yours truly when encountering Tate in the powder room.

"Ah, yes," said Quimby. "You must be Theo Tolstoy."

Evan was stunned. "How do you know—"

"Lady Tate mentioned your wife, Annabel, has enlisted her to plan your grand unveiling. I insist you allow my boys to play dueling tubas at your event." Quimby leaned in close and spoke with a wink. "Generational wealth weighing down those pockets of yours? Not to worry. I'm lining up a book of investors for my latest venture. Strong returns for those who get in on the ground floor."

Evan regained his composure. "Fantastic, mate. I've been seeking ways to squander my wealth. There aren't enough super cars in the world to spend it on."

"Truer words were never spoken."

"Speaking of money, have you received any leads on the whereabouts of your paintings since increasing the reward? I read about it in the paper."

"None yet, though with any luck, when my wife and I return from our upcoming vacation in Majorca, we'll learn our attorney has located the paintings at last." He crossed his fingers. "And if Christmas comes early, we may walk through our front door to discover Julian has slid down the chimney like one of Santa's helpers to rehang them."

Struck by the information, I sought clarification. "If your attorney recovers your paintings, why will Julian rehang them?"

"We'll have a game of musical chairs on our hands that only he can play. In the wake of the thefts, we purchased two paintings from the Titan Gallery's *Decaying Flora* series to hang in our foyer. Only Julian has the vision to select their new location."

"How will Julian access your home if you're not there to let him in?"

"We furnished him with a copy of our house key and the code to our alarm when we acquired a painting of a gutted trout from the Titan Gallery a year ago. My wife and I couldn't agree on where to hang the painting, so Julian hung it for us while we attended our boys' tuba recital. It's a service he's delighted to offer to the gallery's clients, though he prefers to work without an audience."

"Meaning he prefers to hang paintings when the homeowners aren't around?"

"He wouldn't have it any other way."

With wrinkled face concealed by a Moretta mask painted sooty black, the elderly woman from the ladies' room interrupted our conversation to sneak her fingers beneath Quimby's mask and squeeze his cheek. "Byron, you look as though you're two breaths away from presenting yourself to an army of mercenaries. What have you done with your sword?" She snagged him by his cuff. "You're naked without it. Come with me, I'll help you find it."

Quimby called over his shoulder as she pulled him away. "I'll have Domino give me your contact information this evening. We'll talk business on Monday."

"Wait, that won't be necessary," said Evan, words that went unheard as Quimby and his admirer disappeared into the crowd. Evan turned to me with a bewildered expression. "Care to explain how Tate knows about my Theo Tolstoy alias, as well as your real name?"

I hung my head. "Tate put me on the spot, pressing for our identities while staring me down with her skinny pupils. I failed to think of anything original."

Evan was concerned. "News of the Tolstoys will spread through this party like wildfire. Once word makes it back to Domino, he'll put the pieces together and figure out it's us. Then he'll track us down, take us out back, and relieve us of our scalps."

Lyla's eyes bugged out.

"He's not going to take our scalps," I said.

As the words left my lips, two cloaked men costumed in black tricorn hats and white Bauta masks came to hover several paces away.

Lyla motioned toward them. "Ever feel like you're being watched?"

"They're looking for someone else," I said, recognizing the men as the pair from whom I needlessly fled earlier in the night.

"Are you sure? It feels like they're staring right at us, and the whole freemasons-from-the-seventeenth-century thing is creeping me out."

"You're being paranoid."

"Just because I'm being paranoid doesn't mean they aren't watching us."

"I'll prove it to you. Standing behind me is a girl wearing a red sequined dress and an iridescent volto mask. Her long blonde curls have me worked up in a lather of envy."

Lyla moved me aside to look for the girl in question. "Describe her again?"

"Red sequined gown, long blonde curls—"

"The only female wearing red behind you is eighty."

"What?"

"Maybe eighty-five. It's hard to say in this light."

I glanced over my shoulder to find the lone lady in red, old enough to remember the Dust Bowl. Confused, I looked back to the cloaked men and felt my stomach sink as they put swift motion to their feet. Their heavy black cloaks swept across the parquet floors as they charged us at full steam.

Chapter 31

"Ladies and gentlemen," Julian's flowery voice announced into the microphone from upon the stage. "I invite you to join Lady Evelyn Tate and me on the dance floor for the opening waltz to 'Künstlerleben' by Johann Strauss Junior." He offered the audience a genteel bow as Evelyn Tate curtsied beside him. "Find yourself a dance partner and accompany us here before the stage."

Cultivated pairs of men and women took to the dance floor as the violinist set her bow to the strings of her maple instrument, releasing a vibrato hum from within its lacquered core.

Heart pounding in my chest, I dragged my heels as the cloaked men yanked me and Lyla through the crowd. Evan scrambled to grab our outstretched hands, though was stopped in his tracks by an Amazon of a woman wearing a massive bustle.

Writhing and wriggling, we fought to free ourselves from the clutches of the masked men pulling us toward the dance floor, where Domino and Julian were assuming the ballroom position with their partners.

"Let go of us," I said, the sensation of a rug burn nipping at my skin. "We haven't done anything wrong."

"We can't let you go," said the man whose forearm was locked around my waist.

I struggled to shake free. "You don't want to do this. The brothers are bad people."

The men released their grip and bowed before us as we arrived at the dance floor. "What are you talking about? We just need you to stop us from making fools of ourselves."

I blinked twice. "What?"

"If my best man and I can't pull off this waltz, the mother of my fiancée will force us to take ballroom dance lessons," said the man standing before me. He motioned to a platinum-haired dame with a sourpuss planted on her face. "Come on, the music is starting."

As he swept me off through the flock of waltzing couples, I glanced back at Lyla to find her reluctantly agreeing to a single dance. "Just this one," she said to the groom's best man.

From one graceful circle to the next the groom twirled us, the cadence of our movements in line with the music. Ill-practiced in the art of the Venetian waltz—or any waltz, for that matter—I stumbled over my heels and trampled his feet, though he brushed off the misstep with tact.

In a balletic circle he swept us, then rotated us through a series of rhythmic loops, righting me as I tripped through the movements. He spun me beneath his arm, then drew me in and pressed his chest against my back. As he skated us across the dance floor, I appraised the waltzing couples—Julian rotating Tate in a broad ellipse, Domino guiding his partner through a fluid figure eight. My heartbeat quickened as each swaying step brought us closer to their orbits.

When the music softened to a gentle lull—a signal from the string quartet to change dance partners—I tugged my hand from the groom's grip. "Your future mother in law will be proud." Ignoring the formal bow he offered, I turned to hurry off the dance floor, just as the Amazonian woman with the oversized bustle spotted her chance for full frontal contact with the groom and shoved me out of the way. Her elbows slammed into my sternum, a blunt force collision that doubled me over in pain.

Costumed in a velveteen suit of motley colors, a heavyset man wearing a belled jester mask patted me on the back. "Are you all right?"

I raised up and took an elongated breath. "I'm fine."

"Then we must dance." He swept me off my heels before I could protest, the freshly minted pairs of dancers repositioning themselves around us. Effervescent tunes flowed from the musicians' instruments as they resumed their play with "Tales from The Vienna Woods."

"I can't dance with you," I said, pulling my hands free as the stocky jester clamped them tighter. "I've promised this dance to someone else."

"Nonsense." He twirled us across the floor, the brass bells on his jester mask jingling, then tipped me over his forearm like a level on a fulcrum. My pulse spiked as I caught sight of Domino dipping his refined dance partner paces away.

I tried to shake free from the jester's clutches. "I really must be going now."

The jester shook his head with insistence. "As the Yiddish say, *The girl who can't dance says the band can't play.*"

"The band can play fine and I take full responsibility for my rhythmic shortcomings."

"Then zip it and dance. *A silent mouth is melodious*, the Irish say."

"What is it with rich people and proverbs?" I asked, unable to hold my tongue as images of Benjamin Arshile, another overfed collector of proverbs, came to mind. "Wait—" I leaned back to examine the jester's expansive waistline, his large stomach causing the velveteen fabric of his suit to pooch out. "Are you Benjamin Arshile?"

"*Excuse* me?" The man flapped his arms indignantly at his side. "You think I'm Benjamin Arshile?"

"Sorry. My mistake."

"How dare you compare me to that whale." He huffed loudly enough to create a scene. "Third-quarter earnings were horrible, and yes, I've found solace in the gravy boat, but that's no excuse for you to rub it in my face. Find yourself a new dance partner."

As the insulted jester scurried off, a buttery voice spoke into my ear. "Now, now, can't we all just get along?" Frilly white Liberace sleeves brushed across the back of my neck and fluttered my cheeks as I turned to face the man behind the voice. He pulled me close and stared me down from behind the eye slits of his Frombolatore mask, the warm light fuzzy upon its exaggerated features.

I gasped. "Julian."

Chapter 32

As the music shifted to the graceful "Skater's Waltz," Julian laced his fingers around my wrists. The heavy fragrance of his cologne—bergamot, jasmine, and licorice root—assaulted my nostrils without apology. "May I have this dance?"

Made dizzy by the alarming turn of events, I went limp and stared at my feet as Julian, taller than I remembered and grinning obnoxiously, revolved us in a braiding motion through the center of the dance floor.

"Mademoiselle, you look positively *ravissante*," he said into my ear. "I'm ashamed to admit I don't recognize you behind your sequined mask. Would you save me the embarrassment of having to ask your name?"

Petrified, I mumbled the first syllables that came to mind. "Madam Bluh Blar."

"Forgive me, *mon chérie*. I didn't catch that. Tell me again?"

Feeling queasy from his overemphasized pronunciation, I murmured the name a second time. "Madam Bluh Blar."

Julian frowned, the lacy whisk cinched around his neckline

flexing like an accordion. "I apologize, Madam; I simply cannot understand you. Have you had dental work done?"

Frustrated by the man's persistence, I shouted the words. "Madam Bluh Blar!"

"Ah, Madam Lombard," said Julian. "My goodness, *belle,* you look phenomenal. You've shaved twenty years off your age and fifty pounds off your frame." He twirled me on my toes. "The fountain of youth has found you indeed, *ma petite fleur de champs.*" He pressed his chest to my shoulder blades and spiraled us through the crowd as I clomped through the movements. "No more lonely nights for you, Madam Lombard. I must know your secret. Mouse hormones? Infant collagen?"

I nauseated at the possibilities and longed for rescue as he skated me past Evan and Lyla, who were standing anxiously at the edge of the dance floor. I imagined the color draining from their faces as the facts of the situation set in.

"Your transformation will amaze Domino," said Julian, lifting me by my waist. "You're a *papillon* emerged from chrysalis. Spread your wings and fly."

From the corner of my eye, I spied Domino waltzing a red-haired girl half his age in our direction.

"There he is now," chirped Julian. He rolled his fingertips to beckon his brother. "I must present you to him at once."

With a gulp, I searched for a reason to excuse myself. "I need to find the ladies' room. The mouse hormones are disagreeing with my insides—too much field mouse, not enough shrew mouse."

Julian dismissed the emergency with a flutter of his hand. "Don't be silly, *mon cherie.*" He strengthened his grip and pulled me toward Domino at an accelerating pace. "Once my brother sees your magnificent transformation, I shall usher you there myself. The exit is located hazardously close, and should you step through that door by mistake, you'll be funneled into the alley like a rat in a science experiment." He clapped his hand across his mouth. "Can you imagine the horror?"

As the music softened to a lolling whinny, Julian paused to plant a fluffy kiss between my knuckles. He bowed in a courtly gesture, his ruffled pantaloons scrunching between his thighs. Paces away, Domino bid his partner farewell and turned our direction, the warm light from the glowing candles glinting upon the rust-colored horns of his devil's mask. Panicked, I spun on my heel to dart to safety.

"Where are you going, *belle*?" asked Julian.

Domino arrived and examined me with his head tilted. "Who do we have here?"

Julian was giddy. "This is our *fruit de la mer*."

Domino rubbed his chin. "Seafood?"

"No, thank you. I'm stuffed to the gills. The salmon mousse was exquisite."

"I'm not offering you seafood, Julian. I'm telling you *fruit de la mer* means seafood in French."

"You're mistaken. It translates beautifully to jewel of the sea."

"If you wish to say jewel of the sea, *bijou de la mer* are the words you seek."

Julian swept his hand across his chest. "The champagne must be getting to my head." He urged Domino to behold me. "Look at Madam Lombard. Isn't she a magical sight?"

Domino's demeanor changed. "What makes you think this is Madam Lombard?"

"She introduced herself when we shared a dance."

"This is not Madam Lombard."

"Why must you be such a beast, Domino? Of course this is Madam Lombard. She's spent many months perfecting her appearance."

Domino grew tense. "Don't be foolish." He pointed to a golden-haired mare of enormous proportions holding a napkin piled high with mini quiches, stuffed mushrooms, and glazed cream tarts. "*That* is Madam Lombard."

Julian rocked on his heels. "If you aren't Madam Lombard, who are you?"

I froze like a mule deer caught in the high beams. "I'm the wife of Theo Tolstoy, the mild-mannered grandson of a reclusive—"

"No such person exists," said Domino. "Take off your mask."

I inched backward. "I'm suffering from a toxic sunburn. If I remove my mask, everyone will run screaming for the doors, including the dermatologists."

"I'm not buying it," said Domino. "Let's see who you are." He laid his fingers beneath the edge of my mask and plucked it from my face. Unaware of the deception unfolding around them, the waltzing couples swirled blissfully as the musicians transitioned to "Gertrude's Dream Waltz."

I sucked in a frightened breath as my identity was revealed. "I can explain."

Domino seized my arm and dug his fingernails into my flesh. "I told you to stay the hell away from me." He tightened his grip. "Where are the other two, Lyla Finch and the reporter?"

"I have no idea who you're referring to."

"Don't play dumb. I know you wouldn't have come here without them. Dane said you three were inseparable." He reinforced his grip and dragged me toward the double doors marking the entrance. "Sapo should be here by now," he said to Julian. "Fetch him from the sidewalk. Tell him we have three intruders."

"Sapo is here?" I asked.

"How do you know who Sapo is?"

"I know all about Sapo. So do the police. They're investigating him in connection with—"

"You're bluffing. No one is investigating Sapo."

"Don't believe me? Ask the police when they arrive." I craned my neck as if listening for the squad cars that hadn't been called. "If they arrive to find I've so much as skinned a knee while in your custody—"

"These theatrics are beneath you." Domino snapped his fingers at Julian. "Pull Sapo off security. I'll hold onto this one."

Chapter 33

From within the sea of merrymakers, Lyla materialized and rushed across the room to stomp on Julian's feet. "You aren't going anywhere."

Domino growled. "Lyla Finch, I knew you were here. Where's your journalist sidekick?"

A screeching sound like that from a Congolese bonobo in the throes of aggression rang out from the stage. Conversations hushed as the dazed partygoers cupped their ears. A feline-masked server shrieked and spilled her tray of crab cakes.

"Ladies and gentlemen, I apologize for that God-awful sound," a voice announced into the microphone as a spotlight flickered on. It illuminated Evan standing onstage, the device pressed to his lips, his face disguised by the contours of his mask.

Sucking a peanut-sauce-slathered prawn from a skewer, the true Madam Lombard warbled, "Why have you interrupted our waltz, young man?"

"Why, that's Theo Tolstoy," said Byron Quimby from deep within the crowd. "What happened to your British accent, mate?"

"The accent you heard earlier tonight was a phony," said Evan. "Theo Tolstoy is a ridiculous alias that should have never seen the light of day."

"If your name isn't Theo Tolstoy, how do you intend to sign the legal agreements for your investment in my hot dog cart business? My assistant will need this information before we can have the documents drawn up."

"I apologize for misleading you, Byron Quimby. I have no intention of investing in your business."

Quimby slapped his hand across his mouth. "If you're not an investor, who are you?"

"I'm a journalist from the *Seattle Courier*. I've come to warn you all about an imposter floating amongst your ranks."

"I am not an imposter," the high-pitched voice of Evelyn Tate squealed from the edge of the dance floor. Her thick petticoats swooshed over her knees as she stomped her feet. "How dare you make such unfounded accusations."

"You are not the imposter to whom I was referring, Lady Tate."

She straightened her corset and urged Evan to carry on.

"The real imposters are your very own hosts, Domino and Julian."

Domino snarled. "I've heard enough of this." He flung Julian forward by his pillowy sleeves. "Drag him off the stage."

As Julian put swift motion to his feet, Lyla removed her heels and chased after him, her black ponytail bobbing up and down as the fan of silver cockerel feathers bounced above her head.

Domino locked his arms around my shoulders and yanked me toward the stage, hissing in my ear, "You made a big mistake coming here." He called up to Evan as we stopped at the base of the platform. "Get off my stage or I will have you arrested."

Evan ignored his orders and continued addressing the room.

"Domino and Julian have been pulling the wool over your eyes from the moment you met them, hosting lavish parties and feeding your insufferable vanities, all the while plotting to rob you blind."

The crowd gasped like the poetic shot heard 'round the world.

"I will have you sued for defamation," said Domino. He signaled to Julian, who was bounding up the risers to the stage.

Startled by the sound of expensive loafers prancing behind him, Evan whirled around and dodged Julian's outstretched arms.

Julian lurched forward and caught his balance inches from the edge, losing a loafer in the process. He scrambled to retrieve it, the argyle pattern on his socked foot drawing a range of judgments from the crowd.

Evan raced to the opposite side of the stage. "Show of hands, how many of you know who Sapo is?" He scanned the blank faces. "You may not know him by name, but you have likely seen him at the Titan Gallery. He once worked security there. We believe Domino ordered Sapo to carry out the thefts from Benjamin Arshile, Byron Quimby, and Evelyn Tate."

"Domino, is this true?" asked a glittery dame wearing an embellished volto mask with an iridescent pattern spread across her face like the wings of a butterfly.

"This is pure fiction," said Domino. He shouted to Julian. "Forget your loafer. Grab the microphone."

Spurred by his brother's orders, Julian dashed toward Evan with one foot inside his loafer, the other inside his sock.

Lyla clamored onstage, hooked her fingers on his ruffled pantaloons, and tackled him to the ground.

Julian yowled and peeled her fingers from the fabric. "Let go of me."

Evan pressed forward. "As the owners of the Titan Gallery, Domino and Julian possessed intimate knowledge about the art

collections of their victims. They knew which of their paintings would sell best on the black market, and they knew how
to access their homes." He gestured to Evelyn Tate, who was
listening with mouth agape. "Lady Tate, you relied heavily on
the brothers when planning your private soirees, including the
expo peinture the night your abstract landscape was stolen. We
suspect the brothers unlocked a window in your conservatory,
then distracted your party guests while Sapo climbed in and lifted
your painting off the wall."

Tate shrieked. "Domino, how could you?"

"Next, we have you, Byron Quimby," said Evan, pointing
to the hot dog entrepreneur, who was slapping the sides of his
cheeks in shock. "When you became a client of the Titan Gallery
a year ago, you supplied Julian with a copy of your house key
and the code to your alarm so he could hang the painting of the
gutted trout. You didn't realize Julian would later provide Sapo
a copy of the key and the instructions for disarming your alarm
to steal your beloved surrealist paintings while you vacationed
in France."

Domino roared. "These are all lies!" He waved to Julian. "Get
Sapo at once."

Julian pulled himself to his toes, bolted off the stage, and
rushed to the double doors leading to the sidewalk. The harlequin
greeters in their patchwork costumes and bulbous Arlecchino
masks jumped as he pushed past them.

"Someone needs to lock those doors before Julian returns
with Sapo," said Evan.

Lyla rose to her feet. "I'm on it."

Evan turned his attention back to the audience. "Finally we
have you, Benjamin Arshile—" he gazed out across the room in
search of the advertising maven. "Where are you, Mr. Arshile?"

In a shriveled voice, an elderly man working his way through the crowd said, "Benjamin Arshile is in the restroom answering the call of nature. Shall I retrieve him?"

"No, it's an important call to answer. We'll proceed without him."

"What motive would I have to rob my own clients?" asked Domino with disbelief.

"Greed," said Evan. "You realized you could profit twice from each theft, first by selling the stolen paintings on the black market, then by selling your victims new paintings from your gallery."

"How would Domino have found a buyer for my painting?" asked Tate. "Few people outside Scotland are familiar with the artist."

"The brothers have a client who hails from the same county in Scotland as the artist who painted your abstract landscape."

"Dumfriesshire?" she asked.

"*Dumfriesshire?*" the crowd said.

"Yes, Dumfriesshire," said Evan. "But don't ask me to spell it. I'll embarrass myself." He cleared his throat and pointed to the Scotsman lingering near the stage. "You, Mr. Napier, hold an immense passion for your motherland of Scotland, particularly your place of birth, Dumfriesshire. You would have done anything to get your hands on Tate's painting, seeing as how it was the work of your fellow countryman."

The Scotsman threw his fist in the air. "What are ye talkin' aboot? Ah never baught a stolen paintin' from anyone."

Evan heard the kilted man's outburst loud and clear. "Of course not. You had no idea the painting was stolen. When presenting you with the possibility of acquiring it, Domino likely spun a tale about a sheep herder from Eksdale who stumbled upon the painting in a farmers' market while peddling skeins of wool."

"My painting was sold in a farmers' market?" asked Tate with horror.

"No, Lady Tate. I was illustrating my point." Evan pressed the microphone to his lips and spoke to Domino. "The one thing we could never figure out was why Sapo mugged Benjamin Arshile outside 18 Laws. Was he settling a personal vendetta on your behalf?"

Domino clenched his jaw.

"I suppose it doesn't matter now. The jig is up."

"Not until the fat lady sings," Madam Lombard yodeled. She burst into a blistering trill of high C that practically shattered the windows.

Seizing upon the distraction, Domino pushed me away with enough force to send me tumbling to my knees. He bounded toward the hallway where the restrooms and exit to the alley were located.

"He's getting away," I cried, pulling myself to my feet.

The Scotsman sprinted after him. "Nae from me, he isn't."

"We need video of this," I said. "Someone call the police while I chase after them." I brushed off my knees, kicked off my heels, clutched them to my chest, and scurried to the hallway. With images of the Scotsman tackling Domino in the alley lighting up in my mind like indicators on a circuit board, I rounded the corner, spotted the green exit sign, and raced out the door.

Deposited in a cement stairwell smelling of pennies and pond water, I shook off the pain of my bare feet striking the concrete and hustled down the stairs to the door through which Julian had accessed Loft 242 two days earlier. Electrified by the chase, I shoved open the door and dashed across the threshold, my toes chilling as they contacted the damp, rough cobblestones. The door swung shut and locked behind me, leaving me standing alone in the dark, empty alley.

Domino and the Scotsman were nowhere in sight.

Silence blanketed the alley, save the mutterings of the pigeons tucking in for the night, the dim light mounted over the back door coated in their droppings. With a mind to return to the scene inside, I put on my heels and reached for the door handle, just as an exchange of low whispers from the thick shadows of a dumpster reached my ears.

"Is someone there?" I asked, glancing over my shoulder.

The whispers stopped.

My nerves frayed. I shook the handle aggressively, though the lock remained engaged.

"I'll take care of this," the gruffer of the whisperers said to the other. "Wait here."

With a gulp, I released the handle and swiveled around to find a barrel-chested man dressed in motorcycle leathers emerging from the darkness.

Chapter 34

"You wouldn't believe how poor the signage inside this building is," I said, looking into Sapo's cold eyes, the dim light creating a menacing play of shadows across the blunt features of his face. "It's worse than Rome."

With a flinty expression, he pulled a box of unfiltered Camels and a Zippo lighter from his coat. He set a cigarette between his lips, generated a spark, and took a long drag. "You got lost?" he said, his voice absent inflection as he exhaled into the air a noxious cloud of gases.

"While looking for the ladies' room," I said. "Someone should alert the owners to the need for better signage. The liability is immense." Fine sheets of drizzle swept down the alley and dampened my bare skin. "Boy, it's cold out here. I should go in. My doctor has advised I maintain an internal body temperature of at least ninety-eight-point-six degrees, though not to exceed ninety-nine-point-seven degrees. Anything above that is urgent care territory. I don't want to mess around with a fever this time of year."

Sapo gestured down the alley, flicking his thumb across the base of his cigarette to send the ashes sailing. "You shouldn't be back here. Go in through the main entrance out front."

"Thanks, I'll be going now." As I turned to follow his directions, a reckless curiosity washed over me. I knew better than to hang around in that dark alley, but I paused to ask a question anyway. "You didn't see Domino and a ten-foot-tall Scotsman out here a few minutes ago, did you? I heard someone else whispering behind that dumpster and I was wondering—"

"Why are you looking for Domino out here?" Sapo sucked in another drag from his cigarette and exhaled an angry plume.

I felt as though the conversation had deteriorated and reached for humor to soften the mood. "That's a great question. It's like, why do people stop their grocery carts in the middle of the aisle when selecting a can of stewed tomatoes? What can you even make with stewed tomatoes other than more stewed tomatoes?" I chuckled to sell it and set my sights on dropping the question in favor of rushing back to safety and warmth.

Sapo's expression was unchanged. "You need to leave." He motioned down the alley with the finger holding the cigarette, the burning tobacco glowing at the tip.

As I prepared to shut my mouth and do that very thing, a bedraggled homeless man shuffled down the alley, muttering to his imaginary companion, an unidentifiable garment dragging along the greasy cobblestones behind him. He kicked through a pile of cardboard and halted his footsteps near the dumpster concealing the second whisperer. He dropped his tattered cargo and gazed into the shadows. "Magggic hat."

With unprovoked aggression, Sapo shouted, "Get out of here, old man!"

Deep in conversation with the wind, the displaced nomad ignored Sapo's command and stared into the darkness.

"Did you hear me, old man? I said get out of here."

Deaf to Sapo's orders, the man stammered, "Magggic hat." The stutter in his speech conjured a memory of the homeless man who had yanked Julian's houndstooth coat from his cherry convertible. *Purrrty coat* the vagrant had called it, the discovery of its absence causing Julian to bleat like a pastured sheep facing a hungry wolf disrupting its meal of clover.

With mounting impatience, Sapo tossed his cigarette to the ground and snuffed it out with his boot. He unzipped his leather coat and removed a handgun. "Some people just won't listen."

Shocked by his hostile reaction, a fight-or-flight response to run coursed through my system, followed by an inclination to back away slowly. In the realm of the wild where predators roamed free, the wrong method of retreat would land one on the prix fixe dinner menu. Lions chased prey that ran. Gorillas did, also. But what about a thug wearing obvious anger issues on his sleeve?

"Magggic hat," the hobo stammered again. He stepped into the shadows of the dumpster, where a distressed whimper echoed out, followed by the sound of hands slapping hands. With a childlike satisfaction, he remerged, a black top hat resting lopsided on his head, tendrils of matted hair sticking out in all directions like a weather vane beneath it.

Sapo cocked his weapon. "You want to see the other side?"

"Wait, don't shoot." Attired in crisp tuxedo and glimmering volto mask, a heavyset man stepped out from behind the dumpster to create a sizeable barrier between Sapo and the homeless man. "This show of force is unnecessary. He means no harm."

"You think so?" said Sapo. "Why don't you take off your mask and show us your butterball face?"

The large man patted the air and opened his hands to form a landing pad. "Hand me your gun."

"You're outta your mind if you think I'm gonna give you my gun."

"Then holster it, young man, and let these innocent people be on their way. Can't you see how frightened they are?"

"Purrrty face," the vagrant stuttered, entranced by the heavy man's sparkling volto mask. He shuffled toward him and reached for the mask with dirty fingers, ripping it free with the force of the barbaric string-tooth-doorknob contraption outlawed everywhere but the backwoods a century earlier.

"How does it feel to be exposed?" Sapo said with mocking laughter as the corpulent face of Benjamin Arshile was revealed. "Arrogant, exposed, and plump like a Christmas goose."

I couldn't believe my eyes as the pieces slid into place. An elderly man inside the party had notified Evan of Arshile's pre-occupation obliging the call of his bladder. If Arshile had taken the door for the exit by mistake, he would have been funneled into the alley. If he had then encountered Sapo while attempting to reenter the building through the locked door, Sapo could have drawn his weapon and forced Arshile behind the dumpster at gunpoint. But for what reason?

As these thoughts revolved through my mind, I looked back to Sapo to find him waving his gun around. I forced myself to swallow my fear. "You seem upset," I said, patting the air. "While your intentions for Mr. Arshile and me are unclear, your best course of action is to put your gun down and let us leave in peace."

He looked at me with a snarl.

"The police have already been called. If they arrive to find you pointing your gun like this, it will confirm their suspicions about your criminal tendencies, as well as your involvement in the art thefts." I released the breath I didn't realize I'd been holding. "It'll make their case against you all the easier to button up."

"What do you mean their case against me?" said Sapo, his voice enraged. He slammed the barrel of his gun against Arshile's sternum. "Did you set me up?"

"Lower your weapon this instant!" Arshile growled. "You're too volatile for this business, Sapo. All bleach and vinegar. No one is investigating you. I only told her that to get her off our backs." He motioned my direction. "She's the one you should be pointing your gun at. Not me."

Chapter 35

Arshile's words hit me like a ton of bricks. I opened my mouth to cry for help, but felt the sound ripped from my vocal chords by fear.

"You should have walked away," said Arshile, smoothing his lapels. The timbre of his voice changed into one of unnerving confidence that made my skin crawl.

"I still can." I gestured down the alley. "Whatever business you two are engaged in back here is none of my business—"

Arshile cut me off with thin regret. "I'm afraid it's too late."

"How can it be too late? I thought we were on the same side. You baked biscotti and invited me into your home."

"You invited yourself. But I must know—is Domino accepting credit for my masterpiece? I heard that journalist on stage fingering the brothers for my crimes, as if those two could ever pull off something so magnificent. Blind mice chasing their tails is all they are."

Shock washed over me. "You were responsible for the thefts from Byron Quimby and Evelyn Tate?"

Arshile clapped. "Ding, ding."

I shivered. "I don't care who was behind the thefts. Frankly I applaud your ingenuity. The way you pulled off the crimes with such panache? Inspiring." I prayed Evan had called the police as I worked to soften the man with an irresistible cocktail of flattery and appeal whose recipe only Lyla knew best. "There's still time to let this end peacefully before the police arrive with sirens blaring to haul you and Sapo off in handcuffs."

"It's entertaining to hear you speak as though you're the one holding the advantage," said Arshile, immune to my flattery. "As the Dutch would say, *One shears sheep, the other shears pigs.*"

"Enough with the proverbs. Why can't you speak in ordinary English? Yes, you have the advantage in this standoff because your muscle is the one holding the gun, but that doesn't mean you must speak in proverb every damn time our paths cross."

"That won't be a problem much longer." Arshile checked his watch and looked to Sapo. "Can I trust you to take care of this? Call me when you're done."

I waved my hands in a halting gesture. "You can't leave yet, Mr. Arshile. You must explain the motives behind your crimes. It's called *obligatory criminal admission.* You'll never forgive yourself if you pass up this opportunity to boast."

"I've never heard of such a thing."

"Just because you've never heard of it doesn't mean it doesn't exist. We both know on the surface the crimes against Quimby and Tate make no sense. You don't need the money from reselling their paintings, and I suspect you don't much care for their taste in art, either."

"Fine, I'll entertain this last request of your. In simple terms, I had to do the job neither Domino nor Julian were willing to do. They were part of the problem—unconcerned with filtering out the interlopers for the want of selling art from their gallery.

Like it or not, a class system exists in our society and it must be upheld. The moment you allow the likes of Evelyn Tate and Byron Quimby to infect the crop, all that is glorious is lost."

"You consider yourself the hall monitor?"

"I built my empire from the ground up. Evelyn Tate? She's an illiterate hillbilly who happened to get lucky playing the lottery. Byron Quimby? He's a fool who's been hemorrhaging his family's fortune on one moronic business venture after the next. Neither should have any place in our society beyond peddling painted seashells by the waterfront."

"Tate worked hard to keep her hillbilly roots hidden," I said. "How did you uncover her secret?"

"She claimed to be a lady with old-money pedigree, but I knew the moment she chopped down her neighbor's oak tree her self-proclaimed pedigree was a sham. Only new money would take such a classless approach to solving their problems."

"Pillaging and plundering your enemies to settle a trivial score *isn't*?"

Arshile smiled disingenuously. "No one is perfect."

"How did you decide which paintings to steal? I assume it was no coincidence you chose the pieces your victims most cherished."

"Evelyn Tate loved to show off her art collection during her ridiculous expo peintures." He mocked the French pronunciation. "It took immense patience to humor the woman as she guided us from one room to the next, blabbering about provenance, a word I doubt she understood. When she showed us the abstract landscape in her conservatory and spoke affectionately of how she came to own it, I knew that was the piece I would steal."

"How did you choose Byron Quimby's paintings?"

"Quimby foolishly believed me to be the willing recipient of his idiotic nuggets of business advice and welcomed me into his home for dinner. The quail was seasoned to my liking, though his boys' table-side tuba performance was torturous." He shuddered. "After watching Quimby get weepy when recounting the story of acquiring the paintings while on honeymoon with his wife, I knew those paintings were the ones I would steal."

"But you didn't steal them yourself," I said, glancing at the thug in motorcycle leathers whose gun was pointed at my chest. Painfully aware he would eliminate me the moment Arshile left, I felt my only play was to make him question Arshile's loyalty. "You had Sapo do your dirty work. You used him to make sure you'd never get your own hands dirty."

"No one was using anyone," said Arshile. "It was a partnership."

"Quimby and Tate are beneath you, but you view Sapo as an equal?"

"Sapo can be rough around the edges, but so can I, and as anyone who's spent time in a mechanic's garage will tell you, aerosol and flames don't mix well, but octane and ethanol sure as hell do."

"How did your partnership come to be?"

"As fate would have it, Sapo was also in the market for revenge. Our paths crossed on the heels of a dispute between him and Domino this spring. While I wasn't looking to take in a stray, it quickly became apparent what an amazing asset this young man would be for me."

"You took advantage of him."

Arshile shook his head. "Sapo was plenty motivated on his own. It was thanks to him we were able to carry out my plans so efficiently. The night I dined with Byron Quimby—the man boasting about his upcoming vacation plans in France while bits of mashed potato settled into the corners of his mouth—he described a painting of a watermelon he had acquired from the

Titan Gallery's spring exhibition. He said Julian would slip into his home to hang the piece while he and his wife attended their boys' tuba recital." He paused to adjust the waistline of his tuxedo pants. "What Quimby didn't realize was that Domino and Sapo had experienced a major falling out that left Sapo infuriated. But rather than firing him straightaway, Domino made the mistake of allowing Sapo to continue helping Julian with customer deliveries. It was during that time Sapo accompanied Julian to Quimby's estate. He committed Quimby's alarm code to memory and kept his house key long enough to have a copy made. Then we waited until Quimby left for vacation." He snapped his fingers. "Easy as cherry pie."

"And the painting you stole from Evelyn Tate?"

"More cherry pie."

"Let's hear it then."

"After the theft from Byron Quimby went off without a hitch, I became enamored with the idea of stealing Tate's painting during her next expo peinture. When she guided her guests into the far wing of her mansion, I unlocked a window in the conservatory for Sapo to climb in, then locked it back up and rejoined the tour after he slipped out with the painting." He grinned with despicable pride. "Tate discovered the theft the following morning and assumed the thief had blended in with her party guests. No one knew how the crime unfolded."

"What did you do with the stolen paintings?" I asked. "Toss them in a dumpster in Chinatown to marinate in orange sauce?"

"Get rid of my trophies? Never."

"Then where are they?"

"The paintings are in my safe, along with the *Spin Marbles* piece stolen from my mansion during the robbery I staged. Next week, a vagrant will find my painting stashed under a bridge. When it's returned the following day, police will call off the investigation."

I was confused. "Why would you stage your own robbery?"

"It had become necessary to show Sapo tough love." He glanced at Sapo to find the man uncocking his gun and placing it in his coat. Arshile squinted and nodded to the subtle bulge formed beneath the leather. "Keep your gun handy, young man. You're going to need it."

"What do you mean by tough love?" I pressed, desperate to buy myself time as I longed to hear sirens screaming down the alley.

"The similarity in plights that united Sapo and me dissolved when Domino experienced a change of heart—overnight, it felt—and offered Sapo a role overseeing logistics for the speak-easy." He shook his head. "It made no sense. Domino and Julian had treated Sapo like an outsider since childhood."

I looked to Sapo to find the man pulling the pack of Camels from his pocket. He laid one on his lip and lit it with his Zippo, his mouth silent, his face pensive. He took a long drag, flipping the lid of the lighter back and forth.

"Upon receiving the news from Domino, Sapo's hunger for revenge evaporated. Sapo was obsessed with the speakeasy, but he'd never say why. I couldn't let him exit our partnership, though. We still had work to do. Much like Edmond Dantès, the Count of Monte Cristo, had three enemies upon whom he exacted his revenge, I had three enemies of my own."

"Alexandre Dumas," I said, recalling the massive portrait Arshile had purchased from the Titan Gallery. "The painting appealed to you because *The Count of Monte Cristo* is a tale of revenge."

Arshile's wicked eyes lit up. "Now you see why I couldn't allow Sapo's reconciliation with Domino to interfere with our plans." He laid a hand on Sapo's shoulder, forcing a thin smile as Sapo shrugged it off. "I suppose we're still reconciling ourselves."

Arshile paused to collect his thoughts. "The night you stumbled upon Sapo and me outside 18 Laws, Sapo was not mugging me. He had confronted me at gunpoint to say he wanted out of our arrangement. He threatened to reveal our crimes to Domino if I didn't back off. Obviously I couldn't take that risk."

"So what did you do?"

"I realized I needed an insurance policy to keep Sapo quiet, so I made myself a victim and set Sapo up to take the fall should he ever divulge our secrets. I removed the *Spin Marbles* painting from my wall, scuffed the area near the nail to make it convincing, and tucked it inside my safe. Then I unlocked the kitchen window, prepared a panicked reaction, and called the police to report the crime. If Sapo refused to help me pull off my final theft, or if he threatened me again, I'd finger him for the armed robbery at my estate and lead investigators to conclude he was behind the thefts from Quimby and Tate, as well."

I was incredulous. "You staged the robbery to show Sapo who was boss? You'd pin the crimes on him if he didn't realign with your crooked cause?"

"I needed him for one last theft."

"And you needed him to stay silent."

"Silence is in everyone's best interest."

"The news said two men were involved in the robbery at your estate. If you intended to frame Sapo as one of the intruders, who would you finger as the other?"

"My driver."

I balked. "You'd throw an innocent man under the bus?"

"Don't be mistaken, young lady. My driver is not innocent. He may be the most tenured employee on my payroll, but he's a hopeless invertebrate who cowers at the first sign of adversity."

"The story you told me about the man's indispensability meant nothing to you?"

"I must look out for number one." He patted his chest.

"You're unbelievable, Arshile. Cold as stone."

"I've heard that before."

"What are you and Sapo doing in the alley tonight, planning your final heist?"

"Gold star to you, Annabel. And with those arrangements we must proceed. I would apologize for your ill fortune, but we both know that apology would be insincere." He turned to Sapo. "Draw your gun, young man."

Sapo tossed his cigarette to the ground, where it extinguished in a puddle.

"Wait," I shouted, flailing my arms as the thug pulled the pistol from his coat. "Listen to me, Sapo. I'm the only person here who's on your side. Arshile plans to pin everything on you, and I guarantee he's been thorough in his preparations. We both know he's a shark who can't be trusted. Odds are he'll turn you in for the hell of it."

Sapo clenched his jaw.

"Unless you can produce a credible witness to tell authorities about Arshile's confession tonight, you'll spend the rest of your life locked behind bars, stamping out license plates. Where's the justice in that?"

The thug flipped his gaze to Arshile. "You're still fixing to turn me in?"

"Don't listen to her," said Arshile, speaking in the gentle voice of one seeking the allegiance of a toddler. "She's trying to turn you against me to save herself." He gestured to the handgun. "Would you feel better if I took care of this chore myself?"

"How do I know you wouldn't frame me for it?"

"You must trust me, young man." Arshile inched forward. "You have to trust me."

Sapo grit his teeth. "I'm done trusting you."

Arshile blew a gale of wind from his lungs. "Then I have no choice but to silence you both." He bounded forward and ripped the gun from Sapo's hands, his belly lurching beneath his pants.

Sapo scrambled for the weapon, but recoiled as Arshile settled his hips into a readied stance.

"Would you look at that!" said Arshile. "I'd be lying if I said it doesn't feel good to do the dirty work myself for a change." He cocked the hammer. "The question is, how do I choose who goes first?" He waved the chamber back and forth between Sapo and me, his alternating targets. "Eeny, meeny, miny, moe." As the gun came to rest upon my chest, he curled his finger around the trigger. "Goodbye, Annabel."

Chapter 36

The back door to Loft 242 flung open and the Scotsman charged out, his ghillie brogues splashing through a greasy puddle. He swept Arshile's knees, grime splattering his cream hose as the advertising maven landed hard atop the wet cobblestones.

"Get off me," said Arshile, squirming beneath the Scotsman's shoe, the gun kicked from his hands. "I was defending myself. I am the victim."

"Nae ye aren't," said the kilted man. "The lass is the victim." He glanced at me, triggering a single teardrop to well in my eyes and slide down my cheek, leaving behind a trail of saline. I wiped it away and laid my hands over my chest, forcing myself to breathe deeply.

Behind me, the back door swung open. Evan and Lyla rushed out, Lyla throwing her arms around my shoulders as Evan clutched me by my waist. My body went limp and I collapsed into their arms. "Never before have I been this happy to see your smiling faces," I said. Tiny tears of joy formed pockets in my eyes. "What happened to your masks?"

"We left them inside," said Lyla. "Are you okay?"

I nodded, urging my pulse to regulate. "We've made a huge mistake. Domino and Julian are innocent. Arshile was the mastermind behind the crimes. He was manipulating Sapo." I turned to face the tattooed thug, but startled to find an empty space where moments ago he stood lighting up his final cigarette. "Where did he go?"

"Where did who go?" asked Evan.

"Sapo. He was just here." I pointed at his handgun lying on the cobblestones. "That's his gun. Moments before the Scotsman charged out, Arshile disarmed Sapo and pointed the weapon at me. He was seconds away from pulling the trigger."

Evan retrieved his phone and snapped a picture of the pistol.

"Look here," the Scotsman exclaimed. He hauled the advertising maven up by his armpits. "Take a picture of me with mah catch of the day." He pinched Arshile's plump cheeks. "Quite the big balloon ye are, even bigger than tha' skate fish ah reeled in off the coast of the Western Isles."

Evan pointed the camera at Arshile's indignant face. "How about a toothy smile? Soon the whole world will know the truth about your dirty deeds."

Arshile shielded his face as the flash illuminated. "Criminal charges will be brought up against you all. This is an unlawful detainment carried out with unreasonable force."

"My apologies, ye little turnip," said the Scotsman. "Perhaps ye'd prefer ah show ye a bit o' tenderness." He thumped his hands upon Arshile's flabby rhomboids and kneaded his back fat like a braid of dough.

"What are you doing, you ape?"

"Ah can't have ye thinkin' me a brute." He squeezed Arshile's trapezius. "Higher or lower?"

Arshile cried out with disgust. "Get your hands off me."

"Ah see ye prefer it mah way." The Scotsman laced his fingers around the man's wrists. "Ah'll keep ye in mah custody."

Arshile hurled me an evil glare. "You may think you've won this time, but I will emerge the victor."

"Despite the story your enormous ego is telling you, you can't talk your way out of this one," I said. "Your confession is burned into my brain, and your prints are all over Sapo's gun." Cold air swept through the alley in a stiff gust as the rain picked up, drops of moisture saturating my hair and beading on my bare shoulders. I wrapped my arms around my core and looked to Lyla to find her doing the same, her black bangs wet and flat against her forehead. Evan slipped out of his suit coat and invited us to huddle inside the warm fabric.

"Don't count your chickens just yet," said Arshile. "We both know I can sell the narrative that I took the wrong door when seeking the lavatory and found myself locked out in this alley with that lawless thug, Sapo. He threatened my life while pointing his gun in my face. I was just lucky enough to disarm him when he paused to smoke a cigarette." He pointed his toe at the cigarette butts lying in a greasy puddle. "His cigarette tumbled from his lips when I yanked the weapon away. Once he realized the tables were turned, he confessed to the thefts. That's when the back door flung open and you, Annabel, stumbled out. Sapo ran off, leaving me here holding his gun, and you, overtaken with fear at the sight of the weapon, refused to listen to my honest account of the terrifying events that had transpired. Then this beastly Scotsman sprinted out behind you and threw me to the ground in a vicious attack."

"This was nae an attack, ye dunderheid."

From the main road in front of Loft 242, the screeching sound of a motorcycle burning off into the night wailed out. Engine roaring like a rocket launching into space, the sportbike raced down the street at a blistering speed, then faded into the hum of the city.

"Sapo's great escape," said Arshile. "Good news for me. He won't be here to defend himself when my narrative unfolds."

"Don't count on it," I said. "The paintings you stole from Byron Quimby and Evelyn Tate, as well as the painting you falsely reported as stolen from your home, are stashed in your personal safe. No clever story can explain that."

Lyla's eyes lit up. "Quimby and Tate are going to get their paintings back? What fantastic news. We should notify them while Quimby's reward is still on the table."

"I'm not sure we should accept the reward," I said, imagining the greater payoff of restoring my professional reputation and reigniting my career. The world of art recovery and insurance investigations needn't be one from which my ban was permanent. Could I step away from my role at the modern art museum so easily, though? It was a gig I had come to love. Decisions would need to be made, but in the interim, I knew I could forgive myself for the Warhol blunder once and for all.

"Why not?" said Lyla. "We're the reason Quimby will be reunited with his paintings. I could really use the money."

"It doesn't feel right."

"My blender is on the fritz and my bathroom faucet needs to be replaced. Three generations of mycobacterium are growing in places even a Q-tip can't reach."

"Our building super will replace your faucet, and I'll buy you a blender for Christmas."

She pouted.

"Then again, Quimby insisted the reward would be ours if we reunited him with his paintings. Maybe it wouldn't be such a terrible thing to accept a small portion."

"Whatever happens with the reward, I'm just grateful you're

262 • ERIKA SIMMS

okay," said Evan, wrapping his arms around me in a giant bear hug.

"What happened inside the party after I left?" I asked. "Why were neither Domino nor the Scotsman in the alley?"

"Domino darted into the men's room to call his attorney and Mr. Napier chased in after him," said Evan, running his fingers through his damp hair. "You missed them by seconds."

"Just my luck. When did you realize I was in trouble? It feels like an eternity has passed since I walked out that door."

"We regret that we didn't figure it out sooner," said Lyla. "For what it's worth, doctors say it's good to spike the pulse from time to time—something to do with reinvigorating the cardiac cells."

"I'm aware of how it works," I said. "Tonight was off the charts. What happened?"

"Julian was the first of the brothers to return to the party, saying Sapo wasn't on the sidewalk where Domino said he'd be. He hadn't checked the alley, though. He didn't want to ruin his sock."

"How did Julian get in? I thought you locked the doors."

"A tipsy server who heard Julian banging on the doors thought the whole thing was a theatrical performance and let him in."

"Are you kidding me?"

Lyla shook her head. "The server wasn't the only one with that impression. Many of the partygoers thought it was a show. We may walk away from the night with tips in our pocket."

"Unbelievable," I said. "What happened next?"

"Several minutes after Julian returned, Mr. Napier marched Domino back into the party," said Evan. "When we saw you weren't with them, the alarm bells sounded. We feared you had taken the exit to the alley and worried Sapo was out here with you. Lyla and I rushed out with Mr. Napier on our heels."

"We acted fast," said Lyla. "The only reason Mr. Napier beat us out here is because his kilt afforded him great freedom of movement when descending the stairs."

"It wasn't mah kilt lass," the Scotsman chimed in. "Ah thought it smelled manky in there."

"It doesn't smell great," I said. "What do we do about the brothers? Once they file a lawsuit against us for defaming their character, we'll be forced to move into a shoebox to pay the legal fees."

"Let's call the police before we worry about that," said Evan.

"You haven't called the police yet?"

"Everything happened so fast." He reached inside his suit coat draped over Lyla and me to retrieve his phone and placed the call. His voice was firm but calm as he spoke with the dispatcher on the other end. "The police are on their way," he said when the call disconnected. "Back to your question about the brothers..." As his voice trailed off in thought, the back door drew open and Domino emerged, his Diablo mask dangling between his fingers by its black satin ribbon.

Chapter 37

Sapphire eyes flickering with fury, Domino marched past us in a strange tunnel vision, his hands balled into fists. He stopped inches from the advertising maven's pudgy face and said, "Is it true, Benjamin? You were behind the crimes, forcing Sapo to do your dirty work?"

Arshile spat out a bitter reply. "Don't act so surprised. We both know Sapo's only future is in a life of crime. You should thank me for cleaning house. Byron Quimby and Evelyn Tate were ruining our privileged class like flies floating in a bowl of punch."

Domino silenced the man. "You're too arrogant to realize you're describing yourself."

Arshile dismissed the insult. "Don't you want to know how I did it?"

"I already know how your schemes unfolded and I don't need to hear it twice, not while a disgusting grin of pride peeks out from your chapped lips."

Lyla leaned into my ear. "When would Domino have learned Arshile was the one pulling the strings?"

"Sapo must have called him when he fled," I said.

Domino crossed his arms and moved closer to Arshile's face. "I hope you get shipped off to an antiseptic prison where flies buzz in the fluorescent lights until their wings fry, and corn chowder from a plastic tray is the highlight of your day."

"Wishful thinking," said Arshile. "We both know I'll prevail."

"Not this time." Domino looked to the Scotsman. "Will you lead our prisoner around front to wait for the police?"

"Aye," said the kilted man. He tightened his grip on Arshile's thick hands and drug him, kicking and hollering, down the alley.

Domino's lips flattened as he gripped the key to the back door. "You three, follow me."

Inside the cement stairwell smelling of pennies and pond water, Domino led us to the top of the risers and paused before the door, where laughter and merriment leaked in through the frame.

"I'm torn on what to do with you three," he said. "You've painted Julian and me as villains and maligned our reputations, giving us legal cause to sue you for every penny you have." He wiped the beads of drizzle from his tuxedo coat. "At the same time, you've revealed Benjamin Arshile as the true culprit, and prevented Sapo from spending the next twenty years behind bars."

"Given the sentiment of everyone inside, I say we agree to call it even," I said. I squeezed the moisture from my hair and braided it behind my head. "Your clients believe our display was a theatrical performance. If we join you and Julian on stage for a bow, you'll look like hosts supreme for arranging such fantastic entertainment."

Domino raised an eyebrow.

"The narrative will be reinforced when news of Arshile's arrest breaks in the morning. Your reputations will sparkle, Sapo will be free, Arshile will be locked behind bars, and we'll all live happily ever after."

Domino processed the suggestion. "The jester you offended has been telling everyone Julian's loafer was meant to fly off, and Evelyn Tate claims the seams in Julian's pantaloons were reinforced so as not to tear when Lyla grabbed hold of them. Even Madam Lombard, the consummate cynic, has suggested the jugglers were in on it. She's looking for the tip jar."

Lyla squeezed my arm. "See?"

"I'm satisfied with your suggestion. But you must do something for me in return."

"Name it," I said.

"If you wish to avoid the wrath of my attorneys, you will say nothing about Sapo when recounting the events that transpired in the alley to the police. No such person was here tonight. You've never heard of him."

I took a step back. "You're asking me to lie to the police?"

"I'm asking you to modify your statement."

"They'll never believe me. Sapo's gun and cigarette butts are in the alley. When the police collect the evidence, they'll find Sapo's fingerprints and know he was here. I'll be caught in a lie and charged with hampering the investigation. Or worse."

"The evidence will be disposed of before the police arrive."

"By whom?"

Domino was silent.

I shifted on my feet as my arches ached in my heels. "What about security cameras?"

"The only cameras are inside the loft. Sapo hasn't been inside." He rubbed his hands together. "What'll it be, Annabel—will you cover for Sapo to protect yourself?"

I exhaled a troubled sigh and felt my morals tested. Unnerving terms like *perjury* and *aiding and abetting* ran hot laps through my mind. I knew if I declined to cooperate, Domino's slick attorneys would bankrupt us faster than the ignition of the Hindenburg. But was the price of avoiding his wrath too high?

Julian stepped inside the stairwell from the party. He offered us little eye contact as he stopped before Domino to receive his orders.

Domino gestured to the alley and handed Julian the key. "Sapo's gun is on the ground near the dumpster, along with his cigarette butts. Dispose of those items and join us on stage for a bow." He motioned to us. "Tonight these three are our performers."

Julian nodded, his amber irises glimmering with a sense of duty. He descended the stairs and exited into the alley.

Domino cleared his throat. "Like I said, the evidence won't be an issue. Whatever claims Arshile makes about Sapo and his role in the crimes are the mad ramblings of a desperate fool anxious to save himself from prison. The lynchpin will be your corroboration."

I shivered as a breeze swept through the stairwell behind Julian. "It'll never work. Arshile made arrangements to pin the thefts on Sapo."

"Benjamin Arshile isn't as cunning as he'd like to believe. The stolen paintings are in his safe. His fingerprints alone are on the frames."

"Sapo's aren't?"

"He wore gloves. He assured me of this when he called after slipping from the alley tonight."

"Even so, when Arshile tells police of Sapo's involvement, they'll be forced to look into him. They'll discover Sapo has no alibi for the nights the thefts went down. Any alibi you supply will be treated with suspicion—of course you'll lie for him; he's your brother."

"Sapo isn't my brother. He's just a kid who grew up down the street from Julian and me when we were young."

I was confused. "That's not what the sales associates at your gallery think."

"You're referring to Bianca. Sapo had a thing for her. I imagine he hoped telling her we were brothers would make him more appealing."

"It doesn't make sense," I said. "If Sapo isn't your brother, why are you protecting him?"

"It's complicated."

"So is the game Battleship to a five-year-old until a parent explains it to them."

"You played Battleship when you were five?" asked Lyla.

"No, Lyla. I'm making the point that we deserve an explanation if we're going to lie to the police."

Domino ran his fingertips across his chin. "When Sapo was fourteen, his father disappeared under suspicious circumstances. His mother was forced to work two jobs and was rarely around. Sapo spent a great deal of time with our family as a result and began to view Julian and me as brothers."

"A sentiment that was mutual?" I asked.

"I'm afraid not."

"Why are you protecting him then?"

"When Julian and I left for university, Sapo stayed behind and went on to do very little. Years later, after enjoying a decade of romping about the East Coast—a successful string of galleries under our belts—Julian and I returned to the West Coast to set up shop in Santa Barbara. Sapo tracked us down a couple years later to share the news he'd inherited the Meland Hotel. He had the notion to revive the speakeasy in its basement with Julian and me his business partners."

I was struck by the information. "How did Sapo come to inherit the Meland Hotel?"

"He's a descendent of the original proprietor."

"You mean the mobster Alfonso Barretto?"

"You've done your homework."

"We learned about Barretto when solving the directions to 18 Laws. He had everyone fooled, even the mayor."

"Barretto's charm was widely known, as was his taste for fine suits and expensive mistresses," said Domino. "His descendants were no exception. Other than the Meland Hotel, which had been deemed valueless, few assets remained in Barretto's estate by the time it trickled down to Sapo. That was one of the problems with his idea to resurrect the speakeasy—his lack of capital."

I leaned against the metal railing to relieve the pressure on my feet. "Benjamin Arshile said Sapo was obsessed with the speakeasy. Now I see why."

"Another problem was Sapo's desire to call the shots. He had the demeanor of an outlaw and no business sense whatsoever. He would have run the speakeasy into the ground. Nonetheless, I promised him we would think about it.

That night, an idea struck me like a bolt of lightning, as if I had the string of a kite twined around my fingers with a skeleton key dangling perilously. Julian and I would return to the Pacific Northwest and open a new gallery. We would resurrect 18 Laws and use it to establish our client base. It would be imprudent to give Sapo a business role in the speakeasy, but I would offer him a security assignment with our gallery."

"But it wasn't enough, was it? Sapo wanted in on the speakeasy business. He felt he deserved it."

"Sapo groaned constantly that we stole his idea for 18 Laws and duped him into selling us the Meland Hotel." Domino shook his head. "After I fired Sapo from the gallery, he disappeared for a few months, only to return with a vengeance. He left threatening notes for Julian and me, saying he'd involve his ties to organized crime if we didn't rectify our business arrangements. The night Sapo barged into our gallery was the last straw. I realized he had no intention of backing down."

"Hence your sudden change of heart," I said.

"When I spoke with Sapo in the alley that night, I offered him a role overseeing logistics for the speakeasy, along with an ownership stake. He was appeased, but said if we ever wronged him again, we'd regret it. And that, Annabel, is the reason I'm protecting him."

"You're afraid of retribution."

"Organized crime has a disturbing knack for making people disappear."

"None of this explains your confrontational demeanor the night we encountered you in your gallery," said Lyla, adjusting her ponytail. "Nor does it explain the mysterious delivery Mr. Napier was there to collect."

"Regarding Mr. Napier, I had located a unique watercolor painting by an up-and-coming Scottish artist and wanted to surprise him with it," said Domino. "As for my demeanor, I heard you'd been asking around about me. I was suspicious of your motives."

"Who told you?"

"First, Dane. He said you'd returned to the Empire in search of information about 18 Laws."

Lyla frowned. "Dane was playing both sides?"

Domino left her question unanswered. He looked to Evan. "I was further agitated when Dane said you seemed like a journalist."

"His intuition was right," said Evan.

"The next evening, Sapo notified me he'd spotted two females searching the grounds of the Meland Hotel. He was there to oversee the delivery of a painting I had purchased for the speakeasy, a reproduction of Picasso's *Woman with a Hat*." He smiled with an unexpected warmth that made his cheeks bunch. "After you two ran off, Sapo checked the brick path and found Lyla's license in the ivy."

Lyla looked to me. "The burrowing rodent was falsely accused."

I patted her shoulder. "It'll never know."

"Days later, I received a call from Byron Quimby saying three amateur gumshoes whose descriptions matched yours had approached him to look into his relationship with my gallery. He said you had implied a potential connection to the string of thefts. When I then found you three snooping around my gallery, I feared you were drawing false conclusions. I realized I needed to investigate the thefts myself."

"Is that why Julian had copies of the insurance appraisals in his convertible?" I asked.

"How do you know about the appraisals?"

"I saw the folder on his passenger seat when he parked in the alley behind this building on Thursday."

A crease formed between Domino's dark eyebrows. "Julian said a vagrant tossed the contents of his convertible. You're telling me it was you?"

"I plead the Fifth."

"Julian is torn up over the loss of his houndstooth coat."

"I can't claim responsibility for that, but I think the coat is crumpled on the ground by the dumpster if Julian wants it. The hobo who took it did quite the number on it."

"Let's hope Julian doesn't find it." Domino turned to Evan. "I imagine you're chomping at the bit to write a spectacular story about tonight's events."

"It's my obligation to report the truth," said Evan. "Once I break this headline, my editor will shower me with latitude and praise."

"Under no circumstances are you to mention Sapo in your story. Do you understand?"

Evan was disturbed and struggled to contain it.

"Describe Annabel's bravery when facing Benjamin Arshile in the alley tonight. Detail what glorious men Julian and I are for hosting lavish events for our clients like this masked ball."

"What happens if I do mention Sapo?"

Domino's face was stern. "You don't want to face the consequences of disobeying my orders."

Evan's shoulders slumped as he felt unable to protest.

"A final order of business before we return to the party—next weekend, you three will present yourselves for an encore at 18 Laws to sell this charade."

I was floored. "You're inviting us back to your speakeasy?"

"Inviting. Ordering. Call it what you like. It isn't optional."

We returned to the party inside and followed Domino to the stage, where we laced fingers and tipped forward in the most theatric bow seen this side of Broadway while the pianist banged out the lively notes to "The Entertainer."

Julian reappeared from the alley and joined us on the platform, his smile gooey, his eyes sparkling with the deceit of one who'd just destroyed evidence. He gripped Lyla's wrists and swirled her in a figure-eight as applause rolled across the room like thunder through a stormy night. Then the pair joined us in a line to deliver another sensational bow, Domino twirling his hand through the air in an embellished gesture.

I leaned into Evan's ear. "If these theatrics are any indication of how our appearance at 18 Laws will unfold, I must ice my hip flexors ahead of time."

He nodded and motioned to the double doors, where two armed officers were waiting in the threshold, their hips weighed down with guns and clubs. "The cops have arrived. Do you intend to bend your morals and cover up Sapo's involvement in the art thefts?"

"Between the consequences of Domino's pit-bull attorneys and Sapo's ties to organized crime, it doesn't seem like I have a choice." I sighed. "Besides, Julian has already disposed of the evidence that puts Sapo in the alley tonight."

"Or has he?" asked Evan, mischief glowing in his almond eyes as he pressed his lips against my ear. "I still have the picture of Sapo's gun lying in the alley on my phone." He raised his finger to his lips. *Shhh.*

Chapter 38

Intoxicating libations and thinly-veiled threats lured us back to 18 Laws as we slinked past the doormen and slipped from our coats.

Fuzzy illumination from antique Edison bulbs warmed the vintage watering hole while the lilting music of 1940s Harlem spilled from the instruments of the jazz quartet, the bass clef and treble clef playing rhythmic teeter-totter. The hum of mingling voices created a lively concerto while the fine aromas of lavender and musk drifted through the room.

We ordered three martinis from the baby-faced bartender and lingered near the bar, awaiting the arrival of our insistent hosts to parade us around like a traveling circus. Properly attired in a cocktail dress the color of a forbidden apple, I tapped my heel on the hardwood floors, wondering what the night would have in store for us.

My handshake was well-rehearsed and as delicate as bone china. My smile was practiced, viscous, and fake. I looked to Lyla in her black satin shift, and to Evan in his guanaco suit, and knew the same could be said of them.

"There they are, my intrepid travelers," said Julian, his voice melodic as he sashayed across the swinging speakeasy to greet us with open arms. His chestnut bouffant was glossy, his amber eyes sparkled, and his lips quivered with pretense. "Before we wet your whistles, Domino wishes to speak with you in our VIP room. Please, follow me." He instructed us to leave our drinks at the bar and guided us to the plush room in which the doormen had once locked us. With an eager breath, he drew open the door and snapped his fingers as if to say *Showtime!*

I realized why at once.

Perched upon a Verner Panton ribbon chair with a gin martini in hand, a strong-jawed man with blond hair trimmed into a tidy crew cut ordered us to enter with a gesture of his fingers. The pinstripes in his jacquard suit were symmetric, the leather of his cap-toed shoes shined and buffed. In shades of black and gray, the tattooed tentacles of an octopus crawled up his throat.

Seated across from him on the hopsack Florence Knoll sofa, Domino sipped from a tulip-shaped brandy snifter. He addressed us in an even tone. "Annabel, Evan, Lyla, you all remember Sapo."

With passing delirium, I spoke an uncluttered salutation— *How do you do?*—or something like that. And then I forced myself to gaze into Sapo's eyes. Cold and black like beetle shells, they seemed to say a thousand words, the loudest of which reminding us to uphold our oath of silence or face what followed the ellipsis: *Keep quiet or else...*

Turned out, those words said that very thing.

Erika Simms spent fifteen years in Corporate America before escaping to write her debut novel, *Flies in the Punch Bowl*. Native to Anchorage and raised in Seattle, she currently lives in Denver with her husband, where she is at work on the next book in the series.

32447379R00175

Made in the USA
San Bernardino, CA
15 April 2019